India in South Asia

South Asia is one of the most volatile regions of the world, and India's complex democratic political system impinges on its relations with its South Asian neighbours. Focusing on this relationship, this book explores the extent to which domestic politics affect a country's foreign policy.

The book argues that particular continuities and disjunctures in Indian foreign policy are linked to the way in which Indian elites articulated Indian identity in response to the needs of domestic politics. The manner in which these state elites conceive India's region and regional role depends on their need to stay in tune with domestic identity politics. Such exigencies have important implications for Indian foreign policy in South Asia.

Analysing India's foreign policy through the lens of competing domestic visions at three different historical eras in India's independent history, the book provides a framework for studying India's developing nationhood on the basis of these idea(s) of 'India'. This approach allows for a deeper and a more nuanced interpretation of the motives for India's foreign policy choices than the traditional realist or neo-liberal framework, and provides a useful contribution to South Asian Studies, Politics and International Studies.

Sinderpal Singh is a Research Fellow at the Institute of South Asian Studies, National University of Singapore.

Routledge Advances in International Relations and Global Politics

1 **Foreign Policy and Discourse Analysis**
France, Britain and Europe
Henrik Larsen

2 **Agency, Structure and International Politics**
From ontology to empirical enquiry
Gil Friedman and Harvey Starr

3 **The Political Economy of Regional Co-operation in the Middle East**
Ali Carkoglu, Mine Eder, Kemal Kirisci

4 **Peace Maintenance**
The evolution of international political authority
Jarat Chopra

5 **International Relations and Historical Sociology**
Breaking down boundaries
Stephen Hobden

6 **Equivalence in Comparative Politics**
Edited by Jan W. van Deth

7 **The Politics of Central Banks**
Robert Elgie and Helen Thompson

8 **Politics and Globalisation**
Knowledge, ethics and agency
Martin Shaw

9 **History and International Relations**
Thomas W. Smith

10 **Idealism and Realism in International Relations**
Robert M. A. Crawford

11 **National and International Conflicts, 1945–1995**
New empirical and theoretical approaches
Frank Pfetsch and Christoph Rohloff

12 **Party Systems and Voter Alignments Revisited**
Edited by Lauri Karvonen and Stein Kuhnle

13 **Ethics, Justice and International Relations**
Constructing an international community
Peter Sutch

14 **Capturing Globalization**
Edited by James H. Mittelman and Norani Othman

15 **Uncertain Europe**
Building a new European security order?
Edited by Martin A. Smith and Graham Timmins

16 **Power, Postcolonialism and International Relations**
Reading race, gender and class
Edited by Geeta Chowdhry and Sheila Nair

17 **Constituting Human Rights**
Global civil society and the society of democratic states
Mervyn Frost

18 **US Economic Statecraft for Survival 1933–1991**
Of sanctions, embargoes and economic warfare
Alan P. Dobson

19 **The EU and NATO Enlargement**
Richard McAllister and Roland Dannreuther

20 **Spatializing International Politics**
Analysing activism on the internet
Jayne Rodgers

21 **Ethnonationalism in the Contemporary World**
Walker Connor and the study of Nationalism
Edited by Daniele Conversi

22 **Meaning and International Relations**
Edited by Peter Mandaville and Andrew Williams

23 **Political Loyalty and the Nation-State**
Edited by Michael Waller and Andrew Linklater

24 **Russian Foreign Policy and the CIS**
Theories, debates and actions
Nicole J. Jackson

25 **Asia and Europe**
Development and different dimensions of ASEM
Yeo Lay Hwee

26 **Global Instability and Strategic Crisis**
Neville Brown

27 **Africa in International Politics**
External Involvement on the Continent
Edited by Ian Taylor and Paul Williams

28 **Global Governmentality**
Governing International Spaces
Edited by Wendy Larner and William Walters

29 **Political Learning and Citizenship Education Under Conflict**
The political socialization of Israeli and Palestinian youngsters
Orit Ichilov

30 **Gender and Civil Society**
Transcending boundaries
Edited by Jude Howell and Diane Mulligan

31 **State Crises, Globalisation and National Movements in North-East Africa**
The Horn's dilemma
Edited by Asafa Jalata

32 **Diplomacy and Developing Nations**
Post-Cold War foreign policy-making structures and processes
Edited by Justin Robertson and Maurice A. East

33 **Autonomy, Self-governance and Conflict Resolution**
Innovative approaches to institutional design in divided societies
Edited by Marc Weller and Stefan Wolff

34 **Mediating International Crises**
Jonathan Wilkenfeld, Kathleen J. Young, David M. Quinn and Victor Asal

35 **Postcolonial Politics, the Internet and Everyday Life**
Pacific traversals online
M. I. Franklin

36 **Reconstituting the Global Liberal Order**
Legitimacy and regulation
Kanishka Jayasuriya

37 **International Relations, Security and Jeremy Bentham**
Gunhild Hoogensen

38 **Interregionalism and International Relations**
Edited by Heiner Hänggi, Ralf Roloff and Jürgen Rüland

39 **The International Criminal Court**
A global civil society achievement
Marlies Glasius

40 **A Human Security Doctrine for Europe**
Project, principles, practicalities
Edited by Marlies Glasius and Mary Kaldor

41 **The History and Politics of UN Security Council Reform**
Dimitris Bourantonis

42 **Russia and NATO Since 1991**
From cold war through cold peace to partnership?
Martin A. Smith

43 **The Politics of Protection**
Sites of insecurity and political agency
Edited by Jef Huysmans, Andrew Dobson and Raia Prokhovnik

44 **International Relations in Europe**
Traditions, perspectives and destinations
Edited by Knud Erik Jørgensen and Tonny Brems Knudsen

45 **The Empire of Security and the Safety of the People**
Edited by William Bain

46 **Globalization and Religious Nationalism in India**
The search for ontological security
Catrina Kinnvall

47 **Culture and International Relations**
Narratives, natives and tourists
Julie Reeves

48 **Global Civil Society**
Contested futures
Edited by Gideon Baker and David Chandler

49 **Rethinking Ethical Foreign Policy**
Pitfalls, possibilities and paradoxes
Edited by David Chandler and Volker Heins

50 **International Cooperation and Arctic Governance**
Regime effectiveness and northern region building
Edited by Olav Schram Stokke and Geir Hønneland

51 **Human Security**
Concepts and implications
Shahrbanou Tadjbakhsh and Anuradha Chenoy

52 **International Relations and Security in the Digital Age**
Edited by Johan Eriksson and Giampiero Giacomello

53 **State-Building**
Theory and practice
Edited by Aidan Hehir and Neil Robinson

54 **Violence and Non-Violence in Africa**
Edited by Pal Ahluwalia, Louise Bethlehem and Ruth Ginio

55 **Developing Countries and Global Trade Negotiations**
Edited by Larry Crump and S. Javed Maswood

56 **Civil Society, Religion and Global Governance**
Paradigms of power and persuasion
Edited by Helen James

57 **War, Peace and Hegemony in a Globalized World**
The changing balance of power in the twenty-first century
Edited by Chandra Chari

58 **Economic Globalisation as Religious War**
Tragic convergence
Michael McKinley

59 **Globalization, Prostitution and Sex-trafficking**
Corporeal politics
Elina Penttinen

60 **Peacebuilding**
Women in international perspective
Elisabeth Porter

61 **Ethics, Liberalism and Realism in International Relations**
Mark D. Gismondi

62 **Law and Legalization in Transnational Relations**
Edited by Christian Brütsch and Dirk Lehmkuhl

63 **Fighting Terrorism and Drugs**
Europe and international police cooperation
Jörg Friedrichs

64 **Identity Politics in the Age of Genocide**
The Holocaust and historical representation
David B. MacDonald

65 **Globalisation, Public Opinion and the State**
Western Europe and East and Southeast Asia
Edited by Takashi Inoguchi and Ian Marsh

66 **Urbicide**
The politics of urban destruction
Martin Coward

67 **Transnational Activism in the UN and the EU**
A comparative study
Jutta Joachim and Birgit Locher

68 **Gender Inclusive**
Essays on violence, men and feminist international relations
Adam Jones

69 **Capitalism, Democracy and the Prevention of War and Poverty**
Edited by Peter Graeff and Guido Mehlkop

70 **Environmental Change and Foreign Policy**
Theory and practice
Edited by Paul G. Harris

71 **Climate Change and Foreign Policy**
Case studies from East to West
Edited by Paul G. Harris

72 **Securitizations of Citizenship**
Edited by Peter Nyers

73 **The Power of Ideology**
From the Roman Empire to Al-Qaeda
Alex Roberto Hybel

74 **The Securitization of Humanitarian Migration**
Digging moats and sinking boats
Scott D. Watson

75 **Mediation in the Asia-Pacific Region**
Transforming conflicts and building peace
Edited by Dale Bagshaw and Elisabeth Porter

76 **United Nations Reform**
Heading north or south?
Spencer Zifcak

77 **New Norms and Knowledge in World Politics**
Protecting people, intellectual property and the environment
Preslava Stoeva

78 **Power, Resistance and Conflict in the Contemporary World**
Social movements, networks and hierarchies
Athina Karatzogianni and Andrew Robinson

79 **World-Regional Social Policy and Global Governance**
New research and policy agendas in Africa, Asia, Europe and Latin America
Edited by Bob Deacon, Maria Cristina Macovei, Luk Van Langenhove and Nicola Yeates

80 **International Relations Theory and Philosophy**
Interpretive dialogues
Edited by Cerwyn Moore and Chris Farrands

81 **Superpower Rivalry and Conflict**
The long shadow of the Cold War on the twenty-first century
Edited by Chandra Chari

82 **Coping and Conformity in World Politics**
Hugh C. Dyer

83 **Defining and Defying Organized Crime**
Discourse, perception and reality
Edited by Felia Allum, Francesca Longo, Daniela Irrera and Panos A. Kostakos

84 **Federalism in Asia**
India, Pakistan and Malaysia
Harihar Bhattacharyya

85 **The World Bank and HIV/AIDS**
Setting a global agenda
Sophie Harman

86 **The "War on Terror" and the Growth of Executive Power?**
A comparative analysis
Edited by John E. Owens and Riccardo Pelizzo

87 **The Contested Politics of Mobility**
Borderzones and irregularity
Edited by Vicki Squires

88 **Human Security, Law and the Prevention of Terrorism**
Andrej Zwitter

89 **Multilayered Migration Governance**
The promise of partnership
Edited by Rahel Kunz, Sandra Lavenex and Marion Panizzon

90 **Role Theory in International Relations**
Approaches and analyses
Edited by Sebastian Harnisch, Cornelia Frank and Hanns W. Maull

91 **Issue Salience in International Relations**
Edited by Kai Oppermann and Henrike Viehrig

92 **Corporate Risk and National Security Redefined**
Karen Lund Petersen

93 **Interrogating Democracy in World Politics**
Edited by Joe Hoover, Meera Sabaratnam and Laust Schouenborg

94 **Globalizing Resistance against War**
Theories of resistance and the new anti-war movement
Tiina Seppälä

95 **The Politics of Self-Determination**
Beyond the decolonisation process
Kristina Roepstorff

96 **Sovereignty and the Responsibility to Protect**
The power of norms and the norms of the powerful
Theresa Reinold

97 **Anglo-American Relations**
Contemporary perspectives
Edited by Alan P. Dobson and Steve Marsh

98 **The Emerging Politics of Antarctica**
Edited by Anne-Marie Brady

99 **Genocide, Ethnonationalism, and the United Nations**
Exploring the causes of mass killing since 1945
Hannibal Travis

100 **Caribbean Sovereignty, Development and Democracy in an Age of Globalization**
Edited by Linden Lewis

101 **Rethinking Foreign Policy**
Edited by Fredrik Bynander and Stefano Guzzini

102 **The Promise and Perils of Transnationalization**
NGO activism and the socialization of women's human rights in Egypt and Iran
Benjamin Stachursky

103 **Peacebuilding and International Administration**
The cases of Bosnia and Herzegovina and Kosovo
Niels van Willigen

104 **The Politics of the Globalization of Law**
Getting from rights to justice
Edited by Alison Brysk

105 **The Arctic in International Politics**
Coming in from the cold
Peter Hough

106 **The Scourge of Genocide**
Essays on reflection
Adam Jones

107 **Understanding Transatlantic Relations**
Whither the West?
Serena Simoni

108 **India in South Asia**
Domestic identity politics and foreign policy from Nehru to the BJP
Sinderpal Singh

India in South Asia
Domestic identity politics and
foreign policy from Nehru to the BJP

Sinderpal Singh

LONDON AND NEW YORK

First published 2013
by Routledge
2 Park Square, Milton Park, Abingdon, Oxfordshire OX14 4RN

Simultaneously published in the USA and Canada
by Routledge
711 Third Avenue, New York, NY 10017

First issued in paperback 2014

Routledge is an imprint of the Taylor & Francis Group, an informa business

© 2013 Sinderpal Singh

The right of Sinderpal Singh to be identified as the author of this work has been asserted by him in accordance with sections 77 and 78 of the Copyright, Designs and Patents Act 1988.

All rights reserved. No part of this book may be reprinted or reproduced or utilised in any form or by any electronic, mechanical, or other means, now known or hereafter invented, including photocopying and recording, or in any information storage or retrieval system, without permission in writing from the publishers.

Trademark notice: Product or corporate names may be trademarks or registered trademarks, and are used only for identification and explanation without intent to infringe.

British Library Cataloguing in Publication Data
A catalogue record for this book is available from the British Library

Library of Congress Cataloging in Publication Data
A catalog record has been requested for this book

ISBN 978-0-415-62530-2 (hbk)
ISBN 978-1-138-88844-9 (pbk)
ISBN 978-0-203-55222-3 (ebk)

Typeset in Times New Roman
by Integra Software Services Pvt. Ltd, Pondicherry, India

Contents

	Acknowledgements	x
	Introduction	1
1	Nehru and the invention of India	12
2	Nehru and the birth of India's regional policy: the case of Pakistan and Nepal	28
3	'The Empress of India': Indira Gandhi and the idea of India	48
4	A 'new' phase in Indian foreign policy: the case of Pakistan and Sri Lanka	65
5	The BJP era and the construction of Indian identity	85
6	A 'Hindu' foreign policy: dealing with Pakistan and Bangladesh	99
	Conclusion	114
	Notes	120
	Bibliography	147
	Index	161

Acknowledgements

This book project began life in a much earlier form as a doctoral dissertation. Therefore, it would not have come to very much without the guidance and support of my two doctoral thesis supervisors, Michael William and Jeroen Gunning. At the most critical periods, Robin Jeffrey's interventions helped to push this project forward. This book owes Robin a huge debt of gratitude. I would like to thank my colleagues at ISAS and NUS for their support and assistance throughout this project. I would especially like to thank Tan Tai Yong, Rajesh Rai, Natasha Hamilton-Hart, Rahul Mukerji, Amitendu Palit and C. Raja Mohan for their inputs and suggestions at various stages of this book project. I would also like to thank my brother Rajpal Singh, whose musings on 'real life' diplomacy serve to constantly question many of my prior assumptions about contemporary global politics. From its very beginning, Kate's contributions to this project are far too many to list here. I thank her for helping to ensure this project reached its final destination. This book is dedicated to Santokh Singh, who first introduced me to the gratifications of reading a book.

Introduction

Foreign policy and domestic identity: India in South Asia

This book explores a key problem in international relations: the extent and manner in which domestic politics affect a country's foreign policy. It focuses specifically on one of the most politically volatile regions of the world, South Asia and the way in which India's complex political system impinges upon its relations with other South Asian states. The book argues that particular continuities and disjunctures in Indian foreign policy are linked to the way in which Indian political elites, within the context of domestic politics, articulate Indian identity. The manner in which these political elites conceive India's region and regional role depends upon their engagement with domestic identity politics, and such exigencies have important implications for Indian foreign policy in South Asia.

Since independence in 1947, Indian elites have argued vigorously about what 'India' means and how the Indian state should articulate such self-representations. This contest over the idea of 'India' had important implications for Indian foreign policy, specifically in relation to other states in South Asia. The idea that India's own struggle against colonialism and its eventual independence bestowed 'special responsibilities' upon the country beyond its own borders is evident early in India's independent history. In 1948, in the midst of debates over the framing of the constitution, India's first prime minister and external affairs minister, Jawaharlal Nehru

> saw the star of India rising far above the horizon and casting its soothing light [...] over many countries in the world, who looked to it with hope, who considered that out of this new Free India would come various forces which would help Asia.[1]

From the early days of independent statehood, 'Indian-ness' contained within it a conception of India's 'natural' regional space and role. The notion that India had a role beyond her domestic boundaries lay in the fact that

> India, not because of any ambition of her own, but because of the forces of circumstances, because of geography, because of history and because

of so many other things, inevitably has to play a very important part in Asia.[2]

Nehru's framing vision of India's larger role beyond its shores would come to structure the approach and perceptions of future Indian political elites.

The argument

This book intends to make one principal argument. It asserts that rival views of what it means to be 'India' and the contests between the proponents of these rival views affect the ways in which the Indian state interacts with other states in South Asia. In effect, it designates the politics of identity-making at the site of the Indian state as a starting point in understanding Indian foreign policy in South Asia. Moreover, it analyses how domestic identity politics plays a key role in India's foreign policy towards South Asia.

Domestic identity-politics refers to contests among political elites over the way in which the Indian state represents its identity to its own people and its neighbours. It denotes the competitive process by which political elites attempt to represent state identity in specific ways. By advocating the explanatory value of domestic identity-politics, the premise is not that domestic identity-politics explains everything concerning the complexities of India's foreign policy. Rather, the premise is that the framework of domestic identity politics helps to explain important links between the domestic realm and foreign policy, links which have been overlooked in the existing literature on India's foreign policy.

The domestic identity-politics framework does not preclude strategically motivated action in a bounded rational sense; rather, domestic identity politics frames how foreign policy is conceived by rival political elites in their domestic contests about 'Indian-ness'. In short, domestic identity politics is the domestic component of India's foreign policy formulation. By itself, it does not explain the full range of motivations and preferences that go into the making of Indian foreign policy, yet it is argued here that no comprehensive attempt to understand Indian foreign policy in South Asia can be complete without consideration of these rivalries and contests.

Indian political elites articulate and represent their understanding of the Indian state via three discourses – secularism, democracy and anti-imperialism. Each is articulated – used and justified – in the cut-and-thrust of domestic politics, particularly the politics of identity.

The relationship between the discourse of secularism and representations of Indian state identity is fundamental due to the purported ideational basis upon which Pakistan was created. The legitimating basis for the state of Pakistan – that the formation of a separate state was necessary to safeguard the interests of Muslims in British India after independence in order to avoid the tyranny of the 'Hindu' majority – has continually confronted Indian political elites with the fundamental issue of defining the role of religion in the Indian state. In such a context, 'secularism' has been a response to multiple religious identities and is itself a proposed form of meta-identity, transcending these seemingly contending religious affiliations. This has been a dominant theme in the process of defining Indian state identity, especially associated with the legacy of Nehru but it has, nevertheless, been persistently contested. The very content and meaning of 'secularism' as it relates to Indian state identity has been contested since 1947. The manner in which the Hindu nationalist Bharatiya Janata Party (BJP) rose to political power exhibits even more starkly the highly disputed nature of the relationship between 'secularism', or at least an Indian variant of it, and Indian state identity. The BJP era in Indian politics, when the party led a coalition Indian government, witnessed a radical attempt at re-negotiating the discourse on secularism as it relates to the identity of the Indian state vis-à-vis different religious groups.

The discourse on democracy and its relationship to the represention of state identity is hardly unique to India, or to politics in the modern era, especially given the centrality of democracy discourses to the nature of the postcolonial state in a general sense. Similarly, as in other postcolonial states, there was deep contestation about the meaning, both in theory and practice, of 'democracy' in the Indian context at the advent of independence at 1947. There were Gandhian inspired ideas of democracy for the reduction of the centralized state's political role and the strengthening of village representative bodies, the Nehruvian inspired ideas of robust parliamentary democracy and secular, constitutional government and, lastly, the religiously informed ideas of Hindu nationalist groups about democracy as a means of safeguarding certain inherent rights of the majority Hindu community within independent India.[3] These three conceptions of democracy and their related discourse of 'Indian democracy' reflected differing understandings of the aims and potential benefits of democracy for independent India. More specifically, these different conceptions and their associated discourses of 'Indian democracy' reflected a deeper contestation over how to order certain critical relationships among competing groups within independent India.

In independent India, the discourse on democracy is crucial to representations of Indian state identity in terms of framing a specific relationship between the state's imperative to carry out the role of economic redistribution versus the role of the state to defend the rights and autonomy of individuals and various groups, defined in religious, ethnic, economic and provincial terms. As the world's largest democracy and given that it has had a popularly elected central government since independence (except for a brief aberration between 1975 and 1977), the discourse of democracy becomes central to any exercise in defining Indian state identity. Furthermore, the discourse of democracy subsumes other discourses and ideas related to Indian state identity, such as the type of socialism and federalism that India should imbibe. Therefore, it is via contesting discourses on democracy that Indian political elites have framed questions concerning the role of the Indian state as an agent of socio-economic change, versus the imperative of protecting individual and group rights within Indian society and allowing for genuine regional autonomy within the Indian Union.

The genesis of India's independent statehood via a long and bitter struggle for political independence from British imperial control has consequently led to discourses on anti-imperialism to be related crucially to representations of Indian state identity. Thus Indian political elites relate ideas of national autonomy, national honour and freedom to conceptions of Indian-ness via the discourse of anti-imperialism. In fact, Indian political elites saw India's external role to be an expression of this element of its identity, giving credence to its demonstrated freedom and autonomy. This was especially true in framing India's role within South Asia, which they saw as a stage for India to demonstrate its anti-imperialist credentials. Similarly, although references to the defence of India's territorial integrity have been an important part of political elite discourse, such notions are related habitually to the identity of the Indian state via the broader discourse of anti-imperialism.

Taken together, these three discourses – secularism, democracy and anti-imperialism – are crucial to an understanding of the ways in which different sets of Indian political elites across time have sought to represent Indian state identity. By identifying how different sets of Indian political elites participate in the three discourses within the context of domestic identity politics, it becomes possible to understand how these elites represent the identity of the Indian state in certain specific and definite ways. However, in analysing these three discourses within the context of domestic identity-politics, it is necessary to be clear at the outset how discourse is analysed and employed in this study.

The term 'discourse analysis' has been employed with a variety of meanings across a broad range of academic disciplines to denote various actions.[4] Broadly, one prominent strand of discourse analysis is related to how discourse relates to 'regimes of knowledge' within societies. This work is largely influenced by the work of Michel Foucault, with its more recent incarnation, termed 'critical discourse analysis' (usually abbreviated to CDA), drawing upon the central tenets of the critical theory approach of the Frankfurt School.[5] However, this is not how 'discourse' is employed in this study. Instead, 'discourse analysis' is performed in this study by moving away from the above focus on the power dynamics of discourse and towards discourse analysis as 'the processes of social construction that constitute social reality'.[6] As such, its starting point is the examination of how Indian political elites participate, within the context of domestic identity-politics, in shaping a specific state identity as the dominant social 'reality' via the discourses of secularism, democracy and anti-imperialism. The manner in which such discourses reproduce particular relations of power/domination between certain Indian political elites and other groups of people within/outside the Indian state/society is thus beyond the purview of this study. Instead, it concentrates on how, very specifically, Indian political elites compete among themselves in constructing Indian state identity via these three discourses. The manner in which such constructions of 'India' impinge on India's foreign policy in South Asia can then be traced.

Theoretical contentions

This study begins from the theoretical contention that traditional IR theories – variants of realist and neo-liberal approaches – are inadequate in addressing the impact of state identity on India's foreign policy. These approaches contend that state actors formulate foreign policy on the basis of factors existing predominantly in the external milieu and not in the domestic sphere. Similarly, in instances when the existence of 'identity' factors is acknowledged, these factors are either subsumed within the larger explanatory category of 'national interests', or they are assumed to be variables endogenous to explanations of foreign policy. As Wendt puts it, these theories 'bracket' identity in their explanations of state behaviour.[7] In accordance with such theories of IR, an attempt to look at the domestic realm in explaining state behaviour in making foreign policy is thus rendered 'reductionist'.

These shortcomings therefore challenge any serious observer of Indian foreign policy to explore the ways in which 'identity' is employed elsewhere within IR literature and its applicability in the framing of more comprehensive understandings of Indian foreign policy. Moving the analysis from a predominantly materialist conception of how states conduct their foreign policy, the identity approach emphasizes how ideational conceptions of the material world are crucial in comprehending how states approach their foreign policy. The assertion that states conceive of their actions, and those of others, within a larger framework of 'meaning-making' acknowledges the identity approach as a more sensitive analytical tool for understanding why and how states reflect their domestic socio-political differences within their respective foreign policies.

The use of 'identity' to explain how states approach their foreign policy has been a relatively recent trend within IR, with a growing number of works engaging the debate.[8] A key element in these works is discerning the relationship between identity, political elites and foreign policy. Political elites are vital to a study of identity and foreign policy because of their institutional location within institutions of the state, 'where the allocation of authority and responsibility for the national interest to the state' rests.[9] Therefore, other sets of domestic actors are relatively less important when it comes to propagating state identities in foreign policy. From within this institutional position, these elites assign identities to the state in relation to foreign policy formulation. However, such assignment of identities to the state takes place within certain 'reality' constraints, both internal and external. Internally, these constraints embody themselves in what one writer terms the 'security imaginary', defined as the 'linguistic, cultural and institutional resources' located at the site of the state that contain a 'repertoire of meanings' within which political elites propagate state identities in foreign policy making.[10] Externally, certain events that occur outside the state can impinge critically upon the autonomy of such elites in making foreign policy. Such reality constraints, however, are 'quite loose and [allow] a wide range of sometimes quite dramatically different representations'. This is because

> the meanings produced out of a state's security imaginary are [...] not 'dictated' by real factors since it is instead this meaning which attributes to these 'real' factors a particular importance and a particular place in the universe constituted by a given society.[11]

Such externally generated 'real' factors thus assume significance and meaning largely through the kinds of identities that the state, via political elites, has represented for itself and other entities with which it interacts in its foreign policy.

Book structure and methodology

This book analyses three periods since India's independence – the Nehru (1947–62), Indira Gandhi (1966–77, 1980–4) and BJP (1998–2004) eras. The three periods have been selected on the basis of two main factors. First, an examination of these three periods reveals important differences in how Indian political elites attempted to represent Indian state identity. These three periods, with their contrasting experiences of how Indian political elites sought to represent Indian state identity, afford the opportunity to discern the link between varying representations of Indian state identity and Indian foreign policy across time. A second and related factor is the issue of political elites and the duration of their tenure at the apex of the Indian state. Nehru's tenure as both prime minister and external affairs minister (17 years), Mrs Gandhi's term as prime minister (15 years) and the BJP's duration at the head of a coalition government (six years) mark out these three periods as the longest periods that any one set of political elites have exercised political power as head of the government of India from 1947 to 2004. The significance of political elites' duration as heads of the Indian government in this context is relatively clear-cut. There is a discernible link between duration at the head of government and the ability to negotiate (and re-negotiate) Indian state identity, and for its effects to be discerned in foreign policy. Thus, an analysis of these three periods allows for an application of the domestic identity politics framework in linking these political elites who lead governments, their participation in the negotiation of state identity domestically and tangible Indian foreign policy outcomes.

Besides the length of the tenure, the Nehru era is also crucial in one other respect – its role in defining 'Indian-ness' at the point of India's inception as an independent state. This period witnessed the birth of the Indian state and the beginnings of the process of framing Indian state identity. Second only to M.K. Gandhi as the most influential personality in the Indian nationalist movement and the Congress Party, Nehru's central role in defining the tenets of Indian identity, coupled with his towering influence, especially after Gandhi's death in 1948, makes a study of this period crucial. In several ways, all three discourses had their genesis within the nationalist movement against British colonial rule, yet it was during this period that Nehru gave all three discourses specific meaning and content by linking them to representations of Indian state identity. His tenure in office also marked the beginning of independent India's foreign policy, which in the early part was impacted significantly by Nehru's projection of India's global role in the international politics of the post-Second World War world. However, as I argue in Chapter 2, there was a distinct shift in India's foreign policy approach from the mid-1950s as India's foreign policy in South Asia became a more autonomous part of its overall foreign policy, reflecting Nehru's perception of external events as they were mediated through his conception of India's regional space and role.

The Indira Gandhi period has been chosen because it has come to be seen as one of fundamental change within India domestically, specifically with regard to how Indian state identity was re-negotiated in relation to the Nehru era. The imposition of the Emergency in 1975 and the suspension of democracy is only one example of the fundamental domestic changes that took place within India during this time. Indira Gandhi's re-negotiation with the discourses of democracy and secularism meant that by the end of her tenure, the Indian state came to embody a specific type of democratic populism with political power migrating from the federal units of the Indian Union towards the central government in Delhi.

With regard to Indian foreign policy in South Asia, this period ushered in certain significant changes. For example, the discourse of anti-imperialism became increasingly infused with notions of defending territorial space and this guided India's approach towards Sri Lanka in the early 1980s. With regard to Pakistan, increasing centralization of political power at the central state level led to specific conceptions of India as a status-quo power in South Asia, thus informing Indira Gandhi's approach to the Simla Summit of 1972 in the aftermath of the 1971 war between the two countries.

The BJP period has been selected largely because of the manner in which the party, as a part of the larger Hindu nationalist movement (commonly known as the *Sangh Parivar*, or 'Family of Associations'), has traditionally represented itself, and its vision of 'Indian-ness', as the ideological challenger of the Congress Party. In this regard, the BJP's stated agenda – even before it came to power and in its earlier incarnations – to re-define radically the central idea of India, especially via its own specific discourse on secularism and its links to Indian state identity make this period crucial within the context of this study. With its ostensible 'Hindu' nationalist agenda, backed with a history of ideas that stretched back into the colonial era, the BJP era is therefore vital to an examination of how the idea of India came under such radical contestation in comparison to the earlier two periods under scrutiny in this study.

8   *Introduction*

In terms of Indian foreign policy in South Asia, the BJP-led government came to perceive the actions of both Pakistan and Bangladesh via the prism of its own conceptions of India's regional space and role, which in turn were informed crucially by its own domestic construction of Indian state identity. By representing India's role in South Asia largely through its specific representation of India as a 'Hindu' state, the BJP-led government formulated Indian foreign policy towards both Pakistan and Bangladesh as a response to what it perceived was India's perennial challenge: the challenge of Muslim imperialism towards 'Hindu' India.

The next issue concerns how each of the three periods are analysed. One approach often employed in analysing Indian foreign policy within discrete historical periods is to perform a general, broad-brush survey of Indian foreign policy across a particular historical period. However, for the purposes of this book, in attempting to discern the links between negotiations of Indian state identity and specific foreign policy outcomes in each of the three periods, a more directed methodology is employed. As the central aim is to explain specific outcomes in Indian foreign policy within South Asia, an approach that structures an examination of the three periods via specific foreign policy episodes in each period is required. In addition, the basis upon which these foreign policy episodes are selected in each period also need to be made clear.

The foreign policy episodes used in each of the three periods are divided into two categories. The first category comprises episodes of Indian foreign policy involving Pakistan and the second category relates to Nepal, Sri Lanka and Bangladesh. In the first category, one specific Indian foreign policy episode involving Pakistan will be analysed in each of the three periods. For the second category, one foreign policy episode will be analysed with regard to the case of Nepal in the Nehru period, Sri Lanka in the Indira Gandhi period and Bangladesh in the BJP period.

Specific case studies of Indian foreign policy in relation to Pakistan accomplish two things. First, they allow for an examination of a relationship which has preoccupied Indian foreign policy since its inception as an independent nation. Scrutinizing distinct foreign policy episodes vis-à-vis Pakistan in this regard is essential for demonstrating how, via the domestic identity-politics framework, representations of Indian state identity inform India's foreign policy in its principal inter-state relationship within South Asia in each of three different historical periods. Second, on a comparative level it helps to discern patterns of continuity/divergence in India's foreign policy towards Pakistan in relation to the profound transformation in India's domestic realm from the Nehru to the BJP period.

The second category of cases achieves two objectives. First, an examination of India's interactions with other countries in South Asia besides Pakistan will give empirical depth to this study as India's foreign policy in South Asia is clearly more than just the sum of its interactions with Pakistan over time. In order to make reasonable claims about specific outcomes in India's foreign policy in South Asia, it is imperative therefore to look beyond its bilateral relationship with Pakistan. Second, specific regional episodes between India and each of these countries provide the basis upon which empirically verifiable links between domestic identity-politics and Indian foreign policy can be advanced.

An analysis of the manner in which Indian political elites negotiate domestic identity-politics, their conceptions of India's regional space and regional role(s) and how these lead to specific outcomes in Indian foreign policy requires an understanding of the thoughts, beliefs and ideas of these political elites. This requires a consideration of the discourse, both public and private, of these sets of individuals. As Jutta Weldes points out in her study of US foreign policy during the Cuban Missile Crisis, the 'primary locus of analysis is therefore statements in which foreign policy decision makers explain the goals of US foreign policy'.[12] In a similar way, understanding how Indian political elites come to input particular conceptions of India's regional space and its regional role(s) into specific forms of foreign policy requires the researcher to analyse their statements, both public and private. The comparison of these different sources of discourse, both public and private, then allows for a more nuanced understanding of how these elites negotiate and contest the central discourses linked to Indian state identity, how their contestations and negotiation led them to take on particular conceptions of India's regional space and regional role(s) and, lastly, how these impact specific outcomes in Indian foreign policy in South Asia.

In the specific case of the three periods chosen for this study, a further note needs to be added about how specific discourses are analysed in this book. The study of the three periods entailed a focus upon different types of discourses for an understanding of how Indian state identity was framed and represented and how it impacted Indian foreign policy.

In the Nehru period, given the dominance of Nehru's personality and influence amongst the post-independent Indian political elite in framing and representing Indian state identity, this study concentrates largely on the public and private discourses of Nehru himself. Nehru's public speeches, his official correspondence with his ministers and other party members and his more private ruminations on framing Indian state identity thus form the core of the discursive analysis during this period. This includes analysing the contestation that Nehru faced from within his own party, specifically from his deputy in government, Sardar Patel, as well as specific elements outside his government, namely groups like the Hindu Mahasabha. By analysing Nehru's response to these contestations, the process by which domestic identity-politics helped frame a specific idea of Indian state identity can then be observed.

The Indira Gandhi period lends itself to a similar concentration on the discursive analysis of a dominant prime minister, Mrs Indira Gandhi. The process by which Mrs Gandhi initially sought to frame Indian state identity in the face of strong contestation from other Indian political elites within the Congress Party is analysed by looking at both her public speeches and addresses as well as her private exchanges with her advisers, other members in her party as well as her close personal acquaintances. More specifically, in her later years as India's prime minister, it also becomes important to analyse the contestations that she faced from political elites outside her party and how she attempted to negotiate such elite contestations in her framing of Indian state identity in both words and deed.

The BJP period presents a relatively different challenge in terms of locating the material sources that point to contestations in the framing of Indian state identity. Unlike the Nehru and even the Indira Gandhi period, the prime minister of the BJP-led government, A.B. Vajpayee, did not enjoy the same degree of dominance within his party as much as the former two did. As a result, for this period more attention needs to be paid to a larger circle of political elites as important framers of Indian state identity. More specifically, various senior politicians and leaders within the BJP party, as well as its associated Hindu-nationalist organizations, played very significant roles in their capacity as party spokespersons in the framing and negotiation of Indian state identity during this period. Besides the official publications of the BJP and its associated organizations, as well as official parliamentary exchanges, the manner in which these different individuals, in their capacity as spokespersons of these various organizations, articulated their representations of Indian state identity via the mass media is also crucial.

Chapter layout

Chapters 1 and 2 will examine the Nehru era with Chapter 1 exploring how Nehru participated in the formulation, definition and negotiation of Indian state identity in the formative years of the Indian state. Chapter 2 first examines India's foreign policy towards Pakistan within the context of the war over Kashmir in 1947–8. It then moves on to analyse India's foreign policy towards Nepal through the lens of two principles which guided Indian foreign policy towards Nepal in the 1950s – 'reciprocal relations' and India's 'special relationship' with Nepal.

Chapters 3 and 4 look at the Indira Gandhi period with Chapter 3 assessing how Mrs Gandhi's ascent to power signalled a fundamental re-negotiation of the identity of the Indian state. Such re-negotiation, it will be demonstrated, can be traced usefully by probing the discourses of democracy, secularism and anti-imperialism and their relationship to the identity of the Indian state. Chapter 4 looks firstly at the Indian state's approach towards Pakistan within the context of the Simla Agreement of 1972. It will show how specific conceptions of India's regional space and role, impacted by the changing representations of Indian state identity, led to specific Indian foreign policy outcomes towards Pakistan. The second part will analyse how such domestic identity politics impacted upon India's posture towards Sri Lanka vis-à-vis the latter's ethnic conflict in the 1980s.

Chapters 5 and 6 examine the BJP period with Chapter 5 detailing how the BJP sought to actively and fundamentally re-negotiate the idea of India in comparison with the two earlier periods via its ostensibly 'Hindu' idea of India. The manner in which such notions of 'Hindu' India were articulated by way of the three discourses will be outlined. Chapter 6 examines firstly India's perceptions towards Pakistan in relation to the 1999 Kargil War. The second Indian foreign policy episode will involve analysing the Indian state's conceptions of Bangladesh within the context of the dispute over illegal migration and terrorism in 2002. In both cases, the analysis will seek to trace how a fundamental re-negotiation of Indian state identity impacted upon the Indian state's conception of its regional space and its regional role, leading to specific foreign policy outcomes in the case of the two sets of regional relationships discussed during the BJP era.

1 Nehru and the invention of India

Judith Brown is one of the leading authorities on the history of the Indian nationalist movement and on Nehru in particular. In her authoritative biography on Nehru, she notes that in the early days after the independence of India in August 1947, the 'new' India was a deeply divided polity, along the lines of ideology, religion, class and language. In this context, Brown notes that, for Nehru, defining 'India' and 'Indian-ness' was highly problematic and as a result, 'the definition of being Indian was a critical and reopened question'.[1] Nehru, in his role as India's first prime minister, ventured to address this crucial question, along the way negotiating the problematic and contested nature of his own representations of 'India' and 'Indian-ness', sometimes against strong opposition from influential elements both within and outside his Congress Party. Despite the contestations, Nehru's overwhelming influence over the formulation and framing of the identity of the nascent Indian state is best summed up by Sunil Khilnani, when he observes that 'in the years after independence, the nationalist elite came to be dominated by a vision most closely associated with one man, Nehru'.[2] From 1947 until Nehru's death in 1964, the central ideas informing the character of the Indian state would thus be informed largely by India's first prime minister and his representation of 'Indian-ness'. One key aspect of the 'Indian-ness' that he sought to construct as an intrinsic part of the Indian state's identity was the idea of India as a 'secular' state, an idea that was rooted in the context of the painful events leading up to the partition of colonial India into the independent nation-states of India and Pakistan.

Secular nationalism: 'standing above the gods'

The definition of 'secularism', as with so many terms, is deeply contested, both theoretically as well in its actual practice. This is especially the case in the specific instance of India since its independence.[3] However, in its most basic form, secularism, as articulated by Nehru, involved a type of nationalism that was diametrically opposed to what he considered to be 'communal' or 'religious' nationalism.[4] This variety of nationalism translates into the Indian state playing the role of an independent arbitrator between different religious/communal groups and thus affording, in Nehru's words, 'equal protection by the State to all religions'.[5]

This particular representation of the Indian state has its roots in the identity-politics of pre-independent India. From the outset, one of the most obvious reasons for Nehru and the Congress Party to adopt 'secularism' as an elemental core of the party's philosophy was the need to build mass political support. In an undivided, pre-independent India, the Congress Party, under the leadership of Nehru and other political elites, realized that the reality of a multitude of various communal and religious groups within India made it imperative that a secular rather than a more narrow communal ideology was required in order to garner maximum political support under the conditions of universal franchise. More importantly a secular, non-communalist ideology was also pragmatic because of the nature of its challenge to one of the central rationalizations used by the British colonial authority to legitimize its imperial presence in India. This was the assertion that in a communally divided India, imperial authority was crucial in holding the country together, without which the different religious communities would not be able to live together peacefully within the same political unit.[6]

It was within this context that the Congress Party espoused the idea of secularism as a central tenet of Indian identity. For the purposes of claiming to speak for the whole of India in its struggle against British colonial rule, secularism as a stated party position was perceived as being politically valuable in building mass support for the Congress Party. Nehru and the leading nationalist elite within the Congress Party realized that in order to, first, claim to speak for the whole of India, and second to de-legitimize British colonial justifications for its imperial grip over India, it was politically expedient to articulate a broad, religiously inclusive identity based around secular ideals.[7] The second expedient factor for inscribing secularism as one of the fundamental tenets of Indian identity was the events surrounding the proposed partition of British India into two units – independent India and independent Pakistan.

The claim for Pakistan was made by the Muslim League on the basis of the 'two-nation theory' – that Hindus and Muslims in British India constituted two separate nations and that an undivided India meant the subjugation of the Muslim minority to the tyranny of the Hindu majority population.[8] Nehru and other leaders of the Congress Party sought to address such sentiments on the part of the Muslim League and the Muslims they represented by way of espousing 'secularism' as the basic tenet of a single united, independent India, that the Hindu majority would not subjugate Muslim and other minorities and minority rights would be zealously safeguarded within a 'secular' India.[9] For Nehru, such a 'secular' framing of India would reflect an ethos where 'religion, culture, language, the fundamental rights of the individual and the group, were all to be protected and assured by basic constitutional provisions in a democratic constitution applying essentially to all'.[10]

Such a representation of Indian secularism would first treat all identified groups (framed as majority and minority religious groups) as equal through the guarantee of democratic constitutional provisions. Second, it would also protect the unique and separate identity and needs of these minority groups. The dual underlying interests of demolishing the purported necessity of British colonialism, and the imperative of ensuring the inheritance of a united, single independent India from Britain, made this particular framing of the secularist idea central to Nehru's political strategy and aims in the period just before 1947.

The basis of Nehru's representation of secularism as a basic tenet of Indian identity and the newly independent Indian state began to gradually alter with the onset of the traumatic events accompanying the early years of independent India. In 1947, with the partition of colonial India into the independent states of India and Pakistan, predominantly Muslim populated regions were territorially partitioned to form the new state of Pakistan – the homeland of the Indian Muslims that was claimed by the Muslim League before the advent of the independence of India. In the midst of this, there occurred the greatest migration of people in history, Muslims moving from India to Pakistan and Hindus and Sikhs from Pakistan to India.[11] As a result of this migration, violence between the different communities occurred on a scale seldom seen before and there was widespread killing and looting by the Hindu, Muslim and Sikh communities in several cities.[12] Many senior Congress Party leaders, who before the partition had joined Nehru in articulating 'secularism' as an important tenet of Indian identity, began gradually to articulate Indian identity in a narrower, seemingly more anti-Muslim manner.

For example, Sardar Patel, a senior Congress Party member and Nehru's deputy in the Congress Party and the newly independent government, and India's first Home Minister, felt that since Indian Muslims had succeeded in their claim for a separate state, India should be recognized as a Hindu state and the Muslim minority that remained in India should be made to re-affirm their loyalty to the newly independent Indian state. In fact, Patel insisted that the newly independent Indian state should act in a 'ten eyes for an eye' fashion, that it should expel ten Muslims for every Hindu expelled from Pakistan.[13] Moreover, Patel's radical strategy had strong backing from both within the cabinet as well as within the Congress Party and beyond.[14] The instrumental basis for the continued articulation of an inclusive 'secularism' as a central part of the identity of the new Indian state was becoming less clear.

However, at this juncture, Nehru's interventions against defining Indian 'secularism' in such narrow terms become crucial. In a speech to the Indian Constituent Assembly (the elected body charged with framing India's constitution), four days after India's independence, Nehru re-asserted his dichotomy of secularism versus communalism, declaring that the Indian 'State is not a communal state, but a democratic state in which every citizen has equal rights. The government is determined to protect these rights'.[15]

Even in his personal correspondence, Nehru was adamant that the Congress Party, as the governing party of India, should embody a specific type of secularism, far removed from any kind of 'communal politics' or an alliance, even tacit, with 'communal parties', either Muslim or Hindu, as this would have an adverse impact on the type of secularism he wanted the Indian state itself to embody. For instance, in his correspondence with the President of a regional Congress Party chapter, Nehru was categorical in his rejection of any form of 'seat-sharing' or tacit alliance with 'communal parties' and thus any part of their 'communal' platform, even for the instrumental purpose of winning some political support from sections of the population that might lean towards such 'communal parties'. Such an uncompromising rejection of what he deemed as 'communal' was rooted in the belief that any such compromises, however politically expedient, were 'a flagrant violation of what the Congress stands for and what it has declared' and that such instrumental methods would open the way for others to 'say that we (Congress Party) are pure opportunists and have no principles at all'.[16]

Another example of Nehru's desire to inscribe a specific representation of 'secularism' for the Indian state beyond the imperatives of political expediency can be gleaned from a letter he wrote to all Chief Ministers of the Indian federal states in May 1950. In it, he makes it clear where his idea of 'secular' India was concerned:

> There can be no halfway house and no sitting on the fence [...]There can be no compromise on this issue, for any compromise can only mean a surrender of our principles and a betrayal of the cause of India's freedom.[17]

Nehru's articulations in parliament and in personal correspondence are matched by his public speeches about the need for the Indian state to resist being associated with any form of 'communalism' because it would detract significantly from the imperative to construct 'secularism' as a central aspect of Indian identity. In his address to students at Aligargh Muslim University, long seen as a pre-eminent centre of Muslim scholarship and the Muslim intelligentsia in pre-independent India, Nehru emphasized what he saw as the phenomenon 'in recent years [by] forces [that] have been at play diverting people's minds into wrong channels' and that his own vision for India was one where 'we may adhere to different religious faiths or even to none; but that does not take away from that cultural inheritance that is yours as well as mine'.[18] This specific articulation of Nehru's ideas on the framing of Indian state identity was made in the face of strong voices of opposition from political elites both within and beyond his party. Yet, despite the perceived diminishing value of his secularist discourse within the realm of popular political support, Nehru persisted in framing a specific type of secularism as a constitutive aspect of the identity of the Indian state during this period.

The formation of the independent state of Pakistan played a very important role in fostering Nehru's vision of India's secularist identity and his vision of what a future India should represent. This ideational basis for the formation of Pakistan was as troubling, if not more troubling, than the implications of the territorial partition of British India per se. It was disturbing for Nehru because of what it implied about an India within which the Hindus were the majority religious community.[19] It must be remembered that even after the formation of Pakistan, there was still a sizeable Muslim community left in independent India.[20] In fact, some of Nehru's close associates within the Congress Party, having come to terms with the formation of Pakistan as the homeland of Muslims in the Indian subcontinent, were beginning to articulate a slightly altered conception of what the nascent Indian state should come to represent in the wake of the formation of Pakistan.

The associates of Nehru within the Congress Party elites were becoming increasingly more sympathetic to the ideology of the self-styled Hindu nationalist parties. These Congress Party members (and now senior members of the newly formed Indian government), in fact drew a certain consolation from the horrific events that accompanied the partition of colonial India and the formation of the newly independent state of Pakistan. They saw the whole episode as an opportunity, at its most extreme, to rid independent India of the 'troublesome' Muslim minority and their seemingly uncompromising political demands. In their view, this specific historical juncture had lent India's new political elites the opportunity to fashion independent India as a 'state which symbolized the interests of the Hindu majority [and which] assumed that Muslim officials, even if they opted for India, were disloyal and should be dismissed'.[21] Some of these political elites even saw Nehru's determination to protect Muslim minorities against communal attacks after the partition of colonial India as adversely impacting upon their political standing among the majority Hindu community in India.[22] Therefore, these political elites within the Congress strongly contested Nehru's discourse on Indian secularism and its associated representations of Indian state identity.

Nehru, however, thought otherwise. Even though Nehru did, like some of his close associates mentioned above, see India as Pakistan's ideological opposite, this 'otherness' for Nehru meant dichotomizing Muslim Pakistan with 'secular' India, not a 'Hindu' India.

Nehru's perception of and reaction to the election of P. Tandon to the Congress Party presidency in 1950 provides a clear illustration of his position on the relationship between his brand of secularism and Indian state identity. For Nehru, Tandon's election to the Congress Presidency reflected an unwelcome development. Tandon was largely believed to represent the right-wing fringes of the Congress Party, characterized by its strident Hindu nationalist views.[23] Relations between Nehru and Tandon soured rapidly after the latter's ascendancy as party president, and on 6 August 1951, Nehru tendered his resignation from the Congress Working Committee on account of Tandon having staffed the Working Committee with a preponderance of members favourable to the latter's Hindu nationalist outlook.[24] Nehru's letter to Tandon in the immediate aftermath of the former's resignation from the Working Committee illuminates Nehru's view of the brand of secularism that should define Indian state identity. Nehru felt that under Tandon's leadership, the Congress Party was

> Rapidly drifting away from its moorings and more and more the wrong kind of people, or rather people who have the wrong kind of ideas, are gaining influence in it. The public appeal of the Congress is getting less and less. It may, and probably will, win the elections. But in the process, it may lose its soul.[25]

The Congress Party, for Nehru in this instance, had a duty not only to win popular elections but also to articulate a specific 'Indian-ness' on behalf of the Indian state it now represented. This specific 'Indian-ness' embodied a secularism that, in his view, was the binary ideational opposite of the representation of Muslim Pakistan, a state formed on the basis of a communal religious demand. His determination to challenge influential sections of his own Congress Party, even at the cost of his own position within the party, as illustrated above in the episode over Tandon's appointment, demonstrates the fierce contestations that occurred with regard to secularism as a vital aspect of Indian state identity in these early years after independence. The manner in which Indian political elites attempted to advance contending representations onto the nascent Indian state via such practices of domestic identity-politics would not be limited to this debate over secularism alone. Another much worn idea, 'democracy', would be similarly subjected to the same fierce contestations in the attempt to answer a fairly similar question: what was 'Indian democracy'?

Democracy: the tension within

In his introduction to his widely read book, *The Idea of India*, Sunil Khilnani, commenting on Nehru's legacy for contemporary India, observes that 'the period of Indian history since 1947 might be seen as the adventure of a political idea: democracy' and attributes the entrenchment and persistence of this idea to Nehru.[26] Yet, 'democracy', both as a philosophical idea and as an applied political process, is deeply contested and can have a multiplicity of meanings across both different locales and different periods. The Oxford English Dictionary defines democracy as

> government by the people; that form of government in which the sovereign power resides in the people as a whole, and is exercised either directly by them (as in the small republics of antiquity) or by officers elected by them.[27]

On an ideational level, this has broad similarities with Nehru's understanding of democracy. Nehru saw democracy as an idea that embodied the general will of the people of a country, both in their totality and in their individuality. Democracy was thus both the general collective voice of the people as well as the expression of the varying individual voices of each and every citizen of the state.[28]

On democracy as the collective voice of a people, Nehru viewed it as 'a real people's rule, by the people and for the people', while adding the caveat that he 'did not idealize the conception of the masses [and I] think of them as individuals rather than as vague groups'.[29] On democracy as an applied political practice, Nehru viewed universal adult franchise as crucial for his notion of the 'fullest democracy'.[30] Such a belief was born out of Nehru's disdain, formed during the period before India's independence, for the restriction of universal adult franchise to particular sections of the population in the United Kingdom and would have important implications for Nehru's representation of democracy and Indian state identity.[31]

The discourse of Indian democracy had important links to the discourse of Indian secularism discussed previously. Democracy was not just a formal process of voting within the context of competitive party-politics but rather provided, for Nehru, a mechanism to forge greater equality in how the state treated individuals regardless of their religious, ethnic or socio-economic background.[32] The Indian state, as a secular democracy, according to such a vision, was a guarantor of basic equality for all its citizens and not a mere proxy of the parochial interests of particular groups within Indian society.

Similar to the idea of 'secularism', the idea of 'democracy had its genesis in the Indian nationalists' attempt to confer legitimacy to their struggle against British rule, both vis-à-vis the British colonial authority and in relation to the perceptions of the Indian masses. In fact an important watershed in the nationalist movement was the transformation of the Congress Party, led primarily by Mohandas K. Gandhi, from a party of English educated Indian elites to one that could claim the support and loyalty of the large share of the Indian masses during the British colonial period.[33] The initial instrumentalist logic for embracing democracy for the purposes of conferring greater legitimacy on the Congress Party is apparent in the party's debate about whether to participate in the Constituent Assembly elections called by the colonial authority in 1937.

These elections were meant to effect the devolution of some political power from the colonial authority to Indian representatives as embodied in the 1935 Government of India Act. The Congress Party as a whole and Nehru in particular (he was the elected President of the party for the first time in 1929 and re-elected again in 1936) rejected the 1935 Act as it was seen to have been drafted

> to ensure the ultimate authority of Britain in the affairs of India, through an array of special powers vested in the Viceroy and, to a lesser extent, in the Governors of the provinces.[34]

However, this position posed a major dilemma for the Congress Party. On one hand, by contesting these elections the Congress would be implicitly endorsing the legitimacy of the 1935 Act, yet if it boycotted the elections, it would lose the opportunity to demonstrate its legitimacy via the electoral support it expected to receive from the most significantly increased adult franchise to date.[35]

Nehru's position, which became the Congress position (after some debate), was that the Congress would reject the Act 'in its entirety' while agreeing to contest the elections in order 'to bring the Congress message to the masses'.[36] The decision to contest the elections was made, notwithstanding the misgivings listed earlier, despite the recognition that the odds were stacked against the Congress Party to some extent. The franchise was limited – total adult franchise would have made Congress victory easier, given its mass-based appeal and roots – and separate electorates were set up for Muslims, which were expected to swing votes away from the Congress Party towards the Muslim League.[37] Despite all this, the Congress Party, with Nehru at the helm, decided that it would contest the 1937 elections. In the event, the Congress Party won and its main challenger, the Muslim League, fared poorly at gaining its share of the Muslim vote, despite its contention that it was the sole political representative of Muslims in colonial India.[38]

The 1937 elections, when viewed through the prism of democratic ideals outlined earlier, (that of democracy reflecting the general will of the populace collectively and individually), fell way short. The elections ensured the persistence of the undemocratic character of British colonial authority over India, reinforced the position of the unelected Indian monarchs in the princely states and had a restricted adult franchise. Despite these shortcomings, the Congress Party decided to participate in these elections because of the political legitimacy, however qualified, that these conferred on the party as the principal Indian party in the political struggle against British colonial authority.

With the advent of the partition of British India into two parts – India and Pakistan – the Congress Party, with Nehru at its helm, was installed as the popularly elected representative of the new Indian nation-state.[39] At this juncture, two specific challenges confronted Nehru and the Congress Party in their attempts to define the democratic identity of the Indian state. The first of these was the debate concerning the construction of specific political structures for the newborn Indian state, part of which included the task of drafting a new constitution.[40] The second was Nehru's ideas on socialism and the specific manner in which such socialist ideals were negotiated with democratic ideals and practices in framing the identity of the Indian state.

The place of 'democracy' in pre-independent India, as both a set of ideas and as a procedural form, remained largely influenced by the Congress Party's political strategy of conferring legitimacy upon itself as the chief voice of Indians in its struggle both against British colonial authority and in its opposition to political parties that claimed to represent only certain religious communities. As Khilnani so astutely observes of the period leading up to and immediately after the 1937 elections, 'during these years of slow entry into the portals of the Raj, democracy did not capture its concentrated attention', referring to the 'concentrated attention' of both the Congress Party and the majority of the Indian population towards the idea and practice of 'democracy'.[41] After independence, the Congress Party was faced with entrenching a functional constitutional democracy among a largely illiterate, rural and impoverished population. The inauguration of the Indian Constitution of 1950, by which India became a Republic, would become a reference point for the future discourse and functioning of democracy in the country. It would also outline a vision of the democratic Indian state and the latter's role in this nascent project of Indian democracy. Overall, it represented a commitment on the part of Indian political elites to bestow on the new state 'an ideal of legality and procedural conduct', to infuse the newly independent Indian state with a democratic ethos through the procedural forms of constitutional parliamentary democracy.[42]

For Nehru, the idea of India as a 'democratic' nation-state was synonymous with the idea of India as 'secular' nation-state. This meant that character and practice of 'democracy' should not translate into any form of the tyranny of the majority, with special reference especially to the Hindu majority population vis-à-vis other religious minorities. It was this need to protect minority religious rights and especially Muslim minority rights that prompted the debate on formulating a uniform civil code for all the different religious communities within the constitution of India.

Before independence, the different communities were subject to their own respective religious personal laws when it came to matters such as marriage, divorce and property succession rights.[43] With special attention to the equality of the rights of women in issues of marriage, divorce and succession to property, Nehru expressed his desire for a uniform civil code. However, he was alert to the fact that the establishment of such a code would effectively mean the demise of Hindu and Muslim personal law.[44]

Nehru was aware that any attempt to enact a uniform civil code would be met by strong resistance from the leaders of different religious communities. However, he still attempted to reform Hindu personal law by way of legislation without actually enacting a uniform civil code for the whole country.[45] His attempts were not successful until 1955. By 1955, India's parliament had passed in legislation, as separate legal acts, what has come to be known as the Hindu Code Bills that brought Hindu personal law in line with secular-civil laws based upon the principle of enshrining equality of men and women, as well as reflecting other progressive ideas.[46] In effect, this legal reformulation of Hindu personal law made its content akin to provisions that would otherwise have been contained in a uniform civil code.

However, Nehru moved away from legislating any changes in Muslim personal law. In effect, this meant that Muslims were still subject to the Muslim personal law that they had been subjected to before independence, while the

Hindu community, ostensibly still covered by their own Hindu personal law, were in practice being subjected to a form of personal law hardly different from the provisions of a modern, civil code.[47] Nehru's conception of how such a state of affairs was acceptable is testimony to a specific tension in his framing of the idea of Indian democracy.

On one hand, the Directive Principles within the Indian constitution (that are non-binding but seen as articles to be strived for) assert that the Indian 'state shall endeavour to secure for the citizens a uniform civil code throughout the territory of India'. Yet, on the other hand, under the Fundamental Rights section in the constitution, 'subject to public order, morality and health and to the other provisions of this Part, all persons are equally entitled to freedom of conscience and the right freely to profess, practise and propagate religion'.[48] The former provision while striving to instruct the state – probably at some future point – to enact a uniform civil code in the interests of equality seems to be in direct contradiction to the latter provision pertaining to the freedom to practice and profess religion. This is because if Muslim and Hindu personal law are regarded as an integral part of the practice of an individual's religious practice, they are guaranteed under the Fundamental Rights section of the Indian constitution.

This tension in the construction of a specific type of Indian democracy mirrored Nehru's own conflicting ideas on the role of the Indian state in entrenching democracy. While understanding the potential risks of the state intruding upon the agency of individual citizens, he also saw the state as having a potentially important role to play in aiding various groups within Indian society. In the case of such minority and/or disadvantaged groups, he believed that the Indian state, and the political elites that represent it, must aim to 'produce the sense of absolute security in the minds of the [...] minorities. The majority always owes a duty of this kind to the minority'.[49] This sentiment informed several other provisions that were included in the constitution in 1950.

Various parts of the new Indian constitution thus reflected the divergent pulls on Nehru's conception and discourse of 'democracy' for an independent India. On one hand, he saw the need for the Indian state to act as the catalyst and vehicle for change in the sphere of social justice, given the wide degree of social and economic inequality with the country, whilst on the other, he was at pains to ensure that the Indian state did not intervene excessively in the personal sphere of individual Indian citizens. This tension would also come to characterize Nehru's conception of Indian democratic character over a very important debate: the role of socialist principles in framing the Indian state's identity.

Although the preamble to the 1950 constitution spelt out the imperative for 'justice, social, economic and political' for the newly independent state, the exact manner of achieving 'justice' was deeply contested between Nehru and different groups of political elites.[50] A major point of contention was the issue of enshrining the right to private property as one of the fundamental rights within the constitution. Nehru wanted to imbue the constitution and consequently the Indian state with a socialist, re-distributive ethos via a centralized state initiative to nationalize major industry. He saw the capitalist classes as having

> proved totally inadequate to face things as they are today in this country [...]and the only alternative is to put forward some big thing ourselves and rope in not only these classes but the people as a whole. Otherwise we remain stagnant and at the most ward off catastrophe.[51]

This view was in stark opposition to Sardar Patel, his deputy, who was of the persuasion that 'to remove all stimulus to private enterprise at that juncture in the country's history was to sign the death-warrant of India' and thus opposed Nehru's attempt to saddle the Indian state with any overtly socialist, centralized re-distributive role.[52] In this respect, Patel was not merely expressing his personal convictions but representing a wider body of opinion within the Congress Party who were wary of Nehru's socialist re-distributive ideas.[53] In the end, Nehru was unable to prevent the listing of the right of property as a fundamental right within the constitution but he was successful overall in managing to incorporate the discourse and ideals of centralized, state-directed redistributive policies as a fundamental tenet of Indian democracy with the formation of the National Planning Commission in 1951 (after Patel's death in 1950).

By the mid-1950s, Nehru's public discourse on the type of democracy with which the new Indian state should be identified began to be associated with the term, 'a socialist pattern of society'.[54] For example, in a speech to Parliament in 1954, he proclaimed that 'the pattern of society we look forward to is a socialist pattern of society which is classless, casteless' and, at its sixtiethth session in 1955, Nehru oversaw the adoption by the Congress Party of a resolution 'aiming at a socialistic pattern of society'.[55] The death of Patel in 1950 marked the end of one of the strongest opponents to Nehru within the Congress Party. In terms of identity politics, this meant that Nehru's ability to negotiate the place of socialist ideas within the discourse and practice of Indian democracy was largely enhanced by the waning of the power of the right-wing faction within the Congress Party.[56] By the mid-1950s Nehru's vision of a centralized, socialist-redistributive democracy was unchallenged. Nehru envisioned a particular type of socialism for India, a socialism that was redistributive but not necessarily revolutionary.

For Nehru, this variant of the socialist ideal was an integral aspect of the larger democratic identity of the Indian state, for it emphasized the importance of effecting economic redistribution and thus equality.[57] However, Nehru was conscious of the tensions in the discourse and practice of democracy that this might lead to and consequently in the way Indians and non-Indians perceived the identity of the newborn Indian state. In his public pronouncements Nehru sought to clarify the assumption that any kind of socialism necessarily means authoritarianism. It does not – at least in theory; in practice, I think it depends on how a country will develop.[58]

Such tensions between centralizing tendencies and the creation of a democratic polis that safeguarded the great diversity and difference that characterized independent India became evident in Congress's attempt to craft the relationship between the constituent provincial states and the central government within a federally constituted India. Although Nehru foresaw the constituent states within the Indian Union operating largely autonomously within a federal structure, he was keen to ensure that the central government would not be frustrated by the constituent state governments in the pursuit of his vision of the Indian state embarking on nationwide reformist, social-re-distributive programmes and policies. As a leading observer of Indian politics points out:

> There has been a *basic tension* [emphasis added] in the post-Independence political order, arising in part out of features of the Indian Constitution itself, between authoritarian and democratic tendencies. These in turn overlap with the forces favouring centralization and those favouring decentralization.[59]

This tension would come to characterize the discourse and practice of Indian democracy during and after Nehru's lifetime. Wielding the power of being both prime minister of India and the most influential nationalist leader in India after 1950, Nehru sought to infuse the discourse of democracy with socialist ideals and practices associated with the Indian state. Nehru's vision of the democratic Indian state lay in his the image of India as a socialist-democratic country, signifying its identity as a democracy that championed libertarian ideals while providing an equal socio-economic plane for the true practice of democratic equality among its populace. This complex framing of India's democratic identity at home would come to influence Nehru's vision of India's role in South Asia and India's foreign policy towards its neighbours in this region.

Anti-imperialism: the sanctity of territorial integrity

It has already been noted that that the independence of India brought with it great challenges for the framing of a particular, representative identity of the Indian state, given the sheer range of diversity in India in 1947. As discussed before, opposition to British colonialism formed a durable and effective foundation upon which a conception of being 'Indian' could be articulated and framed. Rather ironically for the Congress Party, independence in 1947 threatened to undermine this foundation of 'Indian-ness'. The more general nature of this predicament is clearly spelt out by Brown when she notes that nations have to go on being constantly re-created in the experience of those who compose them, particularly in the context of decolonization, when the common enemy against which the nationalists defined themselves, the former imperial power, has been removed.[60]

India faced a problem similar to other self-professed nations or nation-states. The idea of India as embodying the struggle against imperialism, in the form of British colonialism, was a key feature in the representation of India's identity before the advent of independence. However, once independence from Britain was gained in 1947, this core tenet of Indian identity became, potentially at least, more tenuous. Nevertheless, the discourse of anti-imperialism was also tied to another crucial notion for India's nationalist elites: territoriality.

Since independence, the specific ways in which the Indian state has zealously guarded its territorial borders as part of its nation-building project has been well documented in the literature.[61] The Indian political elite's preliminary encounter with the issue of territoriality was symbolized in the few years before independence in 1947 by the claim for Pakistan and the status of the Indian princely states. On the issue of the princely states, a brief background is necessary before one can understand how Nehru and other Indian political elites perceived and reacted to this particular issue in both the pre and post independent periods.

After the Indian mutiny of 1857, the British imperial 'Raj' divided India into two constitutionally separate units. One category was termed 'British India' and referred to approximately two-thirds of the area and three-quarters of the population of pre-independent India. The second category was termed 'Indian India' and consisted of about 600 princely states, the vast majority of which were ruled by autocratic monarchs. These ranged widely in terms of size but all of them were linked constitutionally with the British government through the doctrine of paramountcy. This meant that the British government was responsible for their defence, foreign relations and communications, while the feudal rulers remained autonomous in their internal affairs. However, in practice, the presence of a British Resident in each of these states meant that their internal autonomy was limited largely by the contours of the British government's own interests and goals. In effect, the relationship was one of suzerainty of the British Crown over the individual princely states.[62]

For Nehru, in addition to the ideational implications of creating an independent Pakistan, the territorial implications of such a partition threatened the future viability of an independent Indian state in international politics. This weakness would stem from, among other factors, its territorial diminution. In Nehru's own words,

> Whether India is properly to be regarded as one nation or two does not matter, for the modern idea of nationality has been almost divorced from statehood. The national state is too small a unit today and small states can have no independent existence. It is doubtful if even

many of the larger national states can have any real independence. The national state is thus giving way to the multi-national state or to large federations.[63]

The prospect of the territorial diminution of a newly independent India was seen by Nehru, and many in the Congress Party, as a significant setback for the party's political interests and goals in the aftermath of British withdrawal. For Nehru and the Congress Party, the view was that independent India needed to retain the territorial boundaries of the British Raj because, without it, India would descend into a weak state in global affairs, without the influence and sovereign independence it deserved. Besides a reduction of independent India's influence and stature due to its reduced territorial size, territorial partition would weaken India further through disruption of administrative and economic links across India that had been developed during British rule.[64] Nehru was thus of the view that the territorial division of the country 'would be injurious to the defence, development and planning of the country'.[65] The need to be a territorially cohesive political unit was therefore informed by the imperative of ensuring independent India was not weakened in terms of its military defence and its economic development.[66] Any territorial diminution of British India would be a telling blow to independent India's attempt to take its place in world affairs as the robust and prosperous symbol of anti-imperialism that Nehru envisaged.

The eventual partition of India into two independent political units magnified this anxiety over territoriality and India's existence as a durable nation-state amongst Indian political elites, especially those in the Congress Party. This anxiety acutely impacted upon the Congress Party's view on the unresolved issue of the Indian princely states at India's independence in August 1947. Although these princely states were largely expected to accede to either India or Pakistan on the basis of a negotiated settlement, some of the larger princely states held the belief that they could maintain their independence from both of these successor states.[67] By the time of India's independence, the three princely states of Kashmir, Hyderabad and Junagadh had still not been formally incorporated as part of the Indian Union and their respective rulers were determined in their effort to remain independent of the Indian state. Nehru's view towards the incorporation of these three states was equally uncompromising. After the territorial division that led to the formation of Pakistan, any further assault on the territorial integrity of the newly independent Indian state was to be strongly resisted.[68]

The link between the discourse of territorial integrity and the discourse of anti-imperialism is clearly visible in the perceptions of Indian political elites in their response to a proposal of the departing British government, drafted between April and March 1947, for the specific arrangements of transferring political power once the British colonial authority left India. The plan, which came to be known as 'Plan Balkan' amongst the Indian nationalist elites, proposed the transfer of power from the departing colonial authority to various provinces of British India that would then decide whether or not to enter into larger unions to form India or Pakistan.[69]

Nehru rejected the plan completely and strongly, viewing in it the British rejection of the 'basic conception of India' and which ran counter to the notion that, territorially, any transfer of British power must accept that 'the union of India had to be the fundamental premise of any proposals'.[70] The plan, as seen by Nehru, amounted to the British government promoting the 'Balkanization' of India with all its attendant disastrous consequences. One of these was that the small provinces would claim themselves to be independent and involve themselves in 'subordinate alliances' with the British government in order to preserve their existence.[71] This proposal's rejection of the territorial integrity of 'India' by the British was thus linked, in Nehru's perception, to the British government's desire to sustain some form of imperial control over its former colony.

For Nehru, the idea of India was crucially linked to territoriality and the defence of India's territorial integrity was a symbol of India's resistance to any form of imperialism. For Nehru, the discourse of the Indian state as a symbol of anti-imperialism thus became linked very early on with the defence of the territory that he deemed to be 'India'. It was a reflection of this crucial link between territorial integrity and the discourses of anti-imperialism that the constitution of India contains provisions within it not permitting the ceding of territory to another state or power without an amendment of the Indian constitution requiring a majority in the Indian Lok Sabha.[72] This link between the discourse of anti-imperialism, Indian state identity and the need to defend Indian territorial integrity was to persist beyond the Nehru period.

Conclusion

The towering influence and personality of Jawaharlal Nehru within the Indian nationalist movement would come to play a crucial role in defining the idea of India at its birth in 1947. Throughout his tenure, Nehru, sought to represent Indian state identity in a specific and distinct manner. This however, did not mean that his articulations on secularism, democracy and anti-imperialism went unchallenged from different sets of elites both within and outside the Congress Party. Within the context of such contestations inherent in domestic identity politics, Nehru endeavoured to frame Indian state identity in relation to the discourses of secular democracy, whereby the Indian state would balance the imperatives of its role as an agent of social change together with protecting the rights and liberties of individuals within the state. For Nehru, the Indian state represented a proud embodiment of resistance to different forms of imperialism, as well as a democratic state that sought to provide assurances and guarantees for the protection of the rights of religious minorities.

Nehru was not only India's pre-eminent nationalist leader and its first prime minister; he was also the Indian state's most prominent and articulate spokesman when it came to India's foreign policy. Being both the first prime minister and first external affairs minister of India, Nehru did not view, contrary to prevailing opinion, a state's domestic and external realms as two discrete spheres. In such a conception, 'Indian-ness' was as much about how the Indian state interacted with other states as it was about the complexion of the Indian state domestically. This was especially the case when it came to India's immediate region: South Asia.

2 Nehru and the birth of India's regional policy
The case of Pakistan and Nepal

For Nehru, India's independence was a significant moment not only for Indians but for the rest of the world as well because, 'the emergence of India in world affairs is something of a major consequence in world history'.[1] India, in Nehru's view, was destined to play a major role in global affairs and its foreign policy would reflect India's unique contribution to the wider world.

This chapter will consider how such domestically constructed representations of Indian state identity influenced specific regional policy outcomes on the basis of particular conceptions of the Indian state's regional space and role. To make this argument, this chapter will first will briefly discuss the type of role Nehru sought to construct for India in global affairs on the basis of his representation of Indian state identity and how this formed a wider context within which India's regional role was conceived. It will then argue that conceptions of India's regional role, though influenced by, were not derived directly from its wider global role. This will be done by first examining India's core regional relationship with Pakistan within the specific context of the first war between India and Pakistan over the state of Jammu and Kashmir and second its regional policy towards the state of Nepal within the context of its 'special relationship' with the latter throughout the 1950s. In both cases, the analysis will examine the manner in which domestic representations of Indian state identity influenced specific regional policy outcomes on the basis of the Indian state's conception of its own regional space and role.

Nehru as global statesman: conceptions of India's regional roles

Besides being of principal influence within the domestic realm, Nehru was also the chief authority in the formulating of India's foreign policy and constructing India's role within its region and beyond. In his position as India's spokesman to the world, Nehru attempted to frame India's overall foreign policy to reflect the broad 'idea' of India that he had constructed domestically.[2] In such a context, Nehru's conceptualization of India's regional space and regional role was intimately influenced by his conception of India's broader global role. Yet, in many ways, Indian foreign policy in South Asia had its own distinctive character. Nehru's prominent part in the founding of the Afro-Asian and Non-Aligned movements is significant to a consideration of his conceptualization of India's wider global role. His attempts to place the Indian state at the forefront of both movements set the tone for Nehru's conceptualization of India's place in the world and the role it should perform on the global stage.

India's domestic self-conception as a nation that was strongly anti-colonial and anti-imperialist led naturally to Nehru positioning the Indian state as a leader in the resistance to attempts by Western powers to curtail the newly found independence of postcolonial states in foreign affairs. Nehru's instrumental role in founding the Afro-Asian and Non-Aligned movement, and his attempt to establish India's central role within these movements, were largely informed by Indian domestic self-conceptions about India as a symbol of resistance to any form of continued domination from Western states.[3]

Moreover, for Nehru, India presented the possibility for the building of a democratic and secular postcolonial state. The Indian state for him represented a demonstration of the fact that a representative democracy could work effectively in newly independent postcolonial states. Thus Nehru's India was the 'Light of Asia' in this postcolonial space, a symbol of how the democratic imperatives of economic betterment and provision of individual liberty could be accomplished in the newly independent countries of Asia and beyond.[4]

In Nehru's perception, the global role of India lay in playing a leading role within the Afro-Asian, postcolonial space, heading a movement of postcolonial states that refused to be part of Cold War bloc politics, and demonstrating the possibility of building a postcolonial state that could deliver economic development, democratic liberties and equal treatment to its citizens. Such global role conceptions thus provided a context within which Nehru conceptualized India's role within its immediate region, South Asia. Nehru's conception of India's regional role did not however flow directly and unproblematically from such conceived roles at the global level. India's regional relationship with Pakistan during the Nehru era was a key example of how certain perceptions of India's role pertinent to South Asia led to specific outcomes in India's foreign policy within its immediate region.

The two-nation theory: Kashmir, Pakistan and the issue of the princely states

The demand for Pakistan – a separate, independent nation-state and a homeland for Indian Muslims – was articulated most clearly by Mohammad Ali Jinnah, the leader of the Muslim League.[5] His demand for Pakistan, based on the idea that Muslims and Hindus in colonial India constituted two separate nations, was famously articulated in March 1940 as part of the famous Lahore Resolution.[6] This belief in the two-nation theory, in the conviction that the Muslims of India would be dominated by the majority Hindu community once British rule terminated, was to lead to the founding of the independent state of Pakistan on 14 August 1947, a day before India obtained its independence.

The issue of Kashmir as a factor in Indian–Pakistani relations arose at the onset of the birth of the two states in 1947. As discussed in Chapter 1, the status of the princely states within the British Empire after the end of British colonial rule was not defined very clearly. The doctrine of paramountcy, which spelt out the nature of Britain's colonial relationship with the various princely states, was to come to an end with Britain's withdrawal in August 1947, yet the future status of the princely states was not clearly outlined. Stuck between honouring British treaty relations and the guarantees contained therein with the princely states and accommodating the desire of both Indian and Pakistani political elites to incorporate these states as constituent parts of the two new states, the British gave mixed and equivocal directions for the future status of these states. They therefore assured the princes of these states that the British government would not automatically transfer control of their states to an independent Indian or Pakistani government but instead allow the various states a period within which to decide whether or not to enter 'into a federal relationship with the successor government or governments in British India or failing this entering into particular political arrangements with it or them'.[7] This created two sets of problems. First, the basis upon which these states should join either India or Pakistan was not outlined clearly. It was not apparent whether or not it should be based on the religious affiliation of the princely ruler or of that of the majority of the people of the state. Second, some of the princely rulers began to interpret the lack of clarity by the British authorities regarding the future status of the princely states as an opportunity for them to remain rulers of their states independent from both the states of India and Pakistan. Both sets of problems would plague the issue of Kashmir's future and its pivotal place in India–Pakistan relations.

The princely state of Jammu and Kashmir had a Hindu ruler, Maharaja Hari Singh and a majority Muslim population at the time of independence. From the outset, Hari Singh intended to remain independent of both India and Pakistan and was unwilling to accede to any one of the two states.[8] The Pakistani claim to the princely state of Jammu and Kashmir was based upon the notion that it was a Muslim majority area and that it was geographically contiguous to areas that would form the state of Pakistan.[9] Nehru, as the leading articulator of India's position, laid claim to the princely state on the grounds that the people of the state itself should decide on whether they wished to join India or Pakistan. This position was made keeping in mind the Jammu and Kashmir National Conference Party (NC) and its charismatic leader Sheikh Abdullah, enjoying wide support in the state in its opposition to Hari Singh's rule, and the fact that the NC was drawn towards Nehru's brand of secularist politics, rather than Jinnah's notion of a Muslim homeland.[10] At the time of Indian and Pakistani independence, the status of the princely state was still not settled and Hari Singh offered to sign standstill agreements with both India and Pakistan, with the stated purpose of allowing the Maharaja more time to decide which state to join.[11] However, two months later in October 1947 events took a dramatic turn when the first spark of the impending war between India and Pakistan over Kashmir was ignited.

Popular uprising or Pakistani aggression? The first Indo-Pak war over Kashmir

On 22 of October 1947, armed tribesmen entered Kashmir from Pakistan and used force against the local Kashmiri forces to push their way towards the capital, Srinagar. There are two rival narratives of the role that the Pakistani state is supposed to have played in this armed invasion. The Pakistani government claimed that these tribesmen were 'liberators' who had gone into Kashmir in order to free their fellow Muslims from the tyranny of the Hindu ruler, Hari Singh. Although they claimed that their sympathy was with the armed invaders, they insisted that the state was not complicit in the invasion and that all reasonable steps had been taken to prevent the infiltration.[12] The Indian government disagreed with such a version of events. Nehru, in a speech to the Indian Constituent Assembly, pointed out that his government had 'sufficient evidence [...] that the whole business of the Kashmir raid [...] was deliberately organized by high officials of the Pakistani government' and that the Pakistani state had 'supplied them (the tribesmen) with the implements of war, with lorries, with petrol and with officers'.[13]

In any event, four days later Hari Singh asked for Indian military intervention in Kashmir in return for signing the Instrument of Accession and becoming a constituent part of the Indian state. Indian troops arrived, defeated and drove back the armed tribesmen and managed to retain control of the capital Srinagar. Just as the military operation finished, the political dispute began. It was a dispute that would last from that day in October 1947 until the present day.

Kashmir in the idea of India: core and periphery

The brief narrative outlined in the previous subsection of the war between Pakistan and India over Kashmir leads to two important sets of questions. First, within the context of the Kashmir war, in what ways did domestic representations of Indian state identity impact the Indian state's perception of its regional space and regional role? Second, in what ways did these conceptions influence specific foreign policy outcomes towards Pakistan within the context of the Kashmir conflict?

Although in the geographical periphery of the Indian state, Kashmir was always at the heart of the democratic and secular imaginings of India. This element of Indian state identity informed Nehru's initial approach towards perceived Pakistani complicity in the armed challenge to the

Maharaja's rule in 1947. Nehru's reflections testify to the important position of Kashmir within his conception of a secular India. In a personal interview and reflecting on Kashmir, Nehru argued that

> probably in Kashmir, more than anywhere else in India, there has been less of what is called communal feeling, and Hindus and Muslims and others have very rarely quarrelled [...] Their culture is alike, their language, eating habits, and whatever goes to make a culture.[14]

The position of Kashmir according to Nehru's representation of Indian secularism as a binary opposite to what he termed 'communalism' was thus crucial. In Nehru's view, Kashmir and the Kashmiris were historically 'non-communal' and thus 'secular', just as India, in his representation, had historically been 'secular' and not 'communal'. This 'secular–communal' binary in Nehru's view of Kashmir becomes especially important when considered alongside his conception of India's secular disposition as a binary opposite to his view of Pakistan as a communal idea. Kashmir, being ideationally secular, thus belonged within the ideational and territorial boundaries of a secular India.

The crucial place of Kashmir within Nehru's idea of India was also apparent to well-placed non-Indians. In a confidential report to the US Secretary of State, Dean Acheson in August 1949, the then US Ambassador to India, Loy W. Henderson notes that he sensed that Nehru was

> under too deep obligations in Kashmir. He would give the State up, only in case the Kashmir people should freely express their desire not to remain a part of India. The Kashmir issue affected the underlying philosophy of India which was that of a secular progressive state.[15]

The perceived attempts by the Pakistani government to forcibly incorporate Kashmir as a part of the 'communal', two-nation concept of Pakistan were thus viewed through this prism. According to Nehru, the Pakistani state wanted to confirm and reinforce the 'communal' basis of the two-nation idea by demonstrating that Muslim majority Kashmir would reject any union with the Hindu majority Indian state. Therefore, for Nehru it was essential to resist such use of force that would attempt to confirm the 'communal' Pakistan idea and to repudiate the 'secular' idea of India. Thus, Nehru translated a clash over the princely state of Jammu and Kashmir into a battle over two contending identities of statehood – secularism against communalism.

However, another important aspect of Indian identity tempered Nehru's approach towards Indian claims over Kashmir in the aftermath of independence, as well as after the 1947 war with Pakistan. Despite the temptation of authoritarianism in the wake of his overwhelming public support within India as Gandhi's heir, Nehru sought to ensure that democracy was represented as an integral part of the idea of India. In the case of Kashmir, this

Nehru and the birth of India's regional policy 33

democratic ideal also informed Nehru's approach. There is evidence to suggest that even before the signing of the standstill agreement with the Maharaja and the armed challenge to the latter's rule, Nehru was of the view that the Maharajah should make a decision to join either India or Pakistan on the basis of the popular choice. Certain deliberations between Lord Mountbatten, the last Viceroy of colonial India and the first Governor General of independent India, and Maharaja Hari Singh show evidence of this.[16] Mountbatten is quoted as saying that in his discussions with the Maharajah, he advised the latter that he should ascertain the wishes of his people and join either India or Pakistan on the basis of the collective will of the people. More importantly he adds that

> had he [the Maharajah] acceded to Pakistan before August 14, the future government of India had allowed me to give His Highness the assurance that no objection whatsoever would be raised by them.[17]

Thus, there was already some evidence that Nehru was prepared to allow popular, democratic choice to determine the status of the state of Jammu and Kashmir, even if it meant that it might become a part of Pakistan rather than India.[18] Democracy, as one of the central pillars of the new Indian state, was therefore an important influence for Nehru's response to the status of Jammu and Kashmir at this stage.

The influence of the idea of India as a democracy on Nehru's position on Kashmir is further evidenced by events following the signing of the Instrument of Accession in October 1947. Legally, under the terms of the Indian Independence Act, the Indian state could claim the princely state of Jammu and Kashmir as being a constitutive part of the Indian state without further argument.[19] Yet, Nehru was still of the view that a democratic India could only accept Kashmir's accession on the basis of popular, democratic choice and that the princely state's accession to India would be conditional on it being endorsed by the popular will of the people of the state. On the same day as receiving the Maharajah's request and Instrument of Accession, Nehru informed the British Prime Minister, Clement Atlee of the developing situation and endeavoured to

> Make it clear that any question of aiding Kashmir in this emergency is not designed in any way to influence the State to accede to India. Our view which we have repeatedly made public is that the question of accession in any disputed territory or State must be decided in accordance with the wishes of the people and we adhere to this view.[20]

The issue concerned the manner in which the popular will of the people in the state could be ascertained. Talks between Nehru and Liaquat Ali Khan, Ali Jinnah's deputy, failed to achieve a breakthrough on how to move forward in ascertaining the democratic will of the Kashmiri people and thus deciding the future of the princely state. At the suggestion of Lord Mountbatten, the governments of India and Pakistan agreed to refer the matter to the United Nations (UN) to act as an impartial arbitrator.[21] Nehru's agreement to this course of action is significant. Despite the fact that India had legal jurisdiction over Kashmir after the signing of the Instrument of Accession by Hari Singh, Nehru was nevertheless willing to allow the UN to arbitrate between India and Pakistan in order for a democratic decision to be reached on the future of the Kashmir state.[22] Moreover, this to some extent reflected Nehru's broader view that the United Nations was a vehicle with the potential to overcome super-power bloc politics and a forum for the Afro-Asian post-colonial nations to resolve differences amicably without succumbing to the 'new' imperialism of bloc politics.[23]

Anti-imperialism is the third discourse central to defining the Indian state at this juncture and also influenced Nehru's approach to Pakistan in the context of this issue. Nehru's advice to Sheikh Abdullah concerning the appropriate response to Pakistan's demands on Kashmir demonstrates this. In December 1947, Nehru explained to Abdullah the various pressures impinging upon him as a result of his approach towards the war with Pakistan over Kashmir and that

> You well know the situation in Kashmir is extremely complicated [...] Any false step may add to our difficulties. If it was a simple matter of using military force only, that would at least be a straight issue even thought it might be difficult. But everything is so interlinked [...] We are acting now in Kashmir on a world stage and the greatest interest is being taken by other countries [...] especially the Great Powers.[24]

Nehru's primary aim was to ensure that the influence of the two super-powers within the context of the Cold War did not impinge upon India's foreign policy in South Asia. As outlined earlier, Nehru referred the Kashmir issue to the UN on the basis of his representation of that body as a 'symbol of hope', especially for newly independent countries in their pursuit of independence in global and domestic affairs in the face of Cold War bloc politics.[25] Having staked its role in world affairs on the basis of its domestic identity – a secular-democracy that symbolized a resistance to any form of Western imperialism – the Indian state found it difficult to refuse a settlement of the Kashmir issue, subject to the democratic will of the Kashmiri people and the good offices of the United Nations.

However, there was a particular tension between representing India's regional space, its role with within this region and India's role in world affairs during the Nehru period. As Krishna, in his study of postcolonial nationhood in South Asia, notes, during this period Nehru did little to advance Indian claims of regional supremacy, mainly because of a tension between what he terms

> a self-fashioning as a peaceful, non-violent country that represented a genuinely new force in the world and a self-fashioning as a regional power that inherited the British presence in the sub-continent.[26]

Nehru and the birth of India's regional policy 35

This tension had come to the fore by the mid-1950s, due to the manner in which Nehru perceived two developments: the Kashmir issue in the UN was reaching a stalemate without any probability of a satisfactory resolution and Pakistan had decided to join the Southeast Asian Treaty Organization (SEATO).

In the UN, the first significant development in the Kashmir dispute came with the adoption, by the United Nations Commission for India and Pakistan (UNCIP), of a resolution on 13 August 1948 that a plebiscite be held in the state of Jammu and Kashmir in order to ascertain the will of the people in the state and to thus decide the future status of Kashmir.[27] Disagreements arose between India and Pakistan regarding the details of implementation of the plebiscite. The most significant of these pertained to the withdrawal of the armed forces on both sides before conditions suitable for a plebiscite could be ensured. The actual details of the implementation of this plebiscite were dogged by objections and criticisms by both Indian and Pakistani representatives at the United Nations. The crux of the difference was clear: Pakistan wanted itself and India to be subject to the same conditions and restrictions and thus to be treated on an equal footing, while the Indian position was that Pakistan was guilty of aggression and, by virtue of the Instrument of Accession, India had the responsibility to safeguard the defence of the state in any interim stage and thus should not be treated in the same manner as Pakistan.[28] These two sets of outlooks prevented the opportunity for a free and fair plebiscite to be administered in the state. However, events beyond Kashmir were taking place that would in effect mould India's position on the Kashmir issue and the future status of the princely state.

President Eisenhower's announcement in February 1954 that the United States would extend military assistance to Pakistan is often seen, as one writer points out, 'as a sudden break with the past and the beginning of an entirely new era'.[29] Furthermore, Pakistan became a member of the United States-led SEATO (Southeast Asian Treaty Organization) and the Baghdad Pact military alliances in September 1954.[30] For Nehru, this signalled a very perilous development. Pakistan's new memberships heralded the entry of super-power Cold War politics into South Asia and India's dispute with Pakistan over Kashmir more specifically The fact that the Pakistani government was now being provided with military hardware at no cost caused concern in India.[31] Moreover, the very notion that a foreign power could influence events in India's immediate region through a proxy state via a military alliance was seen as a major setback for preserving independent action in India's foreign policy. For Nehru, an attack on the independence of India's foreign policy translated into an assault on one of the central pillars of the Indian state, freedom from imperialism. Evidence of this can be gleaned from one of Nehru's speeches made in the Indian lower house of parliament, the Lok Sabha a few days after Pakistan's decision to join SEATO and the Baghdad Pact. In his speech, Nehru points out that people might remember the old days when the great powers had spheres of influence in Asia and elsewhere. The countries of Asia were then too weak to do anything about it [...] It seems to me that this particular Manila Treaty is inclined dangerously in the direction of spheres of influence to be exercised by powerful countries. After all, it is the big and powerful countries that will decide matters and not the two or three weak and small Asian countries that may be allied to them.[32]

As an example of present-day great powers carving out spheres of influence, Nehru's reference to the Manila Treaty – and Pakistan's membership of this alliance – spoke directly to the danger of India's foreign policy in South Asia being held hostage to the imperialist implications of Cold War bloc politics. The fact that Pakistan, its regional neighbour, could use its membership in the alliance to bring the military and political power of the US to bear on India's regional policy was a direct challenge to the Indian state's sovereignty in international affairs and thus to its self-conception as a symbol of anti-imperialism. In this case Nehru believed that India's own immediate regional space was in danger of being controlled by the great powers like the United States. Constructed domestically, this prism of anti-imperialism coloured Nehru's perception of Pakistan's bond with the US Cold War alliance and its implications for how Indian regional policy should proceed on the question of Kashmir from thereon.

It also coloured Nehru's gradual shift in his perception of the democratic possibilities that a UN sponsored plebiscite on Kashmir could offer. With Pakistan becoming a member of the US Cold War alliance, there was a clear shift in Nehru's earlier representation of the UN as a forum that had the potential to aid newly independent states to facilitate their relations with other states, while retaining their autonomy and freedom from the influence of great-power politics. Increasingly, the UN began to embody the Cold War interests of the US. In fact, from 1954 onwards, the Indian state became steadily less willing to allow the UN to act as a mediating body in the Kashmir issue as it felt that the overwhelming influence of the United States within the Security Council and the Commission responsible for mediating on Kashmir made it an unsuitable body to mediate impartially on the conflict any longer.[33]

As a result, the Indian state moved towards unilaterally installing a Kashmiri government in that part of the state under its control and began to sound less enthusiastic on the prospects of a plebiscite in the contested state.[34] In reply to a question posed to him in 1957 about his position on Pakistan's offer to withdraw its troops from Kashmir if there was a United Nations supervised plebiscite in both parts of the country, Nehru emphasized that

> the only thing I want from Pakistan is to get out of Kashmir. I want no offers from them. [...] We will admit no foreign troops in any spot of India, one inch of India, it does not matter whatever happens to India or

whether you call them United Nations troops or any other troops [...] As for the national plebiscite, it is up to us to decide what is going to happen in Kashmir. We will have two elections in Kashmir – two general elections in our part of Kashmir.[35]

The shift in policy was clear. By this stage, the Indian state had decided that it would determine the democratic will of the people in a manner of its own choosing and would no longer tolerate external involvement. Since the UN was deemed to be no longer able to act impartially in aiding the democratic choice of the people of Jammu and Kashmir, its role was no longer seen as useful.

Also evident was the notion of territoriality within the discourse of anti-imperialism negotiated domestically within India. Nehru, by this time, considered Indian-administered Kashmir as an integral part of India's territorial space. In this respect, Nehru's fervent insistence on not allowing foreign troops on even 'one inch of India' pointed to how he represented the guarding of India's territorial space as an expression of India's autonomy and sovereignty.

The resistance of external great-power intervention into India's affairs in South Asia would become a cornerstone of future Indian policy with regard to its regional policy. The Indian state would come to no longer entertain any notion of external involvement in its relationship with Pakistan. In this, it would be guided by the idea that any form of external involvement, especially by a major power, would amount to a subversion of India's autonomy and independence.

From 'reciprocity' to 'special position': the case of Nepal

The formal relationship of Nepal to India differed from that of the other Himalayan states of Bhutan and Sikkim in the crucial sense that the other two states did not, in letter or in practice, enjoy independence in the conduct of their foreign policy as this responsibility was delegated to India. This was the result of their legal-constitutional position with relation to the colonial government of British India, an arrangement, with minor alterations, that continued with the Indian state after independence in 1947.[36] Therefore, in order to begin to understand the Indian state's relationship with the state of Nepal, it is necessary to understand Nepal's relationship with the British colonial authority in India, as this would have important implications for Indo-Nepal relations post-1947.

One of the earliest and most important treaties governing relations between the British East India Company and the Kingdom of Nepal was the Treaty of 1816 after the defeat of Nepal in the Anglo-Nepali war (1814–16). By this treaty, in letter, Nepal was given 'the status of an independent state as regards relations with the British government of India, while also not prohibiting diplomatic relations with other Asian and European powers'.[37] In practice, the British government did not want the government of Nepal to establish relations with any European power.[38] Nonetheless, Nepal was accorded the recognition of full sovereignty by the British government as a result of this treaty with the small caveat that Nepal treated its relations with the British government with greater priority than its relations with other states. The British government chose not to interfere in the internal politics of Nepal. Internally, Nepal, from 1815 onwards came to be ruled by the powerful Rana line of hereditary prime ministers and the monarchy, although it continued, was rendered a powerless institution, subordinate to the Rana's dominant political power.[39] The British–Nepali relationship remained largely unchanged till the end of British rule in India in 1947. At the time of Indian independence, Nepal thus enjoyed the status of a sovereign state, independent in its domestic politics and largely autonomous in its foreign relations.

The 1950 Treaty of Friendship and India's 'reciprocal' relationship with Nepal

In July 1950, the governments of India and Nepal signed a Treaty of Peace and Friendship. Three articles of the treaty are particularly important to note. Article Two states that

> the two Governments hereby undertake to inform each other of any serious friction or misunderstanding with any neighbouring State likely to cause any breach in the friendly relations subsisting between the two Governments.[40]

Article Three, on the issue of diplomatic representatives, states that

> the representatives and such of their staff as may be agreed upon shall enjoy such diplomatic privileges and immunities as are customarily granted by international law on a reciprocal basis – provided that in no case shall these be less than those granted to persons of a similar status of any other State having diplomatic relations with either Government.[41]

Meanwhile, Article Five, keeping in mind Nepal's land-locked geography, states that the 'Government of Nepal shall be free to import, from or through the territory of India, arms, ammunition or warlike material and equipment necessary for the security of Nepal'.[42]

The above treaty set the foundational basis for the interaction between the independent states of India and Nepal, a relationship based upon the notion of equality and 'reciprocity', rather than one upon which India was the superior power that maintained the policy of the colonial government of British India. Although Article Three on the issue of diplomatic representatives does stipulate that Nepal should not grant any other state diplomatic privileges of a higher standing than those granted to representatives of the

Indian government, the directive applied equally to the Indian government as far as Nepali diplomatic representatives were concerned. The treaty thus set a tone of clear 'reciprocity', rather than favouring disproportionately the much larger and more internationally prominent Indian state.

In his biography of Nehru, S. Gopal notes that 'Nehru had always intended to make it clear that India's strategic frontier lay on the northern side of Nepal and any attack on Nepal would be regarded as aggression on India'.[43] This position has been used as evidence by several writers, beginning in Nehru's period, as the continuance of a strategic tradition inherited from the British imperial policy of treating the South Asian sub-continent as India's exclusive strategic backyard.[44]

This position has its merits but it seems to over-simplify the situation when we look carefully at Nehru's approach to Nepal. Although British imperial strategic ideas may have provided an initial guide, they did not comprise the main set of ideas that informed India's foreign policy towards Nepal during the Nehru era. Rather, it will be demonstrated that Nehru's shifting perceptions of Nepal were driven by the tension inherent in his own representation of Indian state identity. A few months after signing the India–Nepal Treaty in 1950, Nehru stressed in a speech in parliament that independent India would treat its relations with Nepal in a qualitatively different manner from those between Nepal and British India. For him,

> Nepal was an independent country when India was under British rule, but her foreign relations were largely limited to her relations with the Government functioning in India. When we came into the picture, we assured Nepal that we would not only respect her independence but see, as far as we could, that she developed in a strong and progressive country. We went further in this respect; Nepal began to develop other foreign relations, and we welcomed this and did not hinder the process. Frankly, we do not like and shall not brook any foreign interference in Nepal. We recognize Nepal as an independent country and wish her well.[45]

This speech reinforces Nehru's intention for this bilateral relationship to be based upon the principle of 'reciprocity' between the two states. The fact that the much larger and relatively more influential Indian state was framing its relationship on the basis of equality and 'reciprocity' provides evidence of the Indian state's urgency in its need to distance itself from its predecessor, British India, as well as India's aspiration to play a wider global role on the basis of its argument for respecting the freedom and sovereignty of postcolonial states in Asia and Africa. In this sense, the Indian state represented itself to be standing against anything that resembled a form of subordination of one state to another, anti-imperialism being one of the basic pillars of the newly independent Indian state. Nehru's response to two significant events after this treaty was signed demonstrates how representations of the Indian state's anti-imperialist character influenced Indian foreign policy towards Nepal during this period.

The first of these events was the Chinese annexation of Tibet in 1950, a move which brought China's territorial boundaries to the edge of Nepal. Although Nehru had hoped that the Chinese government would come to a negotiated settlement with Tibet over the latter's future status, rather than militarily occupying it, he publicly recognized China's position in Tibet and assured the Chinese government that the Indian government had no claims on Tibet.[46] This marked a distinct shift from British imperial policy that had sought to ensure that Tibet's independence served as a buffer between British India and China.[47] Also, Nehru's position on Tibet challenges the idea that independent India unproblematically inherited the strategic imperatives of its predecessor, as far as relations with states within its immediate region were concerned. Challenging the new Communist regime in China over Tibet would make relations between India and China unnecessarily acrimonious as far as Nehru was concerned. It would damage the vision of peaceful co-existence that Nehru championed between two large Asian states that had recently thrown off the shackles of imperialism. In his view, China's historical struggle against imperialism made its occupation of Tibet understandable, especially since it was Western imperial power that had severed China's historical position of suzerainty over Tibet. For Nehru, the expansion of British influence in Tibet was underlain by imperialist motives and it thus 'embarrassed him to lay claim to the succession of an imperial power which had pushed its way into Tibet'.[48] More importantly, Nehru did not think that such an expansion of China's borders to Nepal's northern frontier should necessitate a shift in India's relationship with Nepal.

The second event occurred on 7 November 1950, when the Nepali Prime Minister Maharaja Mohan Shumsher Rana removed the nominal monarch, King Bir Bikram Tribhuvana from the throne. A few days later the king fled to India and Nepalese Congress insurgents began military operations along Nepal's southern frontier.[49] Nehru was of the opinion that the Nepali Congress's demand for a democratic political system should be respected by the Rana regime and the monarch should be allowed to return to Nepal to co-ordinate moves towards such an end by assuming the position of a constitutional monarch. Shortly after these events in a speech in parliament, Nehru stressed the link between democracy in India and the desire to see democracy take root in Nepal. He pointed out that, in his discussion with the Nepali government,

> we added that because in the nature of things, we stood not only for progressive democracy in our own country, but round about also. We talk about it not only in Nepal but also in distant quarters of the world and we are not going to forget it when our neighbouring countries, when a country on our doorstep was concerned. But our advice was friendly, and was given in as friendly way as possible.[50]

The representation of the Indian state domestically as a democratic polity had important implications for Nehru when it came to dealing with Nepal. On one level, the Indian government's advocacy of the democratic ideal in the global realm, based upon its own conception of India as a democratic state, would lack credibility if regionally, within South Asia, it did not attempt to lend its weight to democratic forces in its foreign policy.

However, even though Nehru's sympathy was with the Nepali Congress and its bid for democracy, it was just as important that India's actions within its region were not construed to be interventionist and imperialist. In a letter to Nehru, Jayaprakash Narayan, a close contemporary and follower of Mohandas Gandhi during the independence movement and a respected figure across all cross-sections in India criticized Nehru for not actively supporting the democratic revolt in Nepal. Narayan was referring to a particular incident and Nehru's response to it. The incident arose when the leader of the Nepali Congress came to Delhi to seek Indian military support from Nehru against the Rana regime. Nehru declined to see the representative but informed him, through Indian officials, that he wanted to prevent civil war in Nepal just as much he would like a representative government to be formed in Nepal. This earned Nehru Narayan's ire. In his letter, Narayan noted,

> so this is how you wish to treat a democratic revolution in a neighbouring state! [...] You are destroying yourself. One by one you are destroying your noble ideals. You are compromising, you are yielding.[51]

Nehru's reply to Narayan's letter is illuminating for an understanding of the importance that he attached to ensuring that India would not be accused of acting in a dominant, bullying fashion towards its much smaller immediate neighbour. In his reply to Narayan, he claimed that he was

> distressed at the lack of understanding you have shown and I am more than distressed by the astonishing stupidity of some of the things that the leaders of the Nepal Congress have been responsible for [...] I quite agree with you that the opportunity for securing freedom for Nepal has come and that the trump cards are there [...]. Nothing can stop the success of the revolution in Nepal except the folly of those who are supporting it [...]. Widespread propaganda is being carried out by our opponents abroad to show that this is just an example of Indian imperialism and that we have engineered all this. This obviously can do a great deal of harm to the whole movement. We cannot ignore external forces at work against us. What Koirala suggested would have put an end to the idea of an indigenous movement and made it just an adventure of the Indian government.[52]

This letter demonstrates the tension, as Nehru saw it, in conceptualizing India's role within South Asia and the specific forms of foreign policy that should spring from such conceptions. On one hand, the Indian state's commitment to the democratic ethos meant that Nehru was strongly supportive of the democratic efforts of the Nepali Congress. On the other hand, he was aware that any Indian intervention to aid the forces of democracy would be likely to be construed outside India as a sign of India asserting its domination and imperialist designs on a smaller neighbour. Even at the explicit request of democratizing forces within Nepal, military support by the Indian state would challenge the legitimacy of India's professed role as a protector of the independence of the postcolonial states. However, India's image was about to change. Events in 1951 would begin to signal a gradual change in Nehru's stance towards Nepal and they would have implications for India's self-perceived role within its immediate region.

The claim for India's 'special position': India's changing perceptions of Nepal

In February 1951, the Rana regime's long hold on power in Nepal came to an end. As a result of international and specifically Indian pressure, King Tribhuvana took his place as a constitutional monarch and appointed a government within which the Ranas and the Nepali Congress would come to share power.[53] However, it was only in 1959 that the first general elections were held. The period between 1951 and 1959 saw a lot of political instability and a succession of different civilian governments alternating in political office.[54] Moreover, this period witnessed an important shift in the Indian state's approach towards Nepal.

The main issue precipitating this shift was the Indian state's increasing anxiety that other states beside itself, especially China and to a lesser extent the United States, were trying to establish relations and develop influence in Nepal in competition with India. Within this context, Nehru agreed to the Nepali king's request to send an Indian military mission to Nepal in February 1952. Its aim was to reorganize and train Nepalese army personnel and all Indian officers would function in a strictly consultative capacity vis-à-vis the Nepalese government. It was seen as a way of helping Nepal build its own defence capabilities without the temptation of looking for great-power military aid.[55]

The first real sign of concern, expressed by Nehru, emerged when the Nepali Congress, appointed by the king as the ruling party in the ruling coalition cabinet, began to discuss plans to establish diplomatic relations with China. At a press conference, a reporter questioned Nehru's previous assertion that 'Nepal never had independent diplomatic relations except through independent India and, before that, the British government in India'. The reporter asked Nehru whether or not he believed 'that relationship will continue or change'.[56] In reply Nehru said that

> India's relationship is far more intimate and important to Nepal than that of any other country. If any other country's relationship is in conflict with India's, naturally we will not like it.[57]

This statement was to signal the beginning of a shift in Nehru's earlier stance in which he considered that the Indian state should not want to hinder Nepal in its establishment of diplomatic relations with states other than itself and should in fact welcome such development of foreign ties between Nepal and other states. The tone of an equal, 'reciprocal' relationship was beginning to slowly unravel. Instead, Nehru sought increasingly to underline India's 'first among equals' position as far as Nepal's external relations with other states were concerned. This changing Indian stance would become more evident by the time Nepal and China finally established diplomatic relations in 1955.

In early 1954, certain opposition parties (groups that did not find themselves within the ruling government coalition during this politically turbulent period), such as the Nepali Congress began delivering anti-Indian speeches within Nepal. In response, in his note to the Indian Ambassador to Nepal at that time, B.K. Gokhale, Nehru expresses his frustration at these anti-Indian speeches by noting that

> Nepal, or rather some people in Nepal, can be mischievous and do us harm. But if they go too far, they are likely to injure themselves much more. If it comes down to a final test, we can, if we so choose, prevent Americans and others from functioning there. I would not hesitate to do so if matters come to a crisis [...] because of this I do not see why we should go out of our way to ask the Nepal government how long they want our military mission there. The military mission is there and will continue there [...]. I am prepared to object to the British setting up a wireless transmitting station in East Nepal and yet to maintain our own wireless transmitters near the Nepal border. We have made it perfectly clear to every country that *we have special interests in Nepal* and that we are not going to tolerate other countries' special interests there [...] I am convinced only a firm policy will pay. Therefore I am opposed to any withdrawal from our check-posts, or our military mission, or our trade agents or our wireless instruments or in any other way. *They will have to put up with us even if they do not like us* [emphasis added].[58]

This classified note reveals a discernible shift in India's perception of the nature of its relationship with Nepal. For Nehru, in the light of what he perceived to be the aim of the US and other states to further their own parochial objectives, India's 'special interests' had to be respected by Nepal and these other states as well. In this view, as far as Nepal was concerned, there could be no legitimate claim of similar 'special interests' by any other state. To exemplify this point, at a press conference in New Delhi, on 13 November 1954, Nehru declared that 'India's special position in regard to foreign affairs in Nepal was recognized and that is an admitted fact'.[59] Similar to the case of Pakistan's attempt to involve the US in the India–Pakistan relationship over the Kashmir issue, there was a generally held belief that Nepal was attempting to invite great-power influence into South Asia. The potential effect of such great-power influence in South Asia on the autonomy of India's foreign policy was clear for Nehru.

Furthermore, by late 1954, China's request for full diplomatic relations with Nepal was an urgent issue facing Nehru's government. In Nehru's conversations with Zhou En-Lai, the Chinese premier, Nehru went to great lengths to point out India's 'special' position in Nepal, while offering no explicit objections to China establishing diplomatic relations with Nepal. Nehru made two points clear to Zhou En-Lai. First, that although India did not object to China establishing relations with Nepal, the latter's relations with India should be held as Nepal's most important external relationship. As he explained to Zhou,

> Nepal's foreign affairs are looked after by us [...] but we do not interfere in their internal affairs. But you will understand that traditionally Nepal and India are closely linked together according to the treaty, the foreign policy of India and Nepal are to be co-ordinated.[60]

Second, having demonstrated India's 'special' position in Nepal vis-à-vis China, Nehru pointed out that it was American, rather than Chinese intentions and actions that could adversely impact India's 'special' position in Nepal. He was therefore agreeable to China establishing diplomatic relations with Nepal but emphasized that he would not want a Chinese embassy in Kathmandu, Nepal's capital. Rather, he suggested, the Chinese ambassador to India should be accredited as Nepal's ambassador, as was the case with the French and the Americans. Nehru explained that a Chinese embassy in Kathmandu would give the Americans a 'reason to do so too' and that this would be detrimental to India's interests, given that he believed that the Americans were 'spreading anti-Indian propaganda' in Nepal. Zhou agreed with Nehru's assessment at this point and agreed it would not be a good idea to set up an embassy in Kathmandu in order to 'not allow the US to have any excuse' to further their influence in Nepal.[61]

This feat of balancing the wish to entrench India's position as Nepal's most important bilateral relationship with the concern to not represent as objectionable China's attempts at opening relations with Nepal reflected the tension between balancing India's regional and global roles. However, both of these roles were intimately informed by the construction of the Indian state's identity domestically. Thus, on one hand, Nehru suspected American activity in Nepal to be inspired by its own parochial Cold War calculations, which he regarded to be the more recent incarnation of Western imperialism and which had to be resisted within India's immediate region. Within its own regional space, the perils and dangers of such forms of Western imperialism were especially clear and present given the Indian state's own domestically constructed notions of territorial integrity and anti-imperialism. Yet, on the other hand, the core of Nehru's representation of India's global role rested heavily on a close and friendly relationship between the other major Asian state,

Nehru and the birth of India's regional policy 45

China, as well as on mutual respect and reciprocity in terms of the autonomy of the smaller states in India's region, such as Nepal.

Nepal's subtle attempts to move towards a more independent foreign policy began to test this balancing act within Indian foreign policy. With this, the 'reciprocity' principle in Indian–Nepali relations was strained further. In the treaty signed in 1950, both sides agreed to 'consult' each other on their respective foreign affairs and this was seen to be the cornerstone of the 'reciprocal' principle that initially governed their relations. In May 1954, in meetings with Nepalese leaders, Nehru discussed formalizing India and Nepal's relationship on foreign affairs even further. As a result of these meetings, Nehru's draft memoir explicated that 'the Government of India would consult the Government of Nepal on all matters relating to Nepal and the Nepalese Government would consult the Government of India in matters relating to Tibet and China'.[62] On 15 October 1954, the Nepalese government forwarded a modified version of the aide mémoire. The Nepalese draft argued for reciprocity in terms of consultations with regards to 'matters regarding relations of Nepal and India with countries on the border common to both'.[63] This meant that the Nepalese government was seeking to introduce a greater element of reciprocity in its relations with India than that outlined by Nehru in his memoir. In effect, the Nepalese government wanted the Indian government to consult it over the latter's affairs with China just as the Nepalese government was being asked to consult the Indian government over its affairs with China. T.N. Kaul, Joint Secretary in India's External Affairs Ministry at that this time, suggested to Nehru that the revised draft should be accepted and that the Indian side need not 'quibble too much about the phraseology'.[64]

However, Nehru disagreed strongly with Kaul's view and was not prepared to accept the proposed variation on the earlier memoir prepared by him. For Nehru, the proposed changes were more than just semantic and did not adequately recognize India's more important and influential role especially after China's annexation of Tibet and its growing efforts to open diplomatic relations with Nepal. Nehru's views are spelt out clearly in a note to Kaul and R.K. Nehru, the foreign secretary, in which he notes,

> I do not mind reciprocity in regard to paragraphs (2) and (3) of my draft [...] but it is obvious that the government of Nepal are not concerned with all the innumerable contacts we have with other countries while whatever contact they may have with a foreign country is a matter of concern to us.[65]

Nehru's India was moving from a position of benign reciprocity to one in which it insisted upon an asymmetrical position for itself vis-à-vis Nepal. The idea that India had a 'special' claim over Nepal's foreign relations (especially in relation to China), without any corresponding reciprocity began to be more strongly asserted over time. In this respect, Nehru's private sentiments regarding the need to assert India's prerogative to keep out any external powers from South Asia was matched by his public statements. In a press conference in November 1954, Nehru was asked, after his talks with Zhou, whether 'China has accepted that Nepal was in the sphere of influence of India', to which Nehru replied that in

> so far as Nepal is concerned, it is a well known fact and it is needless for me to state it. It is contained in our treaties and in our other agreements with Nepal that we have a special position in Nepal – not interfering with their independence, but not looking with favour anybody else's interfering with their independence either [...] India's special position in regard to foreign affairs in Nepal was recognized and that has been an admitted fact.[66]

This particular exchange signalled, once again, a distinct shift in Nehru's conception of the nature of Nepal's obligations to India. It reinforced the sense that, for Nehru, Nepal was in India's 'sphere of influence' and the bilateral relationship had morphed from one of benign reciprocity to one of qualified Indian suzerainty over Nepal's affairs. From this point on, relations between India and Nepal deteriorated even further. India's attempts to cement its right to be consulted over Nepal's foreign relations were increasingly resisted by the latter. The government of Nepal achieved this by trying to secure the establishment of a Soviet Embassy at Kathmandu, as well as secretly exchanging notes on various matters with the United States.[67]

In reaction to these steps, Nehru responded with greater pressure by informing the Chinese Government in August 1956 that any move by them to sign a treaty of friendship with Nepal, 'would, from India's viewpoint, be inopportune'.[68] By 1960, relations between Nepal and India were coming under even greater strain as a result of the deteriorating relationship between India and China. It was felt within senior Indian policy circles that Nepal was being pressured by China into reaching boundary agreements over Tibet that were 'manifestly being aimed at India'.[69] From the Indian perspective, more worrying was the decision between Nepal and China to sign a non-aggression treaty in the near future. Nehru went to great lengths to explain to the Nepalese prime minister that he believed such a treaty could only be aimed against India and to strengthen China's diplomatic position in the brewing border dispute between India and China.[70] The change from the earlier position of benign reciprocity was thus clear. A significant shift had taken place in the manner in which the Indian state conceived its immediate region of South Asia, its role within it and, through such a shift, its regional policy towards Nepal.

Conclusion

It is perhaps unsurprising that the Nehru years were characterized to a large extent by the Indian state's aspirations to play a global role in international affairs. Conceptions of India's global role had a significant impact upon India's foreign policy in South Asia. Even though India's view of its global and regional roles were shaped intimately by the specific character of the Indian state, it was regionally, in South Asia, where Nehru's complex negotiation with Indian state identity led to significant shifts in Indian foreign policy. More specifically, the impact of Indian state identity was more evident within its regional policy, with conceptions of India's regional space and regional role forming an important link between domestic state identity and certain outcomes in Indian regional policy.

In the case of its regional policy towards Pakistan, specifically in case of the dispute over Kashmir, the three different discourses, secularism, democracy and anti-imperialism which framed Indian state identity informed shifting conceptions of India's regional role. These shifting conceptions led to conflicting interpretations of certain events relating to the Kashmir dispute and thus created tension in the formulation of Indian foreign policy in South Asia. This tension was apparent in the Indian state's shift of its position from viewing UN's role in the determining the future of the Kashmiri people as desirable to rejecting any form of UN or extra-regional involvement as detrimental. In this case, Indian regional policy was influenced significantly by the way in which particular events in the regional and global realms were filtered via the prism of its own conception of India's regional space.

In the case of Indian regional policy towards Nepal within the context of the 1950 Treaty of Friendship, it was evident that the Indian state's self-representations, transposed onto both on the global and regional levels, drove the Indian policy of balanced reciprocity in its relations with its much smaller neighbour. However, over time, Indian regional policy moved from this position to one in which it claimed a 'special position' in the conduct of Nepal's foreign policy. Once again, the manner in which the Indian state perceived various events and developments, both regionally and beyond, through its conception of its role in South Asia contributed significantly to this shift in Indian regional policy.

In both cases, Indian regional policy during the Nehru period revealed significant shifts in the perception of the role and motivations of 'external' involvement within South Asia, India's immediate region. By the mid-1950s, the Indian state began to progressively view the possibility of any form of external involvement in South Asia as highly detrimental to Indian interests. Even after Nehru's death, this view would come to structure one of the fundamental principles of Indian foreign policy to date.

3 'The Empress of India'
Indira Gandhi and the idea of India

Indira Nehru Gandhi, the daughter and only child of Jawaharlal Nehru, was prime minister of India from 1966 to 1977 and from 1980 to 1984. During this span of 14 years, including her years out of office (1977–80), Indira Gandhi was arguably the single biggest influence in Indian politics.[1] At the peak of her mass popularity, she was described in India as 'the greatest leader India ever had',[2] while the foreign press called her the 'new Empress of India'.[3] The tenure of Indira Gandhi as India's leader is represented by various writers as being both a period of continuity as well as significant change, a continuation of some aspects of Nehru's ideas and policies, as well as a radical departure from others.[4] This chapter will look at how the three central discourses associated with the identity of the Indian state – secularism, democracy and anti-imperialism, framed during the Nehru era – were implicated in negotiating the idea of India during this period.

The first two sections of this chapter will analyse the manner in which Mrs Gandhi negotiated the discourse of secularism in an examination of the specific case of her approach to the Jammu and Kashmir state elections in 1983. The following three sections will examine how Mrs Gandhi radically reshaped the central notions of democracy that had been framed in the Nehru era. In an examination of her two early policy decisions as prime minister – the devaluation of the Indian rupee and bank nationalization – as well as the implications of the imposition of the Emergency in 1975, it will be shown how Mrs Gandhi fundamentally recast the democratic idea associated with the Indian state. Mrs Gandhi's engagement with the discourse of anti-imperialism will be examined in the penultimate section in an examination of her response to the civil war in East Pakistan and India's subsequent military involvement in the crisis.

Indian secularism: the second phase

The discourse of secularism was an important element in the construction of Indian state identity during the Nehru era. In Nehru's discourse on 'Indian-ness', secularism was represented as the binary opposite of a 'communal', religiously based, national identity. Indira Gandhi inherited this legacy when she became the leader of the country in 1966. In her early years as prime minister, Mrs Gandhi persisted with the Nehruvian representation of the place of a specific type of secularism within the larger idea of India. It was in fact during her term in office that the word 'secular' was inserted into the Preamble of the Indian Constitution.[5] At this early stage, in a manner apparently similar to Nehru, she was particularly concerned that the Indian state should not be associated with any explicit religious symbols or expressions. Mrs Gandhi's uneasiness at the provincial state government of Mysore in 1972 organizing a Hindu festival procession is just one small example of her attitude to the type of secularism that the Indian state should represent at this juncture.[6] However, by the end of her tenure in 1984 she had redefined the discourse of secularism as a fundamental aspect of Indian state identity. Mrs Gandhi's assassination in 1984 by her trusted Sikh bodyguards would be a clear testament of the profound effect of this re-definition of secular India.

The manner in which the Indian state during Mrs Gandhi's tenure as prime minister had to face an increasing challenge to its political authority from the Indian-administered state of Jammu and Kashmir has been well documented.[7] An examination of Mrs Gandhi's attitude to the state of Jammu and Kashmir offers an interesting insight into her negotiation and re-definition of the discourse of secularism. As has been pointed out in Chapter 1, the state of Jammu and Kashmir has been critical to representations of Indian secularism since 1947 since it symbolized the secular credentials of India and the poverty of the communal, religiously inspired idea upon which Pakistan was ostensibly founded. The longer Jammu and Kashmir, a Muslim majority province, remained part of an independent India the more robust was the claim that the Indian state was secular in its identity and not a 'Hindu' state as claimed by proponents of the Pakistan idea. While occupying the territorial fringes of the Indian state, the state of Jammu and Kashmir remained, for Indian elites like Nehru, at the heart of Indian secular imagining and discourse. The secular pillar of Indian state identity rested to a large extent upon how it dealt with its only Muslim majority state within the Indian Union. Mrs Gandhi's approach to, and policies for, Jammu and Kashmir thus assume significance in this context.

'Playing God': secularism and the politics of communal fear in Jammu and Kashmir

In 1963, in Srinagar, the capital of Jammu and Kashmir, riots broke out after news that the hair of the Prophet Muhammad had been stolen from the reliquary of one of the city's principal mosques. Although no Hindus were implicated in the theft, this event marked one of the early signs of the Jammu and Kashmir Muslim community's disenchantment with the perceived indifference and neglect shown towards them by the Indian central government.[8] Approximately ten years later, in 1973, another incidence of unrest broke out in Jammu and Kashmir, again the result of the Muslim community's belief that their religious sentiments had not been respected. The issue concerned the discovery, by a student in his college library, of a classic British encyclopaedia for children that contained a drawing of the Prophet Mohammad to whom the Archangel Gabriel was dictating the Holy Quran. There was widespread outrage within the Muslim majority at the existence of this text in a college library. Demonstrations and widespread unrest resulted in the state, with police firing on the demonstrators and eventually arresting hundreds.[9] The Muslim community's disenchantment with the central government was growing steadily. There was a sense that Muslim religious sentiments and interests were not being respected as was expected in Nehru's secular India. Yet, such misgivings about Indian secularism in Jammu and Kashmir were relatively minor in comparison to the impact created by Mrs Gandhi's approach towards the state beginning in 1982.

After the death in 1982 of the influential Kashmiri leader, Sheikh Abdullah, his son, Farooq Abdullah, was sworn in as his successor as the chief minister of the state of Jammu and Kashmir and head of the ruling Kashmiri National Conference. Farooq insisted upon his party's independence from Mrs Gandhi's Congress (I) Party. This compelled Mrs Gandhi to seek Farooq's removal from his position as chief minister. The manner in which she sought to arrange his removal resulted in her fundamentally recasting the secular identity of the Indian state.[10]

With battle-lines drawn, the 1983 state elections in Jammu and Kashmir became the stage upon which Farooq sought to demonstrate the widespread popularity of his party, the National Conference, in the face of the expected challenge from Mrs Gandhi's Congress (I) Party. In April 1983, Farooq announced early state elections in the state. Mrs Gandhi's response was to campaign personally in Jammu and Kashmir on behalf of her Congress (I) Party, specifically against Farooq and his party. As part of her election strategy, she appealed explicitly for electoral support on the basis of religious fears and suspicions. By harnessing and exploiting inter-community suspicions and fears as part the democratic electioneering process, Mrs Gandhi was gradually contesting and reframing previous representations of Indian secularism. This signalled a redefinition of Indian state identity in terms of its proper relationship to different religious groups within India. The idea of India as a secular state was beginning to be renegotiated.

In Jammu, the Hindu majority province within the state of Jammu and Kashmir, Mrs Gandhi warned the Hindu community 'that a National Conference government in Srinagar would be a disaster for them', with the barely concealed implication that the National Conference would represent Muslim interests to the detriment of the Hindu community in Jammu and Kashmir.[11] When she reached Srinagar, the capital within which Muslims were the majority community, Mrs Gandhi altered her message and tried to pander to Muslim sentiment by making sure that all Congress candidates in Kashmir Valley (the Muslim majority province of the state of Jammu and Kashmir) were Muslims. Renowned reporter Tavleen Singh, who was in

Srinagar at this time, recounts how Mrs Gandhi specifically, and her Congress Party in general, conducted an election campaign notable for its malicious attacks on Farooq, branding him with interchangeable labels such as 'Muslim communal' and 'un-Islamic', depending upon which religious community was the intended audience.[12] One of Mrs Gandhi's biographers notes how the Congress Party's use of religious fear mongering and personal abuse against Farooq 'set a new record in viciousness which often degenerated into downright vulgarity'.[13]

The elections results were a blow to Mrs Gandhi. Although Mrs Gandhi's Congress Party won in the Hindu-majority Jammu province, it was overwhelmingly defeated in the more populous Muslim majority province of the Kashmir Valley. Farooq's National Conference won the state elections and Farooq reclaimed his position as the elected chief minister of the state of Jammu and Kashmir. More importantly, the religiously imbued tenor of the election campaign marked the beginning of a visible change in the discourse of Indian secularism that had been inherited from the Nehru period. By running her party's election strategy on the basis of appeals to different sets of voters on the basis of their religious faith, Mrs Gandhi distinguished between Kashmiris as Hindu Kashmiris and Muslim Kashmiris that needed to be protected from each other. In this discourse, only her Congress Party could provide such protection. Her 'warnings' to Hindus in Jammu and their resultant support for her, coupled with the Muslim community's support for Farooq in the Kashmir Valley, led many to a tentative conclusion: Mrs Gandhi and her Congress (I) Party were the party that represented the Hindu community in Jammu and Kashmir, while Farooq's National Conference represented the Muslim community in the state.

The representation of the Congress Party as the defender of the parochial interests of the Hindu community in India was anathema, in an earlier period, for both Nehru and the Congress Party. In fact, one of the strategies of the Muslim League Party before independence was to insist that the Congress Party be recognized as the representative of only the Hindus in India and could therefore not speak legitimately for the Muslim community in colonial India. Ironically, Mrs Gandhi's election strategy in Jammu and Kashmir, and the nature of the electoral result that it spawned, led many to represent the Congress Party as the increasingly singular voice of the Hindus to the exclusion of the Muslims. In Chapter 1, it was shown how the state of Jammu and Kashmir held a crucial place in Indian self-representations, especially as it related to the secular complexion of the Indian state. At this historical juncture, Mrs Gandhi began to utilize a specific type of identity-politics for gaining electoral support, the type of identity-politics that Nehru had termed 'communalism'. This type of identity-politics was based upon cultivating and exploiting the suspicions and fears that existed between different religious communities and it began steadily to spread beyond the state of Jammu and Kashmir into the discourse and practice of Indian politics. The 1983 state elections in Jammu and Kashmir were just the first act in the process of recasting the notion of Indian secularism and Mrs Gandhi's approach towards Jammu and Kashmir after the elections would serve to further transform the secular identity of the Indian state.

Farooq's National Conference state government was toppled on 2 July 1984.[14] This was caused by two factors. First, the Congress Party, under Mrs Gandhi's instructions, encouraged defections from Farooq's Party, largely through promises of cabinet positions in a new government and, failing that, through monetary bribes.[15] Second, Mrs Gandhi appointed a pliant governor in Kashmir who would be willing to depose Farooq and appoint a new coalition government (with the Congress (I) as one member of the coalition) in its place.[16] There were mass protests in the Kashmir Valley against Farooq's dismissal, in support of a leader that enjoyed overwhelming support in this Muslim majority province. Mrs Gandhi's response to the protests was to send troops to restore law and order in the state.[17] Mrs Gandhi and her Congress (I) Party were viewed increasingly as not only the representative of the Hindu community in Jammu and Kashmir but also as the representative of an Indian state that had refused to accept the legitimacy of the elected representatives of the Muslim community in Jammu and Kashmir.

In Nehru's discourse of Indian secularism, the secularism of the Indian state was the binary opposite of 'communalism'. By the 1980s, while still claiming to have stayed faithful to the Nehruvian representation of Indian secularism, Mrs Gandhi, through her practices and via her discourse, fundamentally altered how the 'secularism' of the Indian state was being increasingly perceived. The Nehruvian discourse of Indian secularism as the binary opposite of 'communalism' had become less obvious and persuasive by the end of the Indira Gandhi period, as the specific example of the case of Jammu and Kashmir demonstrates. Instead, by attempting to win popular political support via direct appeals to the religious suspicions and fears of different religious communities in Jammu and Kashmir, Mrs Gandhi had begun to fundamentally renegotiate the identity of the Indian state.

This exercise in domestic identity-politics had some very crucial implications, both for the character of domestic politics in India and for the way that the Indian state, under Mrs Gandhi, came to perceive its role in South Asia in the light of the altering identity of the Indian state. Domestically, it would lead to broad disenchantment within the Muslim community in the country, who began to view the Indian state and its associated secular pronouncements with growing cynicism. On the other hand, certain sections of India's Hindu community began to perceive the Congress Party's brand of 'secularism' as 'pseudo-secularism', used by political elites within the Congress Party and beyond for the appeasement of the minority Muslim community in a blatant pursuit of political power.[18] The rise in popular support for the Hindu nationalist Bharatiya Janata Party (BJP) in the 1990s would reveal the extent to which declarations of India's seeming secular identity on the part of political elites persisted, while the fundamental understanding of Indian secularism, forged in the Nehru period, would come to be bitterly contested by these same elites.

Democracy: populism and the emergency

One of the most contentious aspects of the Indira Gandhi era is the manner in which the practice and discourse of democracy within India underwent fundamental change. Much of the academic literature on this period regards the Indira Gandhi era to be characterized by the subversion of democratic norms and practices forged in the Nehru era. Some writers perceive this to be the direct result of the insecurity and paranoia that were part of Mrs Gandhi's apparent psychological profile.[19] However, others attribute the damage to democratic norms and practices within the context of an expanding electorate, a growing economy and/or the effect of Mrs Gandhi on weakening political institutions domestically.[20] This academic debate essentially is concerned with *why* there was a unravelling of such democratic norms and principles during the Indira Gandhi era. However, for the purposes of this argument, it is more important to understand *how* Mrs Gandhi, during her term as prime minister, radically altered the notion of Indian democracy through a drastic transformation of the discourse on democracy within India. The manner in which this impacted the identity of the Indian state can then be discerned.

Nehru's tenure was characterized by a representation of Indian democracy as a tension between the rights of individuals as citizens of an independent India versus the socio-economic intervening role of the independent Indian state; between the protection of minorities versus the interests of the majority; and between the role of the Indian state as a strong and competent implementer of national policies versus autonomy for the different states that comprised the Indian Union. This dual-faceted feature of India's democratic identity would undergo significant change during the tenure of Indira Gandhi's leadership. This section will discuss two aspects pertinent to this change: the use of populist rhetoric and policies in pursuit of political power and the implications of the declaration of the Emergency in 1975. A discussion of both of episodes will exhibit the ways in which the idea of democracy came to be fundamentally transformed by the end of Mrs Gandhi's tenure.

A brief account of the events surrounding the manner in which Mrs Gandhi came to occupy the office of prime minister is essential in understanding of the form of the contestations that would take place between her and other politically influential elites within the Congress Party. Such a discussion provides an understanding of how such initial contestations within the Congress Party led to more specific contestations over the identity of the Indian state between Mrs Gandhi and other political elites within the party. More specifically, it locates how this contestation in domestic identity-politics led to Mrs Gandhi's initial tryst with the discourse of democracy, presaging her attempts to re-represent Indian state identity via the use of democratic populism to gain greater political power.

The brief tenure of Lal Bahadur Shastri as independent India's second prime minister came to an end with his sudden death in January 1966. In the aftermath of Nehru's death, Mrs Gandhi was deemed to be one of the potential candidates to succeed Nehru as prime minister but she both publicly and privately refused to put herself forward as a possible candidate for a number of possible reasons. However, she was made a member of the cabinet in Shastri's government as the Minister of Information. The death of Shastri signalled another round of speculation about Mrs Gandhi's possible candidacy for the prime minister's position. At this point, senior members within the Congress Party shifted their allegiance to Mrs Gandhi and supported her appointment to the position of prime minister, a decision motivated largely by the expectation that Mrs Gandhi would be amenable to being a temporary, pliant, prime minister, while they themselves would hold the strings of power.[21] According to this logic, the fact that she was Nehru's daughter could be counted upon to win the Congress Party electoral support at the scheduled general elections in 1967, after which she could be pushed aside for one of the senior Congress Party members to assume the prime minister's position. There is ample evidence to deduce that Mrs Gandhi was aware of this train of thought amongst certain senior party members before and at the time of her assuming office.[22] The leading member of this group was K. Kamaraj, Congress Party president, a former chief minister and former member of Nehru's cabinet. Kamaraj wielded great influence within the Congress Party and especially among other regional chief ministers. He was one of the main orchestrators of Mrs Gandhi's appointment.

The stage was set for a political struggle between Mrs Gandhi and these different political elites within the Congress Party, with implications for the kinds of policies to be pursued by the Indian state. More specifically, this political struggle would come to be known for the manner in which both Mrs Gandhi and her challengers in the Congress Party framed their contrasting policy choices as reflections of their competing ideas of Indian-ness. In her position as prime minister, Mrs Gandhi engaged in the pursuit and legitimization of particular policy choices by framing them within the larger imperative of re-negotiating Indian state identity. The issue of rupee devaluation and bank nationalization would represent Mrs Gandhi's initial attempts to consolidate her political power by framing her policy choices as part of her larger project of re-defining Indian state identity.

Rupee devaluation and bank nationalization: populist democracy

Mrs Gandhi's assumption of the office of prime minister coincided with a difficult period in India's economic history. In 1966, India was experiencing a severe socio-economic crisis. Severe droughts had led to widespread food shortages and famine in large parts of the country. The economy was flagging. There was widespread inflation and a sharp shortage of foreign exchange. With this economic downturn came social unrest in parts of the country.[23] It was within this context that Mrs Gandhi embarked upon two sets of policies, the devaluation of the Indian rupee and bank nationalization. In so doing, she radically transformed the discourse on democracy within India and the identity of the Indian state as a democratic institution.

The issue of rupee devaluation was one of the first and most pressing issues for Mrs Gandhi to address as India's prime minister in 1966. Major global actors such as the World Bank, the International Monetary Fund (IMF) and the US were pressing the Indian state to devalue the rupee as a condition for the continued monetary aid and economic assistance it needed to deal with its domestic economic problems.[24] Within India, Mrs Gandhi was advised by a self-appointed small committee to do likewise for the sake of arresting the downturn in the Indian economy.[25] In the midst of this situation, she scheduled an official trip to the US. Privately, she aimed 'to get both food and foreign exchange without appearing to ask for them'.[26] She persuaded President Lyndon Johnson to agree to give India 3 million tons of wheat and US $9 million in aid in return for India devaluing the rupee. On her return, Mrs Gandhi announced that the rupee would be devalued by an enormous 57 per cent in order for the Indian economy to recover and deal with its domestic economic problems.[27] Most significantly, she did not consult Kamaraj on the decision to devalue the rupee. In part, this might have been because she knew that he was strongly opposed to such a policy.[28]

For Kamaraj, Mrs Gandhi's actions shattered his image of her as a weak and pliant prime minister who would allow senior Congress members, with him at the helm, to wield actual political power. The fact that Mrs Gandhi made the decision to devalue the rupee without consulting Kamaraj, or the rest of her cabinet indicated that from this early stage in office Mrs Gandhi had begun to assume the type of role she would adopt as leader of the country vis-à-vis her cabinet, her party and the Indian parliament. The need to devalue the rupee was something that she felt was necessary to pull India out of its increasing economic slide and, associated with this, its emerging social unrest.[29] However, rather than negotiating such policy in her cabinet, or even the Congress Working Committee, she attempted to circumvent such avenues of democratic decision-making and instead endeavoured to speak and reach out directly to the electorate with her message. Her decision to make the devaluation public via All India Radio before having discussed it with her cabinet pointed to a mode of political practice that Mrs Gandhi had begun to utilize early on as prime minister.[30]

It was the beginning of an attempt to mould a democracy in which Mrs Gandhi, as leader of the country, would appeal directly to the electorate without negotiating and accommodating the various interests and perspectives prevalent within her cabinet and party. Her bypass of the constitutional structures of the Indian state embodied in her cabinet and India's parliament meant that the Indian democracy came gradually to be viewed as one in which political power resided increasingly with the office of the prime minister and, more specifically, with Mrs Gandhi herself. The discourse of 'popular', or 'direct' democracy was the means by which Mrs Gandhi was effecting such transformation in the identity of the Indian state.

Given her relatively precarious position as prime minister in 1966 in comparison to Nehru's position in 1947, Mrs Gandhi's approach was not surprising.[31] Nehru, commanding enormous respect and support within his own cabinet, his party and even from various opposition parties, could and did manage significant policy decisions through the democratic processes of consultation in his cabinet and his party. Nevertheless, one should not assume that Nehru did not at times maintain and ensure his own point of view when it came to particular positions, even in the face of opposition from within his government and his own party.[32] The point here is that despite this, Nehru framed democratic decision-making as a process of consultation, negotiation and sometimes even cajolement of the members of his cabinet and his party on significant policy decisions, rather than deciding upon policies on himself and bypassing his cabinet and his party by informing and rationalizing important public policy decisions directly to the Indian citizenry.

By the manner in which she had made the decision to devalue the rupee and the mode in which it became public information before even the cabinet or the party was taken into confidence, Mrs Gandhi had begun to reframe democratic decision-making in India. Her attempt to imbue Indian democratic practice with a populist hue would have the effect of re-framing the discourse on Indian democracy domestically. It would also reformulate the identity of the Indian state as a democratic institution. Following the devaluation of the rupee, her bank nationalization scheme and her 'Garibi Hatao' ('Remove Poverty') slogan would be further proof, early on in her tenure as prime minister, of the wanton populism that was beginning to characterize Indian democracy during this period.

In 1969, Mrs Gandhi nationalized 14 commercial banks by a presidential ordinance.[33] It occurred in the wake of Congress's smallest margin of victory since independence in both national and state elections.[34] However, Mrs Gandhi had won her seat with an overwhelming majority and, more importantly, Kamaraj and a number of senior Congress Party members had lost their seats. Although Kamaraj still remained president of the Congress Party, these electoral defeats effectively meant that, despite their support within the party, he and other senior Congress members had even less leverage to attempt to remove Mrs Gandhi from the her leadership position. However, Morarji Desai, a senior member of the Congress Party who had always harboured ambitions of becoming prime minister since the death of Nehru, was determined to replace Mrs Gandhi as leader of the country. In the end, a compromise was reached such that Mrs Gandhi would appoint Desai as her deputy prime minister and minister of finance. Mrs Gandhi did this rather reluctantly, aware of Desai's ambitions, yet knowing that he had the support of significant sections of the party.

The first time the issue of bank nationalization arose was during the Congress Party's annual session in October 1967.[35] Earlier in May, the party's working committee had agreed in principle upon the need for social control of banking, nationalization of general insurance and land reform as part of a wider programme of socio-economic reforms. In order to implement the social control of banks, a proposal for their nationalization had been raised during the October 1967 annual party meeting. Desai, given his right-wing leanings and in his capacity as finance minister, vehemently refused to entertain such a proposal and the matter, temporarily at least, was shelved.

However, Mrs Gandhi used the issue of bank nationalization in 1969 to first remove Desai from his post as finance minister and, second, to represent her policy of bank nationalization as an example of 'direct democracy'. Sensing an erosion of her political power – a result of her choice of candidate for the post of president of India having been defeated by Desai and Kamaraj's nominee – Mrs Gandhi removed Desai from his post upon the grounds that his opposition to bank nationalization in his capacity as finance minister stood in the way of her implementing her 'progressive programme'.[36] Four days later, Mrs Gandhi nationalized 14 commercial banks via a presidential ordinance, even though parliament was due shortly to convene. By nationalizing commercial banks through an ordinance, Mrs Gandhi framed the policy as a 'personal act' in her capacity as prime minister. On a national radio broadcast, she explained that 'nobody wants to deny the rights of any person unless these rights are impinging on far more valid rights of a far larger number'.[37]

As in the in the case of the devaluation of the rupee, Mrs Gandhi had made a very important public policy decision without consulting her cabinet, or parliament, even when such avenues were readily available. Instead, she sought to validate important policy decisions by appealing directly to the citizenry, representing herself as the appointed defender of the interests of the general populace. These acts demonstrated the manner in which she negotiated contestations from other political elites over policy decisions, whilst in the process re-negotiating the discourse of democracy within India itself. By legitimating key policy decisions upon the basis of the perceived will of the general populace, and by announcing these policy decisions directly via deliberate public appeals, Mrs Gandhi increasingly related Indian state identity to a discourse of democratic populism. Crucially, she used bank nationalization not as an end in itself but as part of reconstituting the democratic balance between majority, socialist rights and private, individualist rights. She used the issue of bank nationalization instrumentally as a justification for the dismissal of Desai and to thwart any move to topple her from her position, in effect to strengthen her own political power within the party and as prime minister. Increasingly, during her term, making public policy decisions became a means of centralizing political power via the discourse of democratic populism.

Mrs Gandhi's decision to nationalize banks was a means of projecting herself as an ally of the majority of the population, advocating socialist ideals with the higher aim of securing and consolidating her political power. Even in personal interviews, the need to embrace socialist policies because they were politically expedient is clear. She remarked that

> the business community don't understand that there is no alternative, the extreme Right position just has no place in India. The whole mood of the country is Center Left.[38]

This strategy, and the discourse of democratic populism that it utilized, began to diminish steadily the significance of other democratic institutions and processes. Political power began to rest increasingly with the prime minister's office and began to give more attention to its role as an agent of change for the majority of the population, while paying scant attention to the rights of individual citizens. The idea of democratic India was being transformed by Mrs Gandhi's discourse of democratic populism.

As events moved towards a crisis point between Mrs Gandhi and those who opposed her in the Congress Party, senior members of the party held an inquiry in November 1969 on charges of Mrs Gandhi showing indiscipline and disobedience to the party leadership. She was found guilty in absentia and expelled from the party. Mrs Gandhi fought back and managed to successfully sway 297 Congress members of parliament to her side, which constituted a majority of Congress members in the Lok Sabha and caused a split in the Congress Party. The party that had spearheaded the Indian independence movement and, since 1947, had shaped the character of the Indian state under Nehru, was finally dismembered. Mrs Gandhi remained prime minister, being the leader of the party with the largest number of members of parliament in the Lok Sabha. Nevertheless, it was a minority government, having lost its already slim majority in parliament as a result of the party's split. After the Congress Party had split, Mrs Gandhi is famously quoted to have said that her position as prime minister and as a member of the Congress was something inherent and beyond challenge, outside even the realm of law and democratic norms. In her address to the party delegates who had defected to her faction of the split Congress Party,[39] her position was characterized by the reality that

> nobody can throw me out of the Congress. It is not a legal question, nor one of passing a resolution to pronounce an expulsion order. It is a question of the very fibre of one's heart and being.[40]

The centralization of political power seemed to have reached its high point under Mrs Gandhi. She now headed a Congress Party that she would not be obliged to adhere to the procedural forms of inner party democracy that Nehru's Congress Party had viewed as part of its very identity. By dismembering the Congress Party in the service of consolidating her position as prime minister, as well as in response to the deep crisis in India's socio-political realm at this time, Mrs Gandhi radically re-framed the idea of Indian democracy.

The Emergency as domestic stability: reconfiguring Indian democracy

The declaration of the Emergency in 1975 is often seen as one of the most significant events during the tenure of Mrs Gandhi, especially since it remains the only time when the powers of parliament and other associated democratic institutions were suspended. A brief narrative of the events that led to the proclamation of the Emergency will serve as a useful context for an understanding of how and why it shaped the discourse of democracy within India. In this respect, representing the imposition of the Emergency as vital for the requisite 'stability' required for Indian democracy to function effectively recast the discourse of Indian democracy. This, in turn, altered representations of Indian state identity.

In late 1974, a group of politicians led by J.P. Narayan began organizing street protests and demonstrations around the country, calling for the removal of Mrs Gandhi as prime minister for her undemocratic policies and behaviour. This culminated in March 1975 in a demonstration through the streets of the capital, New Delhi. In June 1975, the Allahabad High Court ruled that Mrs Gandhi was guilty of two violations of election law during the 1971 elections, relating to corrupt practice.[41] This meant Mrs Gandhi was to be barred from holding any elected political office for the next six years and thus had to vacate the office of prime minister.[42] On 25 June 1975, Mrs Gandhi declared a state of Emergency in the country and leading opposition members were arrested by the police and imprisoned. The civil rights and liberties sanctioned by the constitution were suspended. The power of the courts was curtailed and censorship on the press was imposed.[43] India had experienced its first concrete interruption in democratic politics and it would come to impact very significantly upon the discourse of Indian democracy.

There is still some debate about whether or not Mrs Gandhi declared the Emergency for the cynical purpose of holding on to political power, or if she actually believed that the country was under threat and the Emergency was necessary to rescue it from such threats.[44] As set out in her letter to the president of India, Mrs Gandhi's official reason to declare the Emergency was that 'information has reached us which indicates that there is imminent danger to the security of India being threatened by internal disturbances'.[45] In a personal interview, Mrs Gandhi claimed that she feared that the country was being enveloped by chaos and that she thought that her leadership was badly needed: 'it was my duty to the country to stay, though I didn't want to'.[46]

Moving away from this debate, the most significant point about the imposition of the Emergency, for whatever reason it was actually imposed, is that it fundamentally challenged earlier representations of the relationship between democracy and the Indian state. In addition to the imperative of 'stability', the Emergency was also touted as 'a programme of national regeneration' and included a 20-point economic programme that laid out policies to make bonded labour illegal, to cancel the debt of poor farmers to moneylenders and to restrict land ownership among the wealthy.[47] Once again, following her decision to devalue the rupee and nationalize banks, Mrs Gandhi sought to represent crucial policy decisions via the discourse of democratic populism.

The notion of Indian democracy, represented by Nehru, as a negotiation of the tension between the protection of the institutions of representative democracy on the one hand, and the nature of the Indian state's role as an agent of social change on the other was coming unstuck. Mrs Gandhi's decision to impose the Emergency and her reasons for it adversely impacted this delicate balance. In consideration of the role of the Indian state, the range of coercive powers accrued by the central government during this period for use against its citizens would continue to haunt Indian politics after the end of the Emergency and even after Mrs Gandhi's death.[48]

The Emergency ended on 20 March 1977 after Mrs Gandhi was defeated overwhelmingly in India's sixth general election. It would be the first time in the history of independent India that the Congress Party had failed to form the government of India. However, she would return as prime minister in 1980 and would reengage with the process of the consolidation of the central government's increase in political power relative to the different constituent states within the Indian Union. One important facet of Nehru's representation of the democratic compact was the need to maintain India's federal complexion. Acting for the Indian state, the central government was expected to balance the imperatives of a strong central government with the autonomy of the constituent states within this compact. Via her discourse of democratic populism and her calculated efforts to accumulate overwhelming political power in the office of the prime minister, Mrs Gandhi would transform this balance by increasing the power of the central government over the affairs of the constituent units of the Indian Union. As Paul Brass notes, the major difference between the Nehru and Indira Gandhi periods was that

> unlike her father, who preferred to deal with strong chief ministers in control of their legislative parties and state party organisations, Mrs. Gandhi set out to remove every Congress chief minister who had an independent base and replace each of them with chief ministers personally loyal to her and without an independent base.[49]

The selection of chief ministers who owed personal loyalty to Mrs Gandhi thus began to transform the nature of the balance between the central government and the governments of the constituent units.[50] The appointment and use of governors in the various states to enact presidential rule, dismiss democratically elected state legislatures under the pretext of bad governance and to restore order was a distinctive feature of the relationship between the central government and the constituent state units during Mrs Gandhi's tenure.[51] It fundamentally transformed an important aspect of Indian democracy framed during Nehru's era. By making regional politics and political elites at the state level highly dependent upon the central government for their political existence, Mrs Gandhi's policies would result in the Indian polity's increasing lack of any form of genuine federalism. This, combined with the effects of the Emergency from 1975 to 1977, would alter radically the discourse of democracy within India, impacting Indian state identity in a similar manner in the process.

Territorial integrity as anti-imperialism

Fiercely safeguarding territory deemed to be part of India's territorial space was a prominent feature of the Nehru period. In the Mrs Gandhi period, the imperative to defend India's territorial space was just as important. Similar to the Nehru era, the imperative was legitimated via the discourse of anti-imperialism. It was especially apparent during one of the most important events to take place in the history of South Asia and India since the partition of 1947, India's role in the formation of Bangladesh in 1971.

The critical role played by India in the formation of Bangladesh has often been acclaimed as the high point of realpolitik and a comprehensive shift in Indian foreign policy from its earlier Nehruvian leanings.[52] This line of reasoning views Mrs Gandhi's approach, from the beginning, to be a calculated endeavour to bring about the eventual territorial division and political diminution of the Pakistani state.[53] As prevalent as this argument may be, it is equally vital to understand Mrs Gandhi's perceptions and actions leading up to and in the aftermath of the 1971 Bangladesh War within the context of the domestic anti-imperialism discourse concerning the defence of the territorial sanctity of India's land borders.[54] A brief account of the events surrounding India's role in this war with Pakistan and the eventual formation of Bangladesh will help to illuminate this argument.

At independence, Pakistan was comprised of two halves, East and West Pakistan that were not territorially contiguous and were separated by Indian territory. Despite being the more populous of the two halves of Pakistan, East Pakistan (later to become Bangladesh) was under-represented in both of the major institutions of the Pakistani state – the military and the senior civil service – and in the political decision-making process. By early 1970, widespread street protests against a West Pakistan-dominated government were taking place in East Pakistan. A crisis point was reached when Pakistani army soldiers (predominantly from West Pakistan) implemented a programme of rape and massacre in order to quell the rebellion in East Pakistan.[55] It led to the displacement of millions of refugees from East Pakistan into the neighbouring Indian states of Tripura, Assam and West Bengal.[56] This created a serious problem for the Indian state. Not only was the movement of such large numbers of refugees into India putting enormous financial strain on the Indian state, it demonstrated the porous nature of India's territorial borders.[57] To add to this, Pakistani generals began to proclaim that guerrilla soldiers who crossed the border into India for refuge after attacking Pakistani soldiers in East Pakistan would be pursued into India and, if necessary, 'the war would be fought on Indian territory'.[58] This was interpreted as a clear and direct threat to the integrity of India's territorial borders.

Despite this clear indication of threat to India, Mrs Gandhi chose not to exercise the military option at this juncture to stop the flood of refugees crossing into India in escape from the Pakistani army's brutal repression in East Pakistan. This course was chosen even though members of various opposition parties, as well as certain Congress Party members, were urging Mrs Gandhi to act in a decisive, military manner in response to the threat. In fact, at this time, Mrs Gandhi even refused to officially recognize 'Bangladesh', the name the government-in-exile had given East Pakistan in the event of it becoming independent, much to the consternation of both opposition members of parliament and some of her close associates.[59]

Nonetheless, important strategic imperatives were behind this hesitation. Both the rising position of Pakistan as an ally of the United States and Pakistan's close ties with China made Mrs Gandhi wary of the potential military intervention of one or both of these countries on the side of Pakistan in the event of a war with India.[60] However, there is sufficient evidence to show that even at a later stage (in August 1971), having sealed the assurance of countervailing Russian support in the event of any war between India and Pakistan over East Pakistan, Mrs Gandhi was still not keen to exercise the military option. Rather, her approach to stem the flow of refugees into India from East Pakistan comprised of appeals to Pakistan's political leadership to stop its campaign of brutal oppression in East Pakistan and to agree to a negotiated settlement with the political leadership of East Pakistan.

Mrs Gandhi delivered a similar private message to Richard Nixon, then US President, that the US should use its influence on the Pakistani government to deliver a negotiated settlement between the leaders of Pakistan and the East Pakistani leadership in order to avert the likelihood of war.[61] Despite such seeming restraint in deploying the military option, Mrs Gandhi could not ignore entirely the implications of such large-scale border breaches. From the Nehru period, defending the integrity of India's territorial space was integral to the discourse of anti-imperialism within India. The crisis in East Pakistan and the resultant violation of India's territorial borders on such a large scale inevitably emphasized the anti-imperialism discourse within India at the time.

In her public speeches, Mrs Gandhi went to great lengths to locate the main source of the threat that the East Pakistan crisis was causing for India. To this end, she declared that

India will have to take whatever steps are necessary for the protection of the security of our *borders* and for the maintenance of our *integrity* and stability [emphasis added].[62]

An analysis of the context of Mrs Gandhi's private and public positions on the East Pakistan crisis casts some doubt upon the conventional interpretation of the eventual Indian military intervention during this crisis as a straightforward case of Indian foreign policy derived purely from inter-state realpolitik considerations. As Chadda points out, accounts that explain Indian intervention in East Pakistan in relation to the realpolitik motivations of Mrs Gandhi's venture to establish Indian hegemony in South Asia 'confuse the outcome with motivation'.[63] Therefore, although

> it was in India's interest to weaken and reduce Pakistan in the region [...] this interest did not translate into action until after March 1971, when Pakistani armed action had sent a torrent of refugees into India. The steady stream of refugees virtually erased the boundaries between India and Pakistan.[64]

The importance of guarding India's territorial integrity as a means of maintaining its sovereign status relate directly to the discourse of anti-imperialism, articulated by Mrs Gandhi in this instance. Therefore, rather than merely pursuing her goal of Indian hegemony in South Asia, Mrs Gandhi approached this particular crisis domestically, focusing upon the challenge of large-scale border transgressions to the Indian state's identity and mediating it through the discourse of anti-imperialism.

Conventional war between India and Pakistan commenced officially on 3 December 1971 with the Pakistani air force launching an attack on Indian bases in India. The Indian army responded and, by 16 December, Pakistani troops in East Pakistan had surrendered.[65] In the midst of the conflict, the US Seventh Fleet was dispatched to the Bay of Bengal in a show of support for the Pakistani military. Within India, the perception that the US was attempting to obstruct India in its effort to defend its territorial integrity strengthened even further the necessity of India's military intervention for the protection of its sovereignty and freedom. This perception is discernible in Mrs Gandhi's reaction to the US deployment. In addressing a public rally in New Delhi and discarding her prepared speech, Mrs Gandhi promised the Indian people that India 'will not retreat' and that 'not by a single step will we [the Indian military] move back'.[66]

The ensuing Indian victory in the face of perceived attempts by the US to intimidate Mrs Gandhi emphasized the importance of defending India's territorial integrity and sovereignty, for the country to defend its freedom as an independent state. Within India, the country's military victory was represented as a defence of one of the Indian state's founding principles: anti-imperialism. The references to Mrs Gandhi within the country as the Hindu goddess of war *Durga* is evidence of the way in which the defence of India's territorial space was represented as a crucial aspect of the reinforcement of one of the Indian state's central identities.[67]

By representing the violation of India's territorial space through the discourse of anti-imperialism, Mrs Gandhi was continuing Nehru's mode of representing any possible intrusion or compromise of Indian territory as an attack upon the identity of the Indian state. The representation of territorial integrity as a central facet of the defence of Indian freedom and sovereignty would continue to be an important facet of the Indian state's identity in the post-Indira Gandhi era.

Conclusion

The Indira Gandhi era witnessed a profound change in the construction of Indian state identity. By rearticulating the notion of secularism within the context of India's domestic identity-politics, Mrs Gandhi profoundly re-defined the discourse of Indian secularism from the binary opposite of religiously driven, 'communal politics' to one in which secularism came to represent the Indian state's appeal to the latent suspicions of different religious communities in order to win and consolidate political power. Mrs Gandhi's implementation of the rupee devaluation, bank nationalization and imposition of the 'Emergency' fundamentally changed the democratic complexion of the Indian state. Through the discourse of democratic populism, the central government increasingly accrued political power within the office of the prime minister. Lastly, Mrs Gandhi continued the Nehruvian discourse of representing the breach of India's territorial space as an attack on the sovereignty and freedom of the Indian state. By framing the discourse of anti-imperialism as a demonstration of the will and ability to defend India's territorial frontiers, Mrs Gandhi reinforced this particular aspect of the Indian state's identity. The next chapter will locate the manner in which these specific representations of Indian state identity informed different conceptions of India's regional space and role during the Indira Gandhi period.

4 A 'new' phase in Indian foreign policy
The case of Pakistan and Sri Lanka

In 1972, the end of the Bangladesh War led to a post-war summit in Simla, India. The division of Pakistan and the impending birth of a new independent state in South Asia potentially marked a new epoch for the region. This particular summit, often referred to as the Simla Summit, between India and Pakistan, was viewed as an historical opportunity to re-structure the relationship between the two countries as a result of the war. This chapter will look at the ways in which Mrs Gandhi's specific representations of the Indian state, forged between 1966 and 1972, impacted upon her view of how this bilateral relationship should be re-structured at this landmark summit. The second part of the chapter will examine India's involvement in Sri Lanka's ethnic crisis in the 1980s. It will trace how certain elements of Mrs Gandhi's representations of Indian state identity drove Indian foreign policy towards Sri Lanka during this period.

Mrs Gandhi's India and Indian conceptions of its regional role

Hailed as the 'Empress of India' in the aftermath of the 1971 war, Indira Gandhi significantly re-framed the identity of the Indian state in contrast to the Nehru era. One key shift was the manner in which the Indian state began to acquire and centralize political power, even as early as 1971, in a mode not seen during the Nehru period. The process of the centralization of political power was legitimized largely through the discourse of democratic populism, or 'direct democracy'. It was coupled with a representation of the Indian state's freedom and sovereignty via an apparently firm resolve to defend the integrity of India's territory, a representation that originated in the Nehru era. Taken together, these factors gave the impression of a politically and militarily strong Indian state, with the will and ability to use such force domestically in pursuit of its representation of Indian state identity.

During this period, the representation of the politically and militarily strong Indian state had implications for the manner in which the Indian state perceived its role in South Asia. The war with Pakistan in 1971 demonstrated the crucial link between the self-conception of the Indian state and its

66 *A 'new' phase in Indian foreign policy*

conception of its role in South Asia. This chapter will proceed from this link to demonstrate how the post-war settlement of the 1971 war came to reflect the ways in which the construction of Indian state identity led to particular conceptions of India's role in South Asia, with significant foreign policy outcomes.

The 1972 Simla Agreement and the establishment of 'bilateralism' in Indo-Pak relations

By 16 December 1971, the war over East Pakistan was at and end and the Pakistani troops had surrendered. After the humiliating defeat to India, Yahya Khan, the military ruler of the Pakistan, resigned and was replaced by an experienced politician, Zulfikar Ali Bhutto.[1] The immediate post-war context was dominated by two different sets of demands by India and Pakistan. In the immediate term, the Indian state demanded that Bhutto recognize the new state of Bangladesh (formerly East Pakistan). In the long term, the Indian state wanted Pakistan to transform the Cease-Fire Line (CFL) in Kashmir into a permanent international boundary between the two countries. Moreover, it wanted Pakistan to commit to conducting its relations with the Indian state on a strictly bilateral basis without any other states, or international organizations mediating relations between the two states.[2] Pakistan, on the other hand, wanted the Indian military to withdraw from those areas that it had occupied during the war and the release of the Pakistani prisoners of war.[3] It was within the context of these divergent demands and expectations that Indira Gandhi and Ali Bhutto met on 28 June 1972 for a summit meeting in the Indian resort town of Simla. The product of this meeting, the Simla Agreement, would have far-ranging implications for India–Pakistan relations beyond the tenures and lifetimes of both leaders.

Whilst both leaders arrived at the summit with divergent demands and expectations, Mrs Gandhi was in the stronger position, given that the Indian military had obtained the surrender of Pakistan's troops. She insisted that Pakistan should accept both India's position on Kashmir and to agree to the principle of bilateralism in its relations with India. Realizing his position of relative weakness in the negotiations, Bhutto was nonetheless anxious about the domestic outcry that an acceptance of India's position on Kashmir would cause. He went to great lengths to explain his domestic pressures to Mrs Gandhi during the negotiations.[4] In the end, just as the situation appeared to have reached an impasse from which no agreement would be forthcoming, a private discussion between the two leaders, in the absence of their respective advisers, led to an agreement that would come to be known as the Simla Agreement.[5]

Certain events that led to the Simla agreement and its aftermath demonstrate the ways in which Mrs Gandhi's approach to Pakistan was mediated through specific representations of the Indian state that she had forged. Two points of the agreement are especially relevant. The first is that the two countries are resolved to settle their differences by peaceful means through bilateral negotiations or by any other peaceful means mutually agreed upon between them [and] neither side shall unilaterally alter the situation and both shall prevent organization, assistance and encouragement of any acts detrimental to the maintenance of peaceful and harmonious relations.[6]

The key word here is 'bilateral'. By getting Pakistan to agree and accept that its relations with India should not be subject to any form of external mediation, arbitration or pressure, Mrs Gandhi had managed to fulfil the task that Nehru had attempted in the mid-1950s when he retracted his offer to settle the Kashmir dispute through a plebiscite to be conducted under the auspices of the UN. On this account, most observers of Indian foreign policy are in concurrence that this point of the agreement strengthened India's role as the pre-eminent state in South Asia. As Sumit Ganguly notes,

> the mention of bilateral negotiations is significant. Since India's ill-fated experience of taking the Kashmir dispute to the United Nations, successive Indian governments had made every effort to limit third party or multilateral initiatives for settling the Kashmir question. Pakistan, as the weaker state in the region, had sought to do precisely the opposite. It had consistently sought to internationalise the dispute and had enlisted the support of various nations in order to bolster its position.[7]

The second component of the Simla Agreement that was especially pertinent to Mrs Gandhi's approach to Pakistan was the reference to the status of the disputed state of Jammu and Kashmir. Both sides agreed that

> in Jammu and Kashmir, the Line of Control resulting from the ceasefire of December, 1971 shall be respected by both sides without prejudice to the recognised position of either side. Neither side shall seek to alter it unilaterally, irrespective of mutual differences and legal interpretations. Both sides further undertake to refrain from the threat or the use of force in violation of this Line.[8]

This agreement effectively meant the conversion of the earlier ceasefire line to a line of control, thus reinforcing the relative permanence of the division of the state of Jammu and Kashmir between India and Pakistan. The negotiations between Mrs Gandhi and Bhutto indicated that this line of control would eventually evolve into a permanent, *de jure* international border between the two countries.[9] Of course, this was seen to be very beneficial to India's position in Jammu and Kashmir. By the mid-1950s, Nehru had sought to freeze the ceasefire line in Kashmir and attempted to transform it into a permanent international boundary. Once again, Mrs Gandhi had apparently managed to realize Nehru's aims in India's dealings with Pakistan over Jammu and Kashmir.

However, many Indians argued at the time, and some still argue now, that Mrs Gandhi could and should have pushed Bhutto further on the issue of Jammu and Kashmir. During the negotiations at Simla, Mrs Gandhi's personal advisers advocated strongly the position that nothing short of Pakistan's 'categorical and formal agreement' to recognize the dividing line between the two countries in Jammu and Kashmir as a *de jure* international boundary would do. They believed that the release of Pakistani prisoners captured during the war and the vacation of occupied Pakistani territory by the Indian military should be conditional to Pakistan's acceptance of this demand.[10]

Bhutto claimed that his agreement to such recognition of Jammu and Kashmir division would result in a huge backlash against him domestically, especially in light of the perceived humiliation of Pakistan's defeat and its impending dismemberment. Instead, according to the accounts of several Indian bureaucrats privy to the discussions at Simla, Bhutto agreed in private that there should be a *de jure* border in Jammu and Kashmir between India and Pakistan at some point in the near future but he could not, for domestic political reasons, agree to it in public at that moment.[11] In the end, for the present at least, Mrs Gandhi decided to not make the signing of the Simla Agreement contingent upon Bhutto's official acceptance of the permanent division of Jammu and Kashmir.

The Simla Agreement: Mrs Gandhi as arch-realist?

Mrs Gandhi's ability to secure an Indian victory whilst dismembering Pakistan is often viewed as the quintessential illustration of realpolitik in Indian foreign policy. Such a view came from no less a person than the president of the United States, Richard Nixon. In Henry Kissinger's memoirs, the *White House Years*, he recounts Nixon's personal views on Mrs Gandhi's approach and intentions. Kissinger notes that

> Nixon had no time for Mrs Gandhi's condescending manner. Privately, he scoffed at her moral pretensions, which he found all the more irritating because he suspected that in pursuit of her purposes she had in fact fewer scruples than he. He considered her indeed a cold-blooded practioner of power-politics [he] had admitted to the Senior Review Group that in Mrs. Gandhi's position he might pursue a similar course.[12]

According to this logic, winning the war, dismembering Pakistan, coercing Pakistan into agreeing to the bilateralization of India–Pakistan relations and moving slowly but surely towards the permanent division of the state of Jammu and Kashmir was evidence of Mrs Gandhi's ability to pursue India's national interest through the practice of realist power politics. This is a view echoed in various academic and policy circles and some credence ought to be given to this view.[13] For example, it is difficult to deny the fact that the prospect of dismembering Pakistan by aiding the formation of Bangladesh would have appealed to Mrs Gandhi because it would allow India to further assert its predominance in South Asia. The Indian army's provision of refuge and training of the East Pakistani Mukti Bahani forces would thus be informed by this objective.[14] Moreover, an unambiguous and overwhelming defeat of Pakistan would demonstrate finally India's military supremacy to Pakistan as its main regional challenger, especially after what were held to be, at best, stalemates in the 1947 and 1965 wars.[15] This argument, although accurate to some extent, comprises an incomplete analysis of the reasons for India going to war in 1971 and for the manner in which Mrs Gandhi approached and negotiated the post-war Simla Agreement.

For example, a realist account cannot explain satisfactorily why Mrs Gandhi, after having achieved a decisive military victory, did not push the Pakistani political leadership to accept the Indian objective of converting the ceasefire line boundary between India and Pakistan in Jammu and Kashmir into an international border. At this time, India was in military control of a part of Pakistani administered Jammu and Kashmir and it was in custody of 93,000 Pakistani prisoners of war. Moving beyond a purely realist account, part of the answer to this question lies in the manner in which Mrs Gandhi publicly represented India's support for the East Pakistanis in their fight against the Pakistani state.

In the run-up to the outbreak of war between India and Pakistan in 1971, Mrs Gandhi represented India's support for East Pakistan's challenge to the Pakistani government through the discourses of democracy and ethnic and religious equality. Mrs Gandhi's criticism of the Pakistani government emphasized its denial of democratic rights to East Pakistanis and argued that religion should not be the only basis upon which people should remain part of the same state. Thus, Mrs Gandhi implied that the people of East Pakistan should be allowed to secede and should not be denied this right simply because they were Muslims and thought to be of one nation with their co-religionists in West Pakistan. On 3 December 1971, in a public address a few hours before the commencement of war with Pakistan, Mrs Gandhi, commenting on developments in East Pakistan, went to great lengths to attack the Muslim basis of the Pakistani nation. She told her audience that,

> religion or language alone cannot be a basis for unity [...] You cannot build a nation on the principle of a single religion. We said this at the time of the formation of Pakistan, but the British and others did not listen to us. From the very beginning, what we have been witnessing in Pakistan is the cruel domination of people belonging to one religion over people belonging to other religions and on other minority groups. But what the world is witnessing today is the victimisation of the majority by a minority professing the same religion.[16]

In the light of this argument, the impending division of Pakistan would demonstrate amply the erroneous basis of the country's existence and the supremacy of India's secular model that seemed to protect different religious and ethnic communities with greater success than that which had been demonstrated in Pakistan. By aiding the resistance movement in East Pakistan and delivering a decisive military victory against the West Pakistan-led military, Mrs Gandhi left Bhutto with little choice but to recognize the independence of Bangladesh as an independent state and, in the process, managed to transform Pakistan's initial 'two-nation' theory into a contemporary three-state reality.[17] This new physical reality had implications for the existential ideational battle between India and Pakistan. The idea of Pakistan as the home of the Muslim nation in South Asia had been undermined, while the idea of secular India as a model for a secular South Asia was gaining currency.[18]

As the previous chapter discussed, the discourse of democracy and its relationship to the identity of the Indian state underwent an important re-negotiation during Indira Gandhi's term. In the case of the East Pakistani crisis, one of the primary reasons given by Mrs Gandhi's government for India's involvement was the defence of the democratic rights of the people in East Pakistan. On balance, it is difficult to ascertain whether or not Mrs Gandhi and her advisers believed genuinely that protecting the democratic rights of the East Pakistani people was the paramount justification for Indian military intervention. Moreover, in three to four years' time, in 1975, Mrs Gandhi would herself impose the Emergency and suspend all democratic processes and practices in India for a period of two years.

However, by utilizing the discourse of democracy as the central driver for India's intervention in the East Pakistani crisis, Mrs Gandhi's government inevitably constrained its own goals in the post-war talks at Simla. One external source of constraint at these talks was the UN. The role of the UN as a credible and impartial body, with the ability to settle disputes between India and Pakistan satisfactorily, had diminished in the perception of Indian leaders such as Nehru from the mid-1950s, yet the UN still impinged and set certain limits on Indian foreign policy. As in the Nehru era, the Indian state had to negotiate with international opinion and the UN was an important institution in this respect. In negotiating international opinion on the East Pakistan crisis, the Indian state strove to ensure that the UN not equate India with Pakistan. In fact, the Indian government protested against suggestions that the East Pakistan crisis was borne out of an India–Pakistan issue, arguing that the Indian state was merely lending its support to the plight of the East Pakistani people and that the real crux of the issue was that the Pakistani government denied legitimate democratic rights to its own population. For example, speaking in November 1971 at an address to the National Press Club in Washington, Mrs Gandhi pointed out that

> in the various capitals I have visited on this tour I have been asked what solution India would like. The question is not what we would like, or what one or other of the great powers would like, but what the people of

East Bengal will accept and what solution would be a lasting one [...] We have taken the biggest possible initiative in remaining so self-restrained and in keeping in check the anger within our country. We have endeavoured strenuously to see that this does not become an Indo-Pakistan issue [...] Pakistan's pleas for observers from the United Nations, for bilateral talks with India, and for mutual withdrawal of troops seemed very plausible at first sight. But these are only methods to divert the attention of the world from the root of the problem to what are merely by-products [...] We cannot have a dialogue with Pakistan on the future of East Bengal, because we have no right to speak for the people of East Bengal.[19]

In negotiating international opinion at forums such as the UN, Indian representatives sought to convince the majority of Third World states that it was engaged solely in upholding the democratic rights of the people of East Pakistan. The aim was to win support for India's position in the UN General Assembly as the outbreak of war between India and Pakistan loomed ominously over East Pakistan. This position was critical, especially because many in the Indian government were convinced that Pakistan would initiate war with India soon in order to implicate India in the East Pakistan crisis and to invite a quick UN intervention that would be beneficial to Pakistan's interests.[20]

Once war broke out, the manner in which Indian representatives at the UN conducted the Indian response demonstrates the manner in which the Indian state sought to frame its war with Pakistan. After the surrender of Pakistani troops, Indian representatives characterized Indian involvement as an act of self-defence through which it had also helped uphold the democratic rights of the people of East Pakistan, rather than a military victory against Pakistan. The implication was that India, as a country committed to democracy as a founding state principle, could not 'stand by and see a whole population liquidated'.[21] It is important to not focus upon the apparently genuine motives underpinning Mrs Gandhi's intervention in East Pakistan at the expense of a consideration of the manner in which she sought to represent India's intervention and the way in which the maintenance of democratic rights were linked to Indian state identity. The decision to represent Indian involvement within the context of India's own democratic identity would have an important impact upon Mrs Gandhi's approach to the post-war negotiations at Simla.

The responses of the major states in the UN Security Council were mixed.[22] China introduced a draft resolution that condemned India and asked it to withdraw its troops from Pakistani territory. It called upon all states to support Pakistan in its just struggle against Indian aggression. The US-drafted resolution asked for an immediate end to all India–Pakistan hostilities and called for an immediate withdrawal of Indian and Pakistani forces from each other's territories. However, the Russian resolution called for a political settlement in East Pakistan that, it believed, would lead automatically to an end of military hostilities. The Pakistani delegation claimed that India was deliberately creating a separatist movement in East Pakistan by providing it open military support.

Due to the Soviet Union and the US exercising their respective vetoes, none of the Security Council resolutions were passed and implemented. The Indian position, made by the Indian foreign minister, Swaran Singh, concerned the reiteration of the point that the present conflict was borne out of the denial of the democratic rights of the people of East Pakistan and was not the result of Indian motivation for territorial expansion. By 16 December, on receiving news that the Pakistani army had surrendered in East Pakistan, Swaran Singh announced India's unilateral ceasefire on all fronts in accordance with instructions that he had received from Delhi. This announcement was meant to demonstrate that India had fought the war for exactly the reasons that its government had stated from the beginning – to help the people of East Pakistan win their battle against oppression from the Pakistani state and to not annex East Pakistan and parts of West Pakistan, despite having achieved a complete military victory in both theatres of war. The private instructions passed by Swaran Singh to the Indian delegates at the UN are indicative of the Indian state's desire to represent its military victory as a victory for democracy within the UN. As J.N. Dixit recounts,

> Swaran Singh came out and conveyed two or three very precise instructions that we were to follow strictly. He said that no Indian delegate should be seen at the bar in the delegates' lounge in the coming 48 hours. He cautioned us not to be boastful or jingoistic in our conversation with other delegates about the victory of the Indian Army and the liberation of Bangladesh [...]He stressed in our responses we should underline that the break-up of Pakistan was a tragedy, that the cause of the tragedy was entirely due to the unreasonableness of the Pakistani military regime, that India's support to the liberation struggle was unavoidable and that India's declaration of a unilateral ceasefire in the western theatre of war was proof it had no aggressive designs.[23]

After the war, the manner in Mrs Gandhi approached the negotiations at Simla exhibited the extent to which representations of India's actions in 1971, mediated through the discourse of democracy, had a significant impact upon the outcome of these negotiations.[24] As highlighted earlier, realist explanations appear unable to account satisfactorily for why Mrs Gandhi did not follow the counsel of her advisors and use the advantage of a clear military victory, the possession of previously Pakistani-controlled parts of Kashmir and the capture of 93,000 Pakistani prisoners of war to ensure that Bhutto agreed to convert the ceasefire line (CFL) in Kashmir into a permanent international boundary. Instead, she agreed formally to the much less desirable result of the conversion of the CFL into a line of control (LOC).

According to realist logic, it would have been advantageous for Mrs Gandhi to extract this crucial concession in order to further cement India's position as the leading state in South Asia, in geopolitical terms at least.[25]

Yet, having represented India's war as a quest to defend democratic rights, Mrs Gandhi could not ignore the fact that Bhutto was Pakistan's first elected leader in more than two decades. On a personal level, Mrs Gandhi was not disposed favourably to Bhutto because of his well-known hard-line views on India. In fact, even within US policy circles Bhutto was widely held to be more of a hardliner on India than his predecessor, General Yahya Khan.[26] Bhutto earned this reputation as a result of what was perceived to be his belligerent stance on India during his term as foreign minister in General Ayub Khan's government. He was removed from the post in 1966 on the basis of his 'egoistical opportunism and excessive ambition'.[27]

The fact that Bhutto was Pakistan's democratically elected leader weighed heavily upon Mrs Gandhi's perception of the terms of the Simla Agreement. As available sources attest, Mrs Gandhi was reluctant to force Bhutto to agree to the permanent division of Kashmir because she wanted, as far as she could, to help Bhutto to consolidate his civilian, democratic rule in Pakistan.[28] Furthermore, Bhutto's claims of a potential backlash that could result in his removal and replacement by a more hardline, more anti-Indian leadership may also have been a factor in Mrs Gandhi's calculations.[29] Nevertheless, Mrs Gandhi saw Bhutto as Pakistan's democratically elected leader and did not want to create conditions for his replacement by a non-democratic regime. She believed that it was in India's interest – that it was pertinent to its self-conception as a democratic state – to ensure that Bhutto as Pakistan's elected leader was not replaced by a representative of Pakistan's powerful military establishment. As she told her personal advisers at Simla, 'we have a vested interest in seeing there is democracy in Pakistan'.[30]

Despite the fact that Bhutto was one of the most anti-Indian political elites in Pakistan at this time, he nonetheless represented democracy in the country.[31] More interestingly, Mrs Gandhi was influenced by a specific discourse of democracy in her approach to Bhutto. It was linked intimately to her own domestic discourse on Indian democracy, one that concerned a direct appeal to the populace, in other words, democratic populism. As she related to her foreign secretary, T.N. Kaul the day after signing the Simla Agreement, Mrs Gandhi did not push Bhutto on Kashmir because

> I wanted to make a gesture to the people of Pakistan with whom we have ultimately to settle this question and live peacefully together. I did not want to keep the 5,000 sq miles of West Pakistan territory. It would have antagonised the people of Pakistan.[32]

In a similar manner to her use of democratic populism at home, Mrs Gandhi believed in appealing directly to the wider populace in Pakistan, rather than to approach these negotiations in the conventional fashion, as negotiations solely between the leaders of two countries. By making this gesture on Kashmir via Bhutto as the recently democratically elected leader of Pakistan, she hoped to make a direct appeal to the Pakistani populace, to convince them that India had no ulterior motive, such as the annexation of Pakistan's territorial space. In a similar fashion to the manner in which it was being shaped domestically through the discourse of democratic populism, the Indian state now was aiming to appeal directly to the people of Pakistan as part of its foreign policy.

The 1971 war and the Simla Agreement also demonstrated Mrs Gandhi's ability to keep, against great odds, great-power influence out of the conflict. As discussed in this chapter, Mrs Gandhi was especially concerned about possible US involvement in the Bangladesh War. To counter this possibility, she signed a treaty with the Soviet Union in the midst of the East Pakistan crisis. The signing of the Indo-Soviet Treaty of Peace, Friendship and Co-operation on 9 August 1971 has often been seen to be evidence of the end of India's non-aligned status and its emergence as a Soviet ally during the Cold War. Article nine of this treaty is often cited as evidence of this. It stipulated that

> in the event that any of the Parties is attacked or threatened with attack, the High Contracting Parties will immediately start mutual consultations with a view to eliminating this threat and taking appropriate effective measures to ensure peace and security for their countries.[33]

This was interpreted in most quarters as a defence pact and the end of India's non-aligned status. For example, even an Indian newspaper, *The Statesman* saw the agreement as 'almost indistinguishable from a defence pact'.[34] External opinion, especially the US administration's view, was similar. Details of a private memorandum exhibit this. On 11 August, two days after the signing of the Indo-Soviet Treaty at a meeting of the Senior Review Group on Pakistan, President Nixon notes that

> the USSR has signed a treaty with India. Some think the Russians want to punish the Pakistanis for their relationship with China. In his [Nixon's] view, the Russians are looking at this situation as they looked at the Middle East before the June war in 1967. The danger is that they may unleash forces there which no one can control.[35]

The view was straightforward: India had allowed itself to become part of the Soviet Union's wider Cold War schemes. Anchored in notions of non-alignment and an autonomous foreign policy forged in the Nehru era, the Indian brand of anti-imperialism was construed to have diminished. In fact, this is an incomplete reading of Mrs Gandhi's decision to sign the Indo-Soviet Treaty of 1971. Rather, it can be argued the main aim of the treaty was not to involve the Soviet Union in the East Pakistan crisis, and thus in South Asia, but to ensure that no external, extra-regional, powers involved themselves in the affairs of South Asia. Mrs Gandhi's government was aware of Pakistan's frequent and overt attempts to involve the US in its crisis with India over East Pakistan. Her government was attentive to the fact that the US administration under Nixon was continuing to supply arms to Pakistan and was ambiguous about whether or not it would intervene on the side of Pakistan in the event of armed conflict with India.[36] Additionally, Mrs Gandhi's government was alert to the growing role of China in the crisis. The Chinese government had come out in strong support of Pakistan and it, too, was ambiguous about the possibility of opening a second front against India in the event of an India–Pakistan war.[37]

The very real possibility of two extra-regional powers intervening in South Asia in the event of an India–Pakistan war was a worrying prospect for the Mrs Gandhi government. The signing of the agreement between the Soviet Union and India in 1971 was thus borne out of an anxiety about possible military intervention by the US and China in the East Pakistan crisis. Clearly, Mrs Gandhi's government was attempting to ensure that the US and China had less incentive to intervene militarily on Pakistan's side, rather than seeking military support from the Soviet Union. The tenet of preventing the involvement of extra-regional powers in the politics of South Asia, both internal and external, originated in the Nehru period. This imperative drove Nehru to ensure that the United States and, to a lesser extent, China, did not become significant actors in South Asia, especially with reference to perceived Indian interests in the region. It was understood by Indian political elites that India had special interests in South Asia and that this required the exclusion of extra-regional influence. In this view, such extra-regional exclusion was critical for the safeguard of India's sovereignty and its autonomous foreign policy, central to the Indian state's conception of itself as a symbol of anti-imperialism. Therefore, it was not surprising that Mrs Gandhi sought to bring about a similar outcome through the 1971 treaty with the Soviet Union. Also, it explains Mrs Gandhi's firm refusal to endorse a long-standing Soviet proposal for an Asian collective security organization, even after signing the 1971 treaty.[38]

Similarly, the motivation for Mrs Gandhi to institutionalize 'bilateralism' in the provisions of the Simla Agreement was informed by the need to prevent third-party intrusions in India–Pakistan relations. Similar to Nehru, Mrs Gandhi believed that in the absence of external, extra-regional intrusion, this bilateral relationship would not be subject to the pressure of Cold War politics. The possibility of the Cold War impinging upon India's immediate region, especially upon India's foreign policy in South Asia, had negative implications for the prospects of India's ability to safeguard its own territorial integrity.[39] From an Indian perspective, Pakistan was always eager to offer itself as an ally to external powers with the sole purpose of correcting its military imbalance with, and existential fear of, India.[40] Bhutto's albeit reluctant agreement to bilateralize relations with India marked an important milestone in India's endeavour to ensure that extra-regional powers were kept out of South Asia. This enhanced the Indian state's confidence in defending India's territorial integrity, a crucial element in the constitution of India's anti-imperial identity. From the Indian perspective, the Simla Agreement had sanctioned a central tenet of Indian state identity: it had delegitimized any imperialist interventions from outside the region that threatened Indian sovereignty and India's territorial integrity. The Indian state's position in South Asia had reached its zenith.

Mrs Gandhi and Sri Lanka – the Tamil crisis and Indian regional policy

From as early as 1979 until Mrs Gandhi's death in 1984, the Indian state intervened in various ways in the ethnic conflict in Sri Lanka. Although the Indian military intervened formally in Sri Lanka in August 1987 via the Indian Peace Keeping Force (IPKF) when Rajiv Gandhi was prime minister, the roots of this military intervention were laid in the Indira Gandhi period. Rajiv Gandhi's decision to send in the IPKF in 1987 was, in many respects, the culmination of his mother's approach to the ethnic conflict in Sri Lanka. Moreover, Mrs Gandhi's approach to Sri Lanka set certain precedents for the kind of role that the Indian state framed for itself, post-1971, within South Asia.

'Love thy neighbour' – Ceylon, Sri Lanka and India's role in the Tamil issue

During the British colonial era, Ceylon was not administered as part of the British Raj and was not part of British India.[41] Instead, it was administered by the British Colonial Office as a Crown Colony.[42] After gaining independence on 4 February 1948, the new Sri Lankan government signed defence agreements with Britain that permitted continued British control over its air and naval bases.[43] Up till the late 1970s, there were few major issues of contention between India and Sri Lanka, with the exception of the status of 'stateless persons' of Indian extraction who had been brought to Sri Lanka during the colonial era to work on plantations.

Two main ethno-religious groups populate Sri Lanka, the majority being Buddhist Singhalese and the minority Hindu Tamils.[44] The Tamil minority is concentrated mainly in the northern part of the country, commonly referred to as the Jaffna peninsula.[45] In the unitary Sri Lankan state, Tamil political parties and later Tamil armed groups felt that they were being subjugated by the Singhala dominated central government. Such a perception led inevitably to more vociferous demands for the greater autonomy of the Tamil areas and generally for Tamils within Sri Lanka.[46]

The plight and demands of the Tamils in Sri Lanka attracted much sympathy in the southern Indian state of Tamil Nadu, whose populace and political elites expressed solidarity with the demands of the Sri Lankan Tamils just across the Palk Strait that separates Tamil Nadu from the Jaffna peninsula. Most, if not all of the regional Tamil Nadu political parties, went to great lengths to exhibit their sympathy and solidarity for the perceived Tamil struggle in neighbouring Sri Lanka.

The year 1979 would mark a defining moment for the relationship between India and Sri Lanka. In 1979, Mrs Gandhi returned to power after being out of office for two years. Meanwhile, in Sri Lanka militancy in Tamil politics was becoming more prominent with several groups pushing the Tamil struggle for greater autonomy and the eventual founding of an autonomous Tamil homeland, or Tamil 'Eelam'.[47] Although a number of diverse groups were part of this broad movement, by 1979 a group known increasingly for its ruthless militancy was beginning to overshadow the other Tamil groups and parties in terms of influence and numbers – the Liberation Tigers of Tamil Eelam (LTTE).

From 1979, ethnic riots and killings continued to rise in Sri Lanka. In 1981, for example, during local district elections the government security forces and the LTTE engaged in a continuous cycle of violence that finally forced the central government to impose a national emergency in Sri Lanka from 4–9 June 1981.[48] It led to widespread protests in the Indian state of Tamil Nadu, with both the ruling regional party and the main opposition party calling upon the Indian government to raise the issue at the UN in order to protect their fellow Tamils from the Sri Lankan government's persecution.[49] The situation came to a head in July 1983 with ethnic riots in Sri Lanka's capital, Colombo on an unprecedented scale. It set the stage for the Indian government's direct interest in Sri Lanka's ethnic conflict.[50]

The riots in Sri Lanka led to widespread outrage in Tamil Nadu. The main regional opposition party in Tamil Nadu called upon the Indian government to launch a 'Bangladesh type' intervention in Sri Lanka.[51] Mrs Gandhi's first reaction was to send her external affairs minister, Narashimha Rao to Colombo after a telephone conversation with the Sri Lankan President on 29 July 1983. Rao's stated task was to obtain first-hand information about the crisis'.[52] Upon his return, Rao, reflecting the Indian government's position, reported in Parliament that the Sri Lankan government could not control the ongoing violence. More importantly, the Indian government perceived, with some alarm, that the Sri Lankan government might be looking to 'foreign powers to deal with their situation'.[53] From this point on, the Indian government's representation of the Sri Lankan crisis and India's role in the crisis became much clearer.

Mrs Gandhi and Sri Lanka – the prevailing arguments

The predominant argument in explanation of the Indian state's approach to Sri Lanka's ethnic conflict has been the apparent need for Mrs Gandhi and her government to pander to the sentiments of its Tamil population in India's

South. According to this argument, Mrs Gandhi's initial decision to send her External Affairs Minister to Colombo and her subsequent actions were based upon her efforts to placate Tamil sentiment in the southern Indian state of Tamil Nadu, especially since she needed the continued political support of this state's governing party for the 1984 Indian general elections.[54]

This argument has a number of strengths. It has been documented that Mrs Gandhi was aware that the Chief Minister of Tamil Nadu, M.G. Ramachandran and his ruling party were providing material support to the increasingly militant LTTE but she did not take steps to stop this assistance. It has been claimed that she even told her close associates that she would 'settle this whole thing after the election', implying that she would attempt to restrain the Tamil Nadu government only after the general elections were over.[55] Further evidence for such an argument is the fact that Mrs Gandhi's government provided unprecedented support for the state-government organized general strike in Tamil Nadu, a general strike meant to show support for the Tamils in Sri Lanka.[56] In this view, Mrs Gandhi's interest in and intervention into Sri Lankan internal affairs was based upon rational domestic calculations of siding with popular opinion in Tamil Nadu in order to improve the chances of Congress and its regional allies in the forthcoming Indian general elections.[57]

Another argument that attempts to explain Mrs Gandhi's actions towards Sri Lanka is based upon the broader argument that India's foreign policy, especially after 1971, was motivated by realpolitik calculations. It argues that in line with certain tenets of realist thought Mrs Gandhi wanted to assert India's role as the regional leader within South Asia.[58] The impetus for Mrs Gandhi's intervention in Sri Lanka was to demonstrate India's intentions and ability to play such a role. Accordingly, Mrs Gandhi's actions were meant to demonstrate India's pre-eminent military-political influence within South Asia to both insiders (the South Asian countries) and outsiders (the major powers, such as the United States and China).

Mrs Gandhi and Sri Lanka – the Mrs Gandhi idea of India

Despite their compelling explanations for Mrs Gandhi's approach to the Sri Lankan crisis, these two arguments cannot answer satisfactorily two key questions. First, although it is hard to deny that domestic political considerations were important for Mrs Gandhi to address, this does not account for how such state-level considerations were mediated at an all-India level and, consequently, how such considerations translated into Mrs Gandhi's approach towards the Sri Lankan civil war.

In the Indira Gandhi era, especially in her second government, the Indian state's role as an independent arbitrator between religious and ethnic groups was diminishing. Instead, it sought increasingly to exploit the fears that various religious and ethnic groups held for each other as an instrument for attaining popular support and maintaining political power.[59] Similarly,

Mrs Gandhi's central government sought to represent the interests of the Indian state with that of the Tamil community within Tamil Nadu in order to maintain political support within the state.

While it would not be incorrect to assert that, in this instance, Mrs Gandhi and her government acted on the basis of narrow domestic political interests, it is significant to acknowledge how foreign policy was impacted by the shifting self-representations of the Indian state. Popular sentiment in Tamil Nadu was an important driver for Mrs Gandhi to intervene directly in the Sri Lanka conflict because, on this occasion, she aligned the interests of the Indian state with those of the Tamil community in Tamil Nadu. This association was constructed via the discourse of secularism that Mrs Gandhi had framed, especially in her second term, at an all-India level. This re-framed discourse of secularism represented the Indian state, at various opportune moments, as the guardian of the narrow interests of specific religious and ethnic communities within India. In this particular case it was the Tamil community in Tamil Nadu. Mrs Gandhi's statement in parliament in August 1983 is indicative of how such a representation made Indian inaction on this issue an unrealistic foreign policy option. India could not stand by and watch the events in Sri Lanka silently because

> India stands for the independence, unity and integrity of Sri Lanka. India does not interfere in the internal affairs of other countries. *However, because of the historical, cultural and other close ties between the peoples of the two countries, especially between the Tamil community of Sri Lanka and us,* India cannot remain unaffected by events there [emphasis added].[60]

Having represented the interests of the Indian state with that of the Tamil community in India, Mrs Gandhi could proclaim without hesitation the 'close ties' between the Tamil community in Sri Lanka and the Indian state. In addition, despite the stated qualification of India not wishing to 'intervene in the domestic affairs of other countries', it was made clear that 'India cannot remain unaffected' by events concerning the Tamils in Sri Lanka. In effect, Mrs Gandhi was not ruling out intervention into Sri Lanka's internal affairs at this stage and actually instigated a policy that would lead to eventual Indian military intervention through the IPKF during Rajiv Gandhi's tenure. A specific discourse of secularism had led to a particular representation of the Indian state's interests and its identity. This identity, as shown in this episode, drove Indian foreign policy in a significant direction even after Mrs Gandhi's period in office.

The second explanation for Mrs Gandhi's approach views her response as a case of archetypal realpolitik behaviour. According to this argument, India wanted to demonstrate to the Sri Lankan government, other neighbouring states, and states outside South Asian region that it was the hegemonic state within its immediate region. For example, De Silva explains India's approach to the Sri Lankan crisis of the 1980s under Mrs Gandhi's government through its wider perception of India's role in South Asia. According to him,

> India decided that small South Asian neighbours like Sri Lanka must take shelter under that [Indian security] umbrella and that a search for an alternative would be regarded as an unacceptable if not intolerable, challenge to the new 'dominant power' (parenthesis added).[61]

Similar to the domestic electoral politics argument, this argument is not without its merits. After the division of Pakistan and the establishment of the state of Bangladesh, there is evidence that the Indian state, under Mrs Gandhi Gandhi, had begun to view itself as the dominant power within South Asia. However, this explanation does not shed any light upon why Mrs Gandhi sought to represent India as the dominant power within South Asia beyond an implicit assumption that all states seek to exert their influence, given the opportunity and the resources to do so. It is largely because this line of argument does not probe the domestic realm in understanding Indian foreign policy. By looking domestically at the Indian state, it would become apparent that certain representations of Indian state identity led to particular ways of conceiving of India's regional role in South Asia. Therefore, such representations of its role as the dominant power in South Asia stem from a deeper conception of the Indian state's self-representation. Reminiscent of India's approach to Pakistan, such self-representation had repercussions for the Indian foreign policy towards Sri Lanka.

In the discussion about India's approach towards the East Pakistan crisis in the previous chapter, the link between the discourse of anti-imperialism and the robust defence of India's territorial borders has already been explored. The section on the Simla Summit in this chapter considered why Mrs Gandhi went to great lengths to institutionalize bilateralism in the India–Pakistan relationship in an attempt to keep the extra-regional powers from involving themselves in the domestic and international politics of the South Asian region. It stemmed from the Indian state's representation of any extra-regional involvement in South Asia as a possible source of impediment to the Indian state's ability to safeguard its largely porous territorial borders with other states in South Asia. It provoked Mrs Gandhi's government to take steps to ensure that countries in South Asia abstained from involving such extra-regional influence in India's regional space. The Indian state's approach to the Sri Lankan ethnic conflict in the 1980s demonstrates how certain domestically negotiated representations of Indian state identity rendered India's conception of itself as the dominant power in South Asia. This notion soon came to have a name – the 'Indira Doctrine'.

Sri Lanka and the 'Indira Doctrine'

After the 1983 riots in Sri Lanka, the Indian government expressed its concern about the presence of foreign powers there. Especially worrying for the

A 'new' phase in Indian foreign policy   81

Indian government was the involvement of Israeli commandos in strengthening the intelligence gathering and operational efficiency of the Sri Lankan security forces.[62] In addition to this, the Sri Lankan government had employed a sizeable number of British ex-SAS commandos as part of a private mercenary agency.[63] Moreover, the Sri Lankan government asked the British and American government for arms and training support at about this time and, although both governments refused to provide any direct support of this kind, the Indian government was quick to realize that the US strategic relationship with Sri Lanka was intensifying. A dramatic example of this was provision of refuelling facilities for American naval ships and the December 1983 agreement to allow the establishment of a Voice of America (VOA) transmission facility. The latter was especially worrisome for the Indian government, as it was perceived that such a facility could be used for espionage purposes by the American government against India.[64] All of these developments took place relatively soon after the July 1983 riots in Sri Lanka.

In both public and in private, Mrs Gandhi expressed India's annoyance at such moves by the Sri Lankan government to enlist external aid. On 5 August 1983 – immediately after the July riots and even before the agreement for the establishment of the VOA facility – Mrs Gandhi stressed in a speech in parliament that

> any extraneous involvement [in Sri Lanka] will complicate matters for both countries. We live in a region where many forces are at work not all of whom wish India or our neighbour well. Hence, we must make every effort to minimise any opportunity for foreign elements to weaken us.[65]

In private, Mrs Gandhi conveyed similar sentiments to the Sri Lankan leader. She made it clear that the arrival of foreign troops in Sri Lanka would be a cause of great concern for the Indian government and that if the Sri Lankan government needed troops for internal security, 'it should ask for Indian help or invite others only with Indian consent'.[66]

It could be argued that such moves on the part of the Indian government were driven by orthodox realpolitik logic in order to dominate its smaller and weaker neighbour. However, it fails to address the question why the Indian state, with its ability to influence the domestic politics and foreign policy of Sri Lanka as a result of its larger size and its preponderant military and economic capabilities, only intervened episodically from 1983 to 1991, even though the conflict in Sri Lanka started before 1983 and persisted for more than two decades after. Moreover, it fails to explain why the Indian government first supported the Tamil militant groups, only to send in the Indian Peace-Keeping Force (IPKF) during the governmentof Rajiv Gandhi to disarm these same Tamil groups.[67]

One important reason for this approach towards Sri Lanka was the way in which the Indian state viewed the prospect of any extra-regional influence. It viewed such a prospect as highly detrimental because of the way in which Indian state self-representations had been constructed. External involvement in South Asia threatened the Indian state's perception of its ability to safeguard its borders from various transgressions. This imperative to safeguard its borders was linked to the discourse of anti-imperialism as a central aspect of the identity of the Indian state. Therefore, instead of a desire to dominate Sri Lanka's domestic politics, or its foreign policy for its own sake, the Indian state's main goal was very specific. It concerned the prevention of any extra-regional involvement that could result from Sri Lanka's ethnic crisis.

It is evident that a major source of India's concern with regard to the Sri Lankan issue stemmed from the fact that there were conditions in Sri Lanka that made the possibility of extra-regional involvement possible. The goal of the Indian state was to take steps to ensure that this possibility was not realized. To such an end, it employed a two-prong policy in Sri Lanka. The first and more public position was to establish itself as the 'principal mediator', rather than a neutral mediator, the former position embodying more 'muscle and power in dispute resolution', and with the ability to force different sides in the conflict to accept it as the only mediator that mattered.[68]

The second and more clandestine move was the use of the Indian Research and Analysis Wing (more commonly known by its acronym, RAW), a part of the Indian intelligence machinery, to infiltrate and lend its support to different Tamil militant groups in Sri Lanka. This move comprised the provision of training facilities and even material support. The main reason for such clandestine support of these groups by RAW was to erode any other external support that these groups might seek, thus increasing their dependence upon the Indian state. It is also argued that control of the militants by RAW was a means of deterring the Sri Lankan government from soliciting external political and military support from any other country in its battle against Tamil militants.[69] Although exact accounts differ, by the end of the Indira Gandhi period it is reasonable to believe that Mrs Gandhi was contemplating Indian military intervention in Sri Lanka's ethnic crisis at this time, either with or without the Sri Lankan government's invitation.[70]

These two separate policies had one aim: to ensure that none of the parties in the conflict, neither the Sri Lankan government nor the different Tamil groups, would attempt to involve any other extra-regional state, or institution to intervene in this conflict. To enable this, Mrs Gandhi made both the Sri Lankan government and the Tamil groups reliant upon the Indian state. India was therefore able to play both the role of 'principal mediator' and principal, albeit clandestine, supporter of the Tamil groups. Another aim of the Indian government was to control the intensity of the conflict so that it would not rise to a level at which international, and specifically super-power, interest would be imminent.

Sri Lanka's permission for a VOA transmission facility, allowing US naval vessels to refuel at its Trincomalee harbour and engaging the services of

Israeli and ex-British commandoes to operate in the country were serious developments from the perspective of the Indian state.[71] Furthermore, there were signs that an escalating ethnic conflict in Sri Lanka had the potential to invite even greater global attention, leading to possible to Cold War competition in India's immediate region, South Asia.[72] To move forward in time, India's unconditional withdrawal of the IPKF in 1991 was seen to be based upon the fact that the Cold War was over and that the US, as sole remaining super-power, had accepted tacitly India's pre-eminent role in the affairs of South Asia.[73]

At the global level, the Indian state sought to represent India's role in two different ways. Diplomatically, it sought to draw global and, in particular, Third World attention 'towards the atrocities being perpetrated by the Sri Lankan armed forces on the Tamils'.[74] In the United Nations, both within the General Assembly and the Human Rights Commission, the Indian state sought to raise the issue of human rights violation in Sri Lanka against the Tamil minority.[75] However, the Indian state went to great lengths to discourage direct involvement in the Sri Lanka crisis by any state, or international organization, including participation in mediation between the Sri Lankan government and the Tamil militants.[76]

The policy to keep extra-regional powers out of South Asia has come to be known as the 'Indira Doctrine'.[77] Yet, as discussed in Chapter 2, it was also an important aspect of Indian foreign policy in the Nehru period. The difference lay in the perception of success. It is agreed generally that Mrs Gandhi's approach to Sri Lanka and her success in containing extra-regional 'meddling' marked the beginning of new era in Indian foreign policy. Mrs Gandhi's approach to the Sri Lankan crisis would be used as a template in Indian foreign policy even after her tenure.[78] As long as the defence of India's territorial borders would continue to be linked to the discourse of anti-imperialism within India's domestic politics, this facet of India's state identity would remain largely unchanged. Ultimately, the 'Indira Doctrine' drove Indian foreign policy to keep extra-regional actors out of its own immediate region, South Asia.

Conclusion

The Mrs Gandhi period witnessed Indian military intervention in the 1971 East Pakistan crisis, followed by the post-war negotiations at Simla. India also played an important role in Sri Lanka's ethnic crisis at this point, leading to Indian military intervention in Sri Lanka in 1988 when Rajiv Gandhi was prime minister. Both of these episodes of Indian foreign policy in South Asia demonstrate the manner in which the identity of the Indian state, under Mrs Gandhi, had an important effect upon India's conception of its role in South Asia. In both cases, one of the central aims of Indian foreign policy was to ensure that extra-regional involvement was kept out of the domestic and international politics of South Asia. This was informed by a key attribute of the Indian state's identity. The link between the discourse of anti-imperialism and the imperative of defending India's porous borders was an important aspect of this feature of Indian state identity.

Mrs Gandhi's approach to Pakistan at the Simla Summit and Sri Lanka's ethnic conflict was also informed by her negotiations with the discourses of democracy and secularism domestically. Her discourse of democratic populism, or 'direct democracy' framed her decision to grant Pakistan certain significant concessions at the Simla Summit. The Indian state under Mrs Gandhi represented itself as the proponent of direct communication with the populace, bypassing conventional democratic institutions and even democratically elected leaders in the case of Ali Bhutto. In Sri Lanka, Mrs Gandhi's discourse of secularism in which the Indian state aligned its interests with those of specific religious and ethnic communities, had specific implications for Indian foreign policy. By aligning the interests of the Indian state with those of the Tamils of Sri Lanka – mainly for the purpose of maintaining the political support of the India's Tamil community – Mrs Gandhi drove Indian intervention in Sri Lanka's ethnic conflict, eventually leading to a full-scale military intervention in 1988.

The Mrs Gandhi era would be followed by the relatively short stint (five years) of Rajiv Gandhi as prime minister of India. In 1989, the Congress Party lost in India's general elections and it signalled the beginning of the Congress Party's diminishing political support in the country. Meanwhile, another force was gaining steady political support in India. In 1998, a new BJP-led Indian government took charge, in the process symbolizing the change that had taken place in India in the 1990s. A new era in Indian politics had emerged and, with it, a new idea of India.

5 The BJP era and the construction of Indian identity

In the Indian general election of February 1998, the BJP polled more than a quarter of the popular vote in India and emerged as the single largest party in India's lower house of Parliament, the Lok Sabha. In March 1998, it formed a coalition government with 12 smaller regional political parties, forming the National Democratic Alliance (NDA), with itself as the main party within this governing coalition.[1] This BJP-led coalition would remain in power until 2004, when the Congress Party re-emerged as the party with the largest number of seats at the national level.

This chapter will discuss how the BJP, in its role as the leading party within the governing coalition from 1998 until 2004, attempted to re-invent the idea of India. It will do so by examining how the BJP attempted to renegotiate the three central discourses related to the identity of the Indian state – secularism, democracy and anti-imperialism. The chapter will analyse how such attempts at renegotiating Indian state identity through the three discourses was subject to the dynamics of domestic identity-politics during this period.

Before discussing this period, it is necessary to explain why this period deserves attention within the larger context of this work. The BJP era is relatively short in duration in comparison with the Nehru and Indira Gandhi periods, the latter two spanning 17 and approximately 15 years respectively, compared to the BJP's six years in power.[2] However, this shorter span of time should not detract from two important reasons for assessing this period of Indian politics. First, although there have been other non-Congress central governments since the defeat of Mrs Gandhi's Congress (I) Party in the 1977 general elections, no government has attempted to re-negotiate Indian-ness as fundamentally as the BJP-led NDA government.[3] The BJP and its predecessor, the Bharatiya Jana Sangh (BJS), obtained their ideological character from a wider movement in colonial India that attempted set itself apart from the ideological moorings of the Congress Party. Until today, the BJP and the BJS have sought continually to challenge the idea of India that the Congress Party, under Nehru and Mrs Gandhi, had sought to invent. As such, the BJP's position in the central government and its attempts to re-negotiate facets of the idea of Nehru's and Mrs Gandhi's India merits detailed attention. Second, the Indian state's perception of its regional role shifted significantly during the tenure of this BJP-led government. This shift, it is argued, can be traced back to the manner in which the BJP sought to reshape Indian-ness during its ministry.

The BJP, and its predecessor, the BJS, are products of a wider family of Hindu nationalist organizations in contemporary India, called the 'Sangh Parivar', that have ideological roots dating back to India's colonial period.[4] In order to understand why and how the BJP attempted to redefine the identity of the Indian state, it is useful to comprehend these ideological roots and examine the extent to which these earlier Hindu nationalist ideas have influenced the BJP since its formation and during its tenure in government. This examination will also help to locate the BJP's perceptions of earlier attempts to frame Indian state identity and the manner in which it sought to position its ideas vis-à-vis these earlier concepts of Indian-ness.

Ideological antecedents: 'Hindu' nationalism and the birth of the BJP

In 1923, V.D. Savarkar wrote an opinion piece entitled *Hindutva: Who Is A Hindu?* The ideas contained in this work have come to be regarded as a handbook for nationalist Hindu thought until the present day.[5] Thus it is crucial in this context to understand Savarkar's ideas as he is held to be one of the chief ideologues of Hindu nationalist thought.[6]

Savarkar's ideas on Hindus as a nation and a race and their relationship to what 'India' represented are outlined clearly in *Hindutva*. In it he remarked that

> the Hindus are not merely the citizens of the Indian state because they are united not only by the bonds of the love they bear to a common motherland but also by the bonds of a common blood. They are not only a Nation but also a race [...]We Hindus are bound together not only by the tie of the love we bear to a common fatherland and by the common blood that courses through our veins [...]but also by the tie of a common homage we pay to our great civilisation – our Hindu culture which could not be better rendered than by the word *Sanskriti*.[7]

Lest he be misunderstood, Savarkar went to great lengths to clarify what he meant by the term 'Hindu'. For him, in the idea of India being a Hindu nation, 'Hindu' meant a signifier wider than just someone who is an adherent of the Hindu religion. For him, other religious groups such as

> Sanyasis, Aryasamajis and Sikhs [who] do not recognise the system of the four castes [...]are ours by blood, by race, by country [...]Its name is Bharat and the people are Bharati [...]We Hindus are all one and a nation because chiefly of our common blood – 'Bharati Santati'.[8]

For Savarkar, the most integral factor in deciding whether or not someone belonged to the Hindu nation of India was not necessarily being Hindu in

The BJP era 87

terms of narrow religious orientation but whether a person regarded India not only as his/her fatherland but also as his/her 'holyland'. In other words, the test lay in whether or not an individual regarded India as 'the cradle land of his religion'.[9]

Therefore, for Savarkar, there were two communities in India that were not Hindu and thus did not belong to the Hindu nation of India – the British and the Muslims. According to this view, India was Hindu, discernible in the common cultural heritage that all Hindus shared and signified by the fact that for Hindus, India was 'Bharat' and Indians were 'Bharatis'.[10] This view stands in sharp contrast to the later Nehru characterization of India's core identity as one of religious-cultural syncretism, forged out of the interaction between different religious groups and practices, and out of which something uniquely 'Indian' was built. In Savarkar's opinion, no such syncretic commonality, or 'dream of unity' between Hindus and Muslims was possible. Hindus were united by race and culture and India had always been and still was the land of the Hindus. This view would have important ramifications for the BJP's approach to the re-negotiation of the discourse of secularism within the context of domestic identity-politics.

To appreciate the influence of Savarkar on the BJP's ideological foundations, it is important to sketch briefly the institutional history of a particular organization, the Rashtriya Swayamsevak Sangh (RSS) and its links with Savarkar and his ideas.[11] As will be shown, the RSS has made and still makes important ideological and organizational contributions to the present day BJP Party in terms of the latter's policies and identity.

The RSS was formed in 1925 in Nagpur by Keshav Baliram Hedgewar. Although the RSS had several antecedent organizations dating back to the 1870s, it was the RSS that came to articulate Hindu nationalist ideology most clearly and forcefully, as well as providing the BJP with its ideological orientation and mobilization prowess.[12] From 1925 until shortly before independence, the RSS articulated through leaders such as Hedgewar and later Golwalkar the idea of India as a Hindu nation. Golwalkar, who became leader of the RSS in 1940, was very clear about how it viewed the idea of India. In his 1939 work, *We, or Our Nationhood Defined*, he states that

> the foreign races in Hindusthan must either adopt the Hindu culture and language, must learn to respect and hold in reverence Hindu religion, must entertain no ideas but those of glorification of the Hindu race and culture [...] or may stay in the country, wholly subordinated to the Hindu nation, claiming nothing, deserving no privileges, far less any preferential treatment – not even citizen's rights.[13]

The RSS was thus furthering the idea, articulated earlier by Savarkar, of India as the nation of Hindus and of India possessing an identity that was Hindu at its core. Consequently, in reflection of Savarkar's ideas, it meant that other nations (the Indian Muslims specifically) could only, at best, occupy a subordinate position within a Hindu India. In the post-independence and post-partition era, such views were in direct tension with Nehru's attempts to construct a much broader and more inclusive secular identity for the Indian state. Although the RSS publicly challenged this aspect of Nehru's idea of India, the RSS as an organization refused to be drawn into the arena of competitive party politics.[14] Instead, the RSS saw itself as a Hindu social grassroots organization, with the stated purpose of building the Hindu nation, or Hindu 'Rashtra' from the grassroots upwards.[15] However, several events made the RSS leadership re-think their principled disavowal of competitive party politics. The murder of M.K. Gandhi in 1948 moved Nehru to ban the RSS organization on 4 February 1948 and order the arrest of Golwalkar, due to the alleged links of the assassins with the organization. This experience made many within the RSS argue that the organization should have some way of influencing the government and that becoming involved in competitive politics and taking part in elections at various levels was the only way to achieve such an end.[16] This is where the story of the Bharatiya Jana Sangh (BJS) begins.

With the initial groundwork done largely by RSS members – ostensibly in their private capacity and not as RSS members – the BJS was formed as an all-India party in October 1951. Although formed and led predominantly by individuals from within the RSS at its inception, the BJS sought to adopt a more 'liberal' outlook relative to the RSS by not restricting membership to Hindus and making the 'party open to all citizens of India irrespective of caste, creed or community'.[17] Despite this, the BJS had, at its ideological core, an essentialist 'Hindu' understanding of Indian identity. Therefore, although it labelled itself as a 'national', as opposed to a 'communal' party, it did not deny that in its definition of *Bharatiya Sanskriti*, it was referring unambiguously to the ancient Hindu culture of India and, by extension, excluding much of the 'foreign' culture brought into India by Muslims and Christians. It expected Christians and Muslims to disavow their apparent extra-territorial allegiances, even though these allegiances were religious and not political in nature. The BJS also expected these communities to accept the heroes and mythology of the Hindu past, despite the fact that such expectations may have been objectionable to the monotheistic beliefs of the Muslim and Christian communities.[18]

The BJS had a clear image of the idea of India – one nation, one culture, one people that it posited as the diametrical opposite of Nehru's composite, secular brand of Indian nationalism.[19] The BJS experienced a turning point during the imposition of the 'Emergency' by Mrs Gandhi in 1975. The BJS was one of several parties that challenged overtly the legitimacy of the Emergency proclamation and several of its leading members were imprisoned as a result. In the 1977 elections, the BJS joined several other parties and individuals opposed to Mrs Gandhi's imposition of the Emergency to form the Janata Party and emerged victorious in the general elections. The BJS became part of the ruling coalition in 1977 with its leader, Atal Bihari

Vajpayee serving as the external affairs minister. However, this governing coalition collapsed as a result of infighting among individuals for the coveted seat of Prime Minister and the Janata Party had to dissolve parliament and call for elections in 1980, an election that it lost overwhelmingly to Mrs Gandhi's Congress Party. Shortly after, there were further tensions within the Janata Party due to the BJS's refusal to renounce its policy of allowing its members to hold dual membership of the BJS and the RSS simultaneously.[20] This led to the formation of the BJP on 5 April 1980 with A.B. Vajpayee as its first president. At its inception, the BJP was nearly identical to its predecessor, the BJS in terms of its ideological outlook, due mainly to the direct influence of the RSS on the party's organization and programmes.[21]

'Positive secularism': 'secularism' BJP style

In the Nehru period, 'secularism' was one of the most recognizable signifiers of the nascent Indian state. Nehru's discourse of secularism reinforced a brand of Indian nationalism that he viewed as being diametrically opposed to what he termed 'communal', or 'religious' nationalism. Various representatives of Hindu nationalist thought have contested persistently this binary representation of their variety of Indian nationalism. However, there are varying degrees of contestation within this ideological camp.[22] This section has two objectives. The first is to discern the extent to which the BJP inherited its own discourse of 'secularism' from the ideas of individuals like Savarkar, the RSS and the BJS. Making this link will also show the extent to which the BJP's discourse of secularism was in a crucial way relational to their perception of the Nehruvian as well and the Mrs Gandhi variety of Indian secularism. The second objective will be to demonstrate how the BJP's discourse of secularism formed the most fundamental aspect of its construction of Indian-ness. At the BJP's first National Convention, held in December 1980, party president A.B. Vajpayee illustrated the party's vision of the significance of secularism in the Indian context. The party rejected the Nehru and Indira Gandhi brand of secularism that it termed 'pseudo-secularism'.[23] For them, 'Congress secularism' represented minority appeasement, particularly the appeasement of religious minorities such as the Muslim and Christian communities within India. Such a brand of secularism had bred a sense of self-loathing for Hinduism as a religion and the Hindu community at large. The BJP thus attacked this variety of 'Congress secularism' as being one-sided, siding with religious minorities and encouraging a climate of anti-Hinduism, which in turn had hindered the Indian nation from discovering its broader and true Hindu identity. For the BJP, the proper relationship of the Indian state to religion was one in which the state

> must not reject or stand above religion but inculcate religious ideals [and] must base itself on the foundation of Indian cultural heritage which is seen as synonymous with 'Hindutva'.[24]

This was a clear rejection of Nehru's model of secularism, in which the state stood above different religious communities and mediated their relationship with each other. However, lest the BJP be accused of being 'communal', its then vice-president and later deputy Prime Minister, L.K. Advani denied the charge that the term 'Hindutva' was necessarily communal and thus not secular. In his rendition, 'Hindutva' signified a different kind of secularism; a 'positive' secularism. Furthermore, he claimed that the BJP did not 'use the word "Hindutva" in religious terms' and that the concept of a Hindu nation, or 'Hindu Rashtra' meant 'Bharatiya Rashtra', or the nation of Bharat, or India.[25] The echoes of some of Savarkar's ideas on 'Hindutva' and 'Hindu' not as religious categories but wider cultural terms of reference are difficult to miss in this instance. Despite this, there was an important difference. The BJP had diluted to some extent the fierce exclusionary ideas of Hindu India evident in Savarkar's and the RSS's discourse on Indian secularism. In the BJP's representation, Muslims and Christians were as 'Indian' as the majority Hindu community because they were 'Hindu-Muslims' and 'Hindu-Christians' respectively and not the second-class citizens that Savarkar and the RSS had represented.[26] This however did not mean that the BJP had moved away from its representation of India as 'Hindu'. Instead, it still represented India as 'Hindu India', with the aid of the same broad arguments used by Savarkar and the RSS, the main difference resting upon the fact that the BJP had stripped the 'Hindu' reference of virtually all of its religious properties in its discourse of secularism.

For the BJP, in tracing its ideological roots back to Savarkar and the Hindu Mahasabha and organizationally back to the RSS, the Nehru and Mrs Gandhi discourses of secularism remained a key reference point. Opposition to this perceived Congress brand of secularism was thus not merely instrumental but a deeply held, constitutive part of the BJP's identity and what it represented. Such opposition, embodied in its doctrine of Hindutva, gave the party its central identity. As L.K. Advani reminded fellow party members,

> Hindutva is not merely a slogan for us. It is the BJP's ideological mascot – the most distinctive feature of its identity and approach [...]the hallmark of the party well before Ayodhya and will continue to be so even after a Ram temple at the birthplace in Ayodha becomes a fact of life.[27]

As Van Deer points out, the BJP did not consider using 'Hindutva' as a mere electoral plank to win electoral support but in fact its core 'Hindutva' identity 'helped it to mark out its own electoral constituency', rather than vice-versa.[28] Therefore, just as Nehru saw his idea of India as inseparable from his discourse of Indian secularism, similarly the BJP saw their idea of India as inseparable from their conception of secularism embodied in their discourse of Hindutva in India. One perceptive observer of Hindu nationalist thought demonstrates how, in contrast to the more belligerent tone of Savarkar and Golwarkar of the RSS, the BJS and then the BJP has been consistent in its use of the term 'Bharatiya', instead of the term 'Hindu'. He translates aptly the term to mean 'Hindian' – a mixture of 'Hindu' and 'Indian'.[29]

In order to understand how domestic identity-politics serves as a useful analytical tool for the comprehension of the BJP's attempts to re-frame this crucial facet of Indian state identity, it is necessary to examine the three perennial 'articles' of faith associated with the BJP: the building of the 'Ram' temple, the enactment of a uniform civil code and the abolishing of Article 370 of the Indian constitution.

The project to build the Ram temple in Ayodha – the site claimed to be the birthplace of the Hindu God, *Ram* (or *Rama*) – led to the demolition of the Babri Masjid, or Babri mosque in 1992.[30] This demolition came about in the aftermath of a rally organized by the BJP and other Hindu nationalist groups to show support for the building of such a temple.[31] To understand the integral place of the *Ram* temple within the BJP's collective identity, it is important to note the BJP's manifesto for the 1996 election, two years before it formed the ruling party within the governing coalition. On the Ram temple, the manifesto unequivocally states that

> on coming to power, the BJP government will facilitate the construction of a magnificent Shri Rama Mandir at Janmasthan in Ayodha that will be a tribute to Bharat Mata. This dream moves millions of people in our land – the concept of Rama lies at the core of their consciousness.[32]

During the elections of 1996, even as the BJP were perceived by many to have downplayed the more radical ideas associated with its Hindutva programme in order to project itself more favourably to a wider electoral constituency, the Ram temple project remained integral to the BJP's plans. The link between 'Rama' lying at the core of the Indian consciousness and the building of the Ram temple follow from the BJP's articulation of India as a 'Hindu' nation. It was therefore not surprising that building the Ram temple became an article of faith for the party.

The second article of faith is the uniform civil code. The issue of a uniform civil code has been fiercely contested issue since the early years of India's independence. Under Nehru's direction, the Hindu Code Bill was first introduced in parliament in 1949 and finally, after much criticism, became part of Indian legislation over the years 1952–7. Its main aim was to provide a civil code in place of the extensive body of Hindu personal law that previously governed matters relating to marriage and inheritance for the majority of Indians. However, Indian Muslims were not covered by this civil code and were allowed to retain their Muslim personal law. Hindu nationalist leaders perceived this as another example of Nehru's appeasement of minorities and application of double standards to the detriment of the majority Hindu community.[33] When in opposition, the BJP in fact tried to push through a private members bill in the Lok Sabha. It was entitled the Constitution (Amendment) Bill, in 1996, which sought to make civil laws common to all citizens throughout the country by replacing the Hindu Code Bill and Muslim personal law with a uniform civil code that would apply to members of all communities.[34] As far back as 1993, L.K. Advani made it plain that

> when the BJP talks of a uniform civil code, it does not contemplate imposing the Hindu law on the country. Our party manifesto has very clearly stated that the BJP would ask the Law Commission to examine the Hindu law, the Muslim law, the Christian law and the Parsi law and cull out the modern, progressive, equitable ingredients of these laws and, on that basis, draw up a common civil code. If some of the laws relating to the Hindus today have to go on that account, they have to go. Whatever has to be done, has to be done for all.[35]

The BJP's position was clear. The Hindu Code Bill made only the Hindu community subject to a civil code, whilst making exceptions for other religious communities. This became a symbol of the Congress's apparent 'pseudo-secularism' and 'appeasement of minorities'. Advani's statement bears testimony to the party's vital stake in the issue of a uniform civil code within which the Muslim community in India should be treated on the same basis as the Hindu community and should not be given special treatment under the provisions of Muslim personal law.

The third article of faith for the BJP was abolishing Article 370 of the Indian constitution. This refers to the 'special status' of the Indian state of Jammu and Kashmir within the Indian Union. It was passed as a supposedly temporary measure by agreement between Nehru and the then Maharajah of Jammu and Kashmir in March 1948. Article 370 restricts the central government to making laws only within relation to defence, external affairs and communications in the state of Jammu and Kashmir. In addition, Jammu and Kashmir enjoys several other liberties that are not extended to any other constituent unit within the Indian Union.[36] This is again represented by the BJP as an example of the Nehru's 'pseudo-secularism' and an attempt to appease the minority Muslim community to the detriment of the Hindu community. In fact the BJS took part in the political agitations in Kashmir between 1952–3 in protest against the consolidation of the 'special status' of Jammu and Kashmir within the Indian Union.[37]

Despite these being three articles of faith for the BJP, the nature of the 1998 general election results presented the party with a dilemma. Despite emerging as the party with the largest number of seats in the Lok Sabha, the BJP did not win enough seats to form a majority in the lower house of the Indian parliament. It therefore needed the support of smaller political parties to stake its claim in forming a coalition government. In consideration of their aim to head an enduring governing coalition, the BJP had to bow, in letter at least, to its coalition alliance partners' insistence that the BJP's three articles of faith were not pursued as the coalition government's policy. In fact, the NDA coalition government had an agreed 'Minimum Common Programme' under which the BJP agreed not to pursue actively the three central articles of faith as part of the governing coalition.[38]

Born out of the RSS's historical impulse to challenge the policies of the Congress-controlled Indian state in the realm of competitive party-politics, the BJP ironically now found itself in government, yet still unable to implement its three central articles of faith into public policy. Its ability to re-invent the idea of India, in this case to replace Congress 'secularism' with 'Hindutva' through its access to the power of the Indian state, as Nehru and Mrs Gandhi had done, was being restrained. However, being at the head of the Indian government still gave the BJP the unrivalled ability to invent the identity of the Indian state through a re-negotiation of the discourse of secularism. Thus the BJP, in its capacity as a political party, continued to articulate its discourse of Hindutva and Hindian secularism publicly even after coming to power in 1998.[39] More significantly, its institutional position at the head of the Indian state allowed the BJP to translate, albeit within certain limits, its own representations of Indian-ness into specific Indian foreign policy outcomes.

Thus a useful means of comprehending the BJP's discourse of secularism within the larger project of constructing Indian state identity is to view it as a discursive contest against the Nehru and Mrs Gandhi discourses of Indian secularism. In a sense, the contest over the idea of secular India had come full circle. Nehru sought to position the Indian state above the gods, Mrs Gandhi made the Indian state manipulate the gods and the BJP wanted the Indian state to represent the identity of specific gods. As was the case in the Nehru and Indira Gandhi periods, such a disposition would have a particular effect upon the way in which the Indian state viewed its role within South Asia, a discussion that is pursued in the next chapter.

'Hindu democracy': the BJP and majoritarian democracy

An important aspect of Nehru's idea of democratic India encompassed a negotiation of a subtle tension between the safeguard of individual rights versus the interventionist socio-democratic role of the state, between the preservation of the rights of different minorities versus the general good of the majority of the populace and between the central government's assumption of the role of a robust and effective executor of national policies versus autonomy for the various constituent units within the Indian Union. By the end of the Indira Gandhi period, this tension ceased to remain subtle. The legacy of the Emergency, Indira's centralization of power and her exploitation of the anxieties of different religious groups to win and consolidate political power had taken their toll on Nehru's earlier negotiation of the Indian state's democratic identity. The BJP's discourse of Indian democracy was in many ways related to the Nehru and Indira varieties of Indian democracy.

In a manner similar to that of Nehru and Indira, the BJP's discourse of Indian democracy was linked intimately to its discourse of Indian secularism.[40] Therefore, it is not surprising therefore that because the BJP had constructed its idea of Indian secularism as the binary opposite of the Nehru–Indira Gandhi 'Congress' brand of secularism, the BJP framed its notion of Indian democracy in opposition to the 'Congress' variety of democracy.

This opposition to the Nehruvian discourse of Indian democracy for the BJP is evident in how L.K. Advani, then BJP President and later Deputy Prime Minister and Home Minister, represented Indian democracy, on the basis that

> democracy and liberalism as preached by Nehru are denuded of their Indianness [...] I believe India is what it is because of its ancient heritage – call it Hindu or call it *Bharatiya*. If nationalism is stripped of its Hinduism, it would lose its dynamism.[41]

In Advani's representation, 'Indian-ness' is linked to certain facets of India's ancient Hindu heritage, rather than the seemingly alien Nehruvian discourse of democracy. Within the context of domestic identity-politics, this is an important discursive approach. On one hand, the BJP required the institutions of competitive party-politics based on universal suffrage to challenge the decades-old hold on the Indian state by the Congress Party. They thus needed to engage in the discourse and practice of 'democracy'. On the other hand, by representing Indian-ness as the product of an ancient Hindu legacy and by characterizing Indian secularism as the necessary acknowledgement of India's essential 'Hindian' nature, the BJP was undermining implicitly the idea of democratic equality in its treatment of various religious communities.[42] The result was a very specific form of majoritarian democracy. In the BJP's discourse of democracy, it became known as 'Hindu democracy'.

In this specific form of majoritarian democracy – in a situation of universal suffrage and competitive party-politics – the religious majority, represented by a party, or parties, should remain the perennial bearers of political power with obvious implications for those not belonging to this majority religious community.[43] When in power, the way in which the BJP employed the discourse of 'Hindu democracy' in the construction of Indian state identity is evident in its approach towards the Gujarat state elections of December 2002. These elections were held nine months after one of the worst outbreaks of communal violence in India seen in recent times, with the majority of the victims belonging to the Muslim community.[44]

The details of the communal violence in Gujarat are well-documented.[45] In brief, 58 people, mainly members of Hindu nationalist organizations, were burnt to death inside a railway carriage returning from the disputed site of Ayodha on 27 February 2002 in Godhra, in the state of Gujarat. The perpetrators were identified as a mob of 2,000 Muslims. A day-long general strike called by the VHP (World Hindu Council, or Vishwa Hindu Parishad) soon descended into a violent backlash against Gujarati Muslims, with killings, rapes and destruction of homes and businesses. In all, there were between 800 and 2,000 estimated deaths over the two-week period of the violence.[46]

The most significant aspect of the violence was the role of the ruling state BJP Party and especially its chief minister, Nerendra Modi. An independent commission found that 'the bulk of the violence that followed was state-backed and one-sided violence against Muslims tantamount to a deliberate pogrom'.[47] More importantly, it implicates the central BJP-led government in noting that

> instead of intervening and taking decisive action against the State government, the Central government has chosen to minimize the seriousness of what has happened [...]without this sustained and consistent support, the Modi government could not have continued in power or have been emboldened to continue its bloody, anti-Constitutional and anti-national activities.[48]

In fact, Modi was quoted to have said that in the midst of the attacks on Muslims in Gujarat, the violence was taking place because 'every action has an equal and opposite reaction', implicitly justifying the revenge killings of Muslims by Hindus in Gujarat.[49] Meanwhile, the BJP president Jana Krishnamurthy, said that the 'the post-Godhra violence, though strongly condemnable, is a result of revulsions after Godhra', lending his voice to the justification of the collective violence against Muslims in Gujarat.[50]

These events led to calls for Modi to resign even from the BJP coalition partners in the central government.[51] However, the BJP refused to call for Modi's resignation and instead called for early elections in Gujarat, sensing the manner in which Modi had become the hero of Hindu nationalists and the increased possibility of him securing an election victory in Gujarat on the basis of parochial appeals to the Hindu community.[52] The BJP's election strategy adopted a strident pro-Hindu tone. It eventually won the state elections, winning the most seats in those areas that were affected most by communal violence in February and March 2002 and in which members of the BJP had been implicated.[53]

The strategy of mass mobilization on the basis of Hindu nationalist slogans and the disparagement of religious minorities demonstrate how the BJP, together with its more radical partners in the Hindu nationalist fold, employed the discourse of democracy and re-invented the identity of the Indian state as a 'Hindu' state. The Gujarat episode, with the BJP supported violence against the Muslim community and its later comfortable win in the state elections, was seen in the Hindu nationalist movement as a 'Hindutva lab', with strategic implications for the utility of a discourse of 'Hindu' majoritarian democracy to win political power for the BJP throughout the rest of the country.[54]

In re-inventing the democratic identity of the Indian state, the BJP contested the discourses of Indian democracy framed during both the Nehru and

Indira Gandhi periods in different ways. In relation to the Nehruvian discourse of Indian democracy, the BJP positioned its discourse of Indian democracy at odds with notions of individual liberties and minority rights and in favour of communal group rights and majoritarian interests. The Indira Gandhi era began the process of framing the discourse on Indian democracy in a populist direction. Her selective appeals to various religious and ethnic communities at opportune moments in order to concentrate political power were meant to appeal to the largest constituency and to increase her political popularity. On some level, the BJP employed a similar strategy.[55] In its discourse of majoritarian democracy, it, too, sought to appeal directly to the largest electoral constituency to win political power. However, there was one important difference. Mrs Gandhi's discourse of Indian democracy was meant to concentrate political power at the level of the central state, with the result that Indian democracy came to be defined as the overwhelming ability of the Indian state to wield power in large spheres of Indian society. The BJP's discourse of Indian democracy was not merely a tool to win and concentrate political power unto the Indian state but to re-invent the nature of the Indian state into a 'Hindu' Indian state. Discourses of 'Hindu' democracy were meant to re-invent the idea of India by making the Indian state a representative of India's 'Hindu' identity.

The 'twin imperialisms' and the resurgence of 'Hindu' India: anti-imperialism and the BJP

The idea that India was a symbol of stubborn resistance to any form of foreign imperialism was an important aspect of the representation of India domestically in both the Nehru and Indira Gandhi periods. The BJP era persisted with this representation but with some important differences. An examination of how BJP leaders framed their discourse of anti-imperialism will demonstrate both the continuities and the changes in the representation of this particular facet of the identity of the Indian state. These continuities and changes in representations of the Indian state would have important ramifications for the tenor of Indian foreign policy in South Asia.

The prolonged and often-times distressing nature of the Indian nationalist struggle meant that Indian political parties from across the political spectrum came, in one manifestation or another, to represent their party's goals in terms of being the most able defenders of India's legacy of resistance to any form of foreign imperialism. In this sense, the BJP, even before coming to power at the central government level, was not much different from most of the other political parties. In its need to win popular support within the arena of competitive party politics, it had always attempted to represent itself as the most able party to protect India from any form of foreign imperialism.

One example of this is the manner in which the BJP has attempted to appropriate particular idioms largely associated with M.K. Gandhi during the nationalist struggle. In the prior discussion it was shown how the BJP and the like-minded organization, the RSS viewed themselves to be the binary opposite of the Congress Party in terms of the way in which they represented India. The fact that Gandhi was associated mainly with the Congress Party through much of the independence struggle did not endear him to the BJP's ideological predecessors, the RSS especially.[56] However, the BJP attempted in several ways to associate itself with Gandhian ideas in order to represent itself, and not the Congress, as the most able defenders of the freedom and sovereignty that India gained as a result of its prolonged nationalist struggle.

At the party's formation, A.B. Vajpayee advocated the adoption of 'Gandhian Socialism' as one of the guiding philosophies of the party. It largely involved a broad vision of replacing capitalism with the principle of co-operatives and a form of trusteeship in all fields of economic activity.[57] This was a clear deployment of Gandhi's legacy into the BJP's social programme in order to link the party with images of India's independence struggle and thus its ability to oppose foreign imperialism. However, this philosophy came under attack early from within the party ranks on the basis that it used the word 'socialism' and thus seemed too close to the ideologies of the communist and Congress Parties.[58] Thus this attempt to use Gandhian idioms troubled party members because it seemed to reduce the party's perceived differentiation from the Congress Party. This differentiation was, of course, crucial to the party's collective self-image. Therefore, on 20 July 1985, the BJP's Working Group presented its report to the BJP National Executive proposing the adoption of 'integral humanism' as the party's basic philosophy. The proposal was accepted and the party's constitution was amended accordingly.[59]

Despite its attempt to associate itself, like other Indian political parties, with idioms and personalities pivotal to the Indian nationalist struggle, the BJP's discourse of anti-imperialism had its own unique attributes. The distinct feature of the BJP's discourse in this respect is well captured by Corbridge and Harris when they observe that, for the BJP, anti-imperialism meant that

> the forces of Hindutva would reclaim Bharat from the 'two imperialisms' – Muslim and British – which were cankers in the body of Hindudom and which had turned the country away from its true and natural course.[60]

The idea that both the British and Muslim encounters in India's history represented the humiliation and subjugation of Hindu India follows closely from Savarkar's reading of India as a Hindu nation and how the two communities, the Muslims and the British, were 'foreigners' in such representations of India during the colonial period.[61] Leading from such a representation, the BJP's discourse of anti-imperialism exhibited a specific understanding and diagnosis of India's historical humiliation and a prognosis of redemption from such imperialisms. Therefore, the BJP's narrative of loss and redemption became a telling critique of a once strong nation of Hindus brought to its knees first by the Muslims and the British and more recently by the Congress and allied pseudo-secularists.[62]

In a sense, for India to be free and to redeem itself from the shackles of imperialism, it needed to acknowledge its genuine identity, that of being Hindu India. This discourse of anti-imperialism was thus 'centrally concerned with notions of national honour' and thus sought to 'ultimately extract a much-desired global recognition of India's place among the leading nations in the world'.[63] In opposition to Nehru and Mrs Gandhi's discourses of anti-imperialism, the BJP version concerned the Indian state's rediscovery of its Hindu identity and, on this basis, gaining the respect it deserved from other nation-states.[64]

Conclusion

The BJP period witnessed a fundamental re-negotiation of Indian state identity. With its discourse of secularism, the BJP attempted to infuse the Indian state with qualities associated with a specific type of Hindu character. This was linked crucially to the manner in which it represented Indian democracy as a majoritarian Hindu democracy, whilst recasting the discourse of anti-imperialism to include notions of Muslim imperialism towards Hindu India. These representations of Indian state identity differed to varying degrees from the Nehru and Indira Gandhi periods but, most significantly, they marked a watershed in the manner in which the Indian state had come to be represented since its birth in 1947.

The BJP's vision of 'Hindu' India had repercussions beyond India's domestic realm. In fashioning India's foreign policy, the BJP-led government came to be guided by particular conceptions of India's role in South Asia, conceptions that were imbued heavily by its domestic representations of Indian state identity.

6 A 'Hindu' foreign policy
Dealing with Pakistan and Bangladesh

Chapter 5 discussed the significance of the BJP era for domestic identity-politics and its effect upon the identity of the Indian state. As was the case in Nehru and Indira Gandhi periods, the BJP-led government's construction of Indian state identity had important implications for the manner in which the Indian state represented its role in South Asia. This representation of India foresaw a self-confident Hindu India, unapologetic about its Hindu civilizational heritage and unabashed about its claims to dominance in the South Asian region. For the BJP, this representation of India contrasted sharply with depictions of earlier (mainly Congress) Indian governments of making India synonymous, in foreign affairs, with 'weakness, insecurity, marginalisation and [a] lack of power'.[1]

This chapter will deal first with India's policy in Pakistan within the context of the Kargil conflict. The second part of this chapter will look at India's policy towards Bangladesh within the framework of the issue of the movement of people across the India–Bangladesh border.

An important starting point in understanding the link between Indian state identity and Indian foreign policy in South Asia during this period is to comprehend the 'sacred' geographical imaginings of India that featured in earlier Hindu nationalist thought and persisted into the BJP era. India's Hindu heritage, according to Savarkar, was manifested by the complementarities of its physical and cultural geography. 'Hindu' India was therefore best viewed through the 'image of a landscape of boundaries, the "natural frontier lines" that both enclose and exclude (the Himalayas, the Bay of Bengal, the Indian Ocean, the Arabian Sea, the Indus and Ganges rivers)'.[2] Inherent in such sacred imaginings is the conception of a wider, 'Greater' India, encompassing an area larger than the landmass of post-independent India. In fact, the above physical–cultural boundaries that Savarkar alludes to approximates to the present-day boundaries of the South Asian region.[3] Thus, although Savarkar was writing much before the independence of India and Pakistan in 1947 and the later formation of Bangladesh, his representation of 'Hindu' India's sacred geographical boundaries approximate to the present boundaries of the South Asian region. The notion of the South Asian region being characterized by its physical–cultural unity was echoed by the then External

Affairs Minister in the BJP-led government, Jaswant Singh, when he stated that 'the Indian subcontinent is recognized as one of the self-contained civilizational areas of the world'.[4] According to this logic, if India was civilizationally and culturally 'Hindu', the South Asian region, as the 'Indian subcontinent', has an essential 'Hindu' civilizational character.

Pakistan has perpetually occupied an important place within Hindu nationalist thought. As it was discussed in Chapter 1, Hindu nationalist ideas about India being a 'Hindu' country were articulated in the early years of independence with reference to the formation of Pakistan. It is therefore not surprising that the BJP's approach to Pakistan was impacted by its own understanding of Indian-ness and the threat that potential Muslim 'imperialism' seemed to pose to such constructions of Indian state identity.

From Lahore to Kargil

In this section, India's approach to Pakistan will be examined within the context of one particular set of events – the Lahore Summit and the Kargil conflict. The two events, taken together as one set of events, took place between 20 February 1999 and the end of July 1999. The manner in which the BJP-led government framed and then responded to the actions of the Pakistani state depended significantly upon specific notions of Indian state identity constructed during the BJP era. This set of events has been selected for two reasons. First, this set of events defined the nature of the India–Pakistan relationship for the tenure of this BJP-led government.[5] Second, although there were other episodes of interaction between India and Pakistan during this period, such as the December 2001 storming of the Indian parliament by terrorists allegedly based in Pakistan, such events that came chronologically after the Lahore summit and the Kargil War were influenced by the BJP's perceptions of Pakistan's actions and intentions at Lahore and in Kargil.[6] This 'Lahore–Kargil' set of events is therefore the most important episode in Indian foreign policy towards Pakistan during the BJP-led government's tenure in office.

The 'betrayal' of Lahore: the 1999 Kargil conflict

Between 20 and 21 February 1999, the prime ministers of India and Pakistan met in Lahore, Pakistan for discussions that later came to be known as the Lahore Summit. A few months later on 6 May, India became engaged in a conflict with Pakistan's military and insurgents backed by the Pakistani military in the Kargil sector on the line of control, located within the Indian-administered state of Jammu and Kashmir. The actual armed conflict lasted approximately until the end of July of that year and involved Indian and Pakistani armed forces being engaged in full-scale military operations against each other.[7] Although ostensibly two separate events, they need to be viewed as one connected set of events because BJP leaders perceived them as such.[8]

A 'Hindu' foreign policy   101

More specifically, they viewed these two events as part of a distinct and calculated set of actions on the part of Pakistani leaders to deceive and lure India into a false sense of complacency vis-à-vis Pakistan's intentions.[9] For example, Vajpayee, in an interview in 2002, pointed out that 'Pakistan's incursions in Kargil were not just an invasion of our territory. It was a betrayal of the trust that I sought to build in Lahore.'[10] Several BJP leaders in fact believed that the Pakistani state was already making plans for the occupation when Shariff was at the Lahore Summit.[11] In this sense, both the Lahore Summit and the Kargil conflict, in the view of the Indian government, comprised two sides of the same coin of Pakistan's duplicity.

It is widely understood that in the wake of the 1998 nuclear weapon tests by both India and Pakistan, the US administration had nudged both countries towards repairing bilateral relations and instilling some confidence building measures.[12] The first manifestation of this process was the initiation of the inaugural and historic Delhi to Lahore bus service by Nawaz Shariff. This attempt to improve confidence in bilateral relations came to be termed 'bus diplomacy' in the media.[13] The Indian prime minister, with senior officials in tow, crossed the border from India into Pakistan at the Wagah crossing in the Indian city of Amritsar on 20 February and was greeted by Nawaz Shariff as his entourage crossed into Pakistan. With this, Vajpayee became the first Indian prime minister in a decade to visit Pakistan.[14] For the next two days, the two leaders had a series of discussions that led to a joint statement and a memorandum of understanding that was collectively termed the Lahore Declaration.[15]

A significant part of the declaration aimed at getting both countries to agree to devise some form of mechanism to '[reduce] the risks of accidental or unauthorized use of nuclear weapons under their respective control', as well as

> to abide by their respective unilateral moratorium on conducting further nuclear test explosions unless either side, in exercise of its national sovereignty decides that extraordinary events have jeopardised its supreme interests.[16]

This was obviously a response to the steadily deteriorating relationship between the two countries in the wake of their respective nuclear weapons tests in May 1998.[17] Two general points made in the Lahore Declaration are of specific interest. Although neither was ground-breaking in any sense, they revealed the attitudes of Indian leaders in this instance regarding Pakistan's apparent intentions. The first is that both governments agreed

> that an environment of peace and security is in the supreme national interest of both sides and that the resolution of all outstanding issues, including Jammu and Kashmir, is essential for this purpose.[18]

Second, recalling the landmark agreement between India and Pakistan in the aftermath of the 1971 Bangladesh War, both leaders reiterated 'the determination of both countries to implementing the Simla Agreement in letter and spirit'.[19]

Taken together, these two statements meant two important things to India's political leadership with regard to Pakistan's commitments. First, although India had agreed to compromise and to include the case of Jammu and Kashmir as an 'outstanding issue', among other unresolved issues between the two countries, this clause committed Pakistan to refrain from altering the status quo in Jammu and Kashmir, especially through any form of force, in the interests of maintaining an 'environment of peace and security'. Preventing the outbreak of a nuclear war between the two countries was also a factor in Indian perceptions. More specifically, the reference to maintaining an 'environment for peace and security' was viewed as a way of ensuring that Pakistan understood that any use of unilateral military force could impact adversely nuclear stability between the two states. In this vein, a retired additional secretary to the Indian government's cabinet, writing in August 1999, remarked that

> it was thought, at least from the Indian side, that Lahore Declaration of 1999 would meet with the interim need of nuclear stability despite testing of more advanced missiles by both countries during this period.[20]

Second, Pakistan's undertaking to continue to abide by the 'letter and spirit' of the Simla Agreement meant that Pakistan agreed to be bound by the clause of 'bilateralism' in its relations with India and that any agreement between the two countries could only be reached on the basis of bilateral discussions and agreement. This had ramifications during the Kargil War. In the midst of the Kargil conflict, on 5 July 1999, the Indian government, in a press release responding to the US–Pakistan Joint Statement issued the previous day, noted that

> our US interlocutors have informed us that 'concrete steps' referred to in the Statement means withdrawal by Pakistan of their forces from our side of the Line of Control in the Kargil sector. We have also noted the sequencing of steps agreed to in the statement, that only after withdrawal is completed will other contemplated steps be initiated. We hope Pakistan will heed this call immediately. We will be watching developments on the ground [...]. One word about the Lahore process. It is direct and bilateral. In this process, there is no place whatsoever for any third party involvement. The same is true for any other aspect of India–Pakistan relations.[21]

In this instance, even though the Indian government valued the role of the US administration in pushing Pakistan to withdraw its forces from areas on the

Indian side of the line of control, the US were mere interlocutors', not a third party that the Indian government would accept in its dealings with Pakistan. As far as the Indian government was concerned, Pakistan had accepted the bilateralism imperative contained within the Lahore Declaration and it intended to hold the Pakistani government to that principle in this instance.

Altogether, the Indian government had specific, yet circumscribed expectations regarding the Lahore Declaration. There was a view within the Indian government that the declaration was significant for its potential to regulate the manner in which India and Pakistan interacted presently and could interact in the future. As Jaswant Singh remarked in Parliament, a few days after Vajpayee's visit to Lahore, the declaration marked

> the most significant engagement between India and Pakistan in over a quarter of a century ... This visit also provided the Prime Minister with an opportunity to emphasize that India and Pakistan must work together to build a comprehensive structure of cooperation, resolve all outstanding issues through peaceful and direct bilateral discussions and negotiations.[22]

The Indian government believed that by getting the Pakistan's leaders to agree to the resolution of its disputes with India through a 'comprehensive structure of cooperation', the latter would be less inclined towards using unilateral force to alter the political and territorial status quo in Jammu and Kashmir. In terms of foreign policy, while stressing bilateralism, the Indian government did not expect Pakistan to involve an external power militarily in its dispute with India. Indian leaders still expected Pakistan's leaders to continue their perennial tendency to attempt to enlist extra-regional powers diplomatically at various fora, such as the United Nations, or the Commonwealth countries' meetings. The more qualified and circumscribed expectation was that Pakistan would stick largely to the diplomatic path, rather than attempt to involve an extra-regional power militarily in any conflict between the two countries.

With such qualifications in mind, the Indian government hoped that the Lahore Declaration would, at the very least, lead to a longer-term process in which Pakistan would view negotiations and not unilateral force as a means to address the status of Jammu and Kashmir. In fact, in early June, after the outbreak of the Kargil War, Jaswant Singh explained again the wider importance of the Lahore Declaration for India. The importance of the Lahore Declaration lay in its role in fostering the 'larger strategic purpose of amity' between the two countries.[23] Such hopes for the Lahore Declaration would be dashed by the onset of the Kargil War. The high peaks of the Kargil sector of the line of control, within the Indian-administered state of Jammu and Kashmir, were manned all year round with the exception of the colder, snowy months due to the difficulty of access for personnel and logistics. However, in early May 1999, as Indian troops were beginning to reoccupy the peaks from which they had pulled back during the winter months, they detected Pakistani troops atop the Kargil ridges.[24] Throughout the months of May and June 1999, Indian military forces sought to push back the intruders. Then, on 30 June, Indian forces launched a major high-altitude offensive against Pakistani military posts along the border in the disputed Kashmir region. To underline the scale of the conflict, it is important to note that the total Indian troop strength in the region had reached 730,000 by the end of June. The build-up also included the deployment of around 60 frontline aircraft.[25] An important watershed was the visit of Nawaz Shariff to Washington to meet President Clinton, during which Clinton asked Shariff to take relevant measures to restore the sanctity of the LOC between India and Pakistan.[26] Finally, in early July 1999, India claimed to have cleared the Kargil sector and declared victory in the Kargil conflict.[27]

Many explanations have been given for the rationale behind the Pakistani, or Pakistani-backed intrusion.[28] It is agreed widely that the aim of the Pakistani leadership was to establish control of key strategic Himalayan heights in the disputed Kashmir region. This objective was to be achieved by cutting off access to the district of Ladakh, part of the Indian-administered state of Jammu and Kashmir, from the rest of India by breaching the main highway between Srinagar and Leh, and to cut off the Indian forces stationed on the contested Siachen Glacier. The Pakistani military could then try to force a stalemate and an internationally induced ceasefire, all of which would force India to renegotiate on the issue of Kashmir on the basis of the territory that Pakistan had newly occupied in the Kargil region.[29]

In the aftermath of the Kargil War, the BJP-led government convened a review committee to probe the reasons for the apparent failure in detecting the intrusions in Kargil.[30] This Kargil Review Committee had two main terms of reference to review the events that led to the Kargil conflict, and to recommend measures seen as necessary to safeguard Indian national security against any such future situations.[31] The full report was made public and consists of 228 pages and several volumes of annexes.

The report made three main points.[32] The first was that the Indian government and its various agencies were caught unaware of a major intrusion in the Kargil sector, even as it was happening. According to the report's findings, there was an inexcusable lack of anticipation, or knowledge of the impending intrusion until there was a serious build-up already in place.[33] Second, after the acquisition of nuclear weapon capability by both states, Pakistan believed that nuclear deterrence gave it an opportunity to wage a proxy war to change the territorial status quo in the disputed region of Jammu and Kashmir.[34] The report held that this was premised upon Pakistan's assumption that the Indian government would not engage in an all-out conventional war for fear of it escalating into a nuclear standoff. This, it alleged, was part of a wider tendency on the part of Pakistan's leaders, since 1947, to belligerent behaviour towards India and not being averse to changing the territorial status quo in Jammu and Kashmir by force, if necessary.[35] Lastly, it recommended that there be a revamp of the way that foreign policy was formulated and for greater institutional co-ordination between different government agencies within the policy making process.[36] Offering to locate Pakistan's perceptions of the Kargil War within a wider historical perspective, the report observed that

> the Pakistani establishment has a long and consistent history of misreading India's will and world opinion. In 1947, it did not anticipate the swift Indian military intervention in Kashmir when it planned its raid with a mix of army personnel, ex-servicemen and tribals under the command of Major General Akbar Khan. In 1965, it took Zulfikar Ali Bhutto's advice that India would not cross the international border to deal with Pakistan's offensive in the Akhnur sector. In 1971, it developed high but totally unwarranted expectations about the likelihood of US–Chinese intervention on its behalf. The same pattern of behaviour was evident this time too. This is presumably the price the Pakistani leadership has paid for its inability to come to terms with the military realities. It has obviously been a victim of its own propaganda.[37]

These three main points and the final observation are important in two respects. First, the findings of the committee found wide agreement within the ruling BJP-led government.[38] The government agreed largely with the report's rendition of Pakistani intentions and perceptions, as well as the manner in which it should respond to similar threats in the future. Second, it reflected the ruling government's view on Pakistan's perennial strategy of attempting to induce 'outsiders' to neutralize perceived Indian military superiority. In this view, with both countries having nuclear weapons, Pakistan would continue to wage low-intensity conflicts like the one in Kargil, attempting to avoid direct conventional war with a militarily superior India by implicit threats to use its nuclear weapons.[39] Forcing a stalemate in such instances would allow Pakistan to involve external powers, especially if it played up the threat of nuclear war with India.[40] The Pakistani state was thus viewed as perpetually aspiring to alter the territorial and political status quo in Jammu and Kashmir, through force if need be.

'The existential Muslim threat': Pakistan in BJP's foreign policy

When the above two reflections of the BJP-led government are seen within the context of the discussion of domestic identity politics in the previous chapter, particular linkages become clear. As outlined in the Kargil Review Committee Report, the first perception of the BJP-led government was that 'the Pakistani establishment has a long and consistent history of misreading India's will'. This perception of the persistent nature of the Pakistani state's challenge to India's territorial boundaries leads to two conclusions. First, the Indian government should never be in doubt about the pervasive need of the

Pakistani state to challenge India's territorial integrity. In the perception of Indian leaders, Nawaz Shariff was trying to convince India and the wider world that it wanted to establish durable peace via initiatives such as the Lahore Declaration at the same time that the Pakistani military, with or without Shariff's prompting or knowledge, was planning the Kargil intrusion. This made the representation of Pakistan's perpetual intransigence and betrayal even more durable in the eyes of Indian state elites.

The second point that it makes, rather implicitly, is that the Pakistani state has been allowed the opportunity to make such challenges to the Indian state as seen in the 1947, 1965 and 1971 conflicts with India. More specifically, past Congress governments had given the Pakistani state these opportunities to make such challenges. Through the Lahore process, the BJP-led government had been guilty, to a limited extent, of allowing itself a similar sense of complacency vis-à-vis Pakistan. However, given the affinity of the committee to the BJP-led government, most of the fault was placed at the feet of the Indian state intelligence agencies.[41] Conversely, the government's success in dealing diplomatically and strategically with the Pakistani threat once the intrusion was detected was praised by the committee.

However, influential voices within the BJP party and the *Sangh Parivar* articulated forcefully the spectre of Pakistan's perennial threat to India and the need for India to deal decisively with such threats. In the midst of the Kargil conflict, the BJP's national president, K. Thakre advocated that the eventual aim of the Indian government should not only be the eviction of the infiltrators from the Kargil area but to take back, by force, that part of Kashmir that was currently under Pakistan's control.[42] The BJP's general secretary, known to be close to L.K. Advani, the deputy prime minister, also hinted at the very real possibility of India using its military might to take back Pakistan-administered Kashmir, since

> if the situation goes on escalating because of Pakistan not adhering to LOC in actuality, the present LOC will end up coinciding with the original border minus Pak held Kashmir.[43]

The BJP's ideological parent organization, the RSS went even further in representing the existential Muslim threat that Pakistan posed and the manner in which Hindu India should respond. In its newspaper, *Panchjanya*, it ran an editorial that urged the BJP to demonstrate Indian resolve in countering Pakistan's aggression, given that

> the time has come again for India's Bheema to tear open the breasts of these infidels and purify the soiled tresses of Draupadi with blood. Pakistan will not listen just like that. We have a centuries-old debt to settle with this mindset. It is the same demon that has been throwing a challenge at Durga since the time of Mahammad bin Qasim. Arise Atal Behari! Who knows if fate has destined you to be the author of the final

chapter of this long story. For what have we manufactured bombs? For what have we exercised the nuclear option?[44]

In this instance, the RSS was rankled by the BJP-led government's various assertions during the Kargil conflict that India wanted to treat the conflict as a 'limited war', not wanting it to escalate into a conventional war in which nuclear weapons could be a potential option.[45] The BJP was involved in a delicate balancing act. Whilst it wanted to limit the conflict, it nevertheless sought to represent itself as the foremost custodian of India's territorial frontiers, unlike

> in 1948 when our forces were on the victory march and needed just a few months to clear today's Pakistan Occupied Kashmir (POK), they were halted by the Nehru government and the matter taken to the UN [while] in 1965 Indian Army captured the strategic Uri-Punch bulge with the strategic Haji Pir pass at its head. Biggest blunder took place by returning it to Pakistan at Tashkent. In 1971, the Indian government captured 93,000 POWs. At Shimla we returned them without getting an inviolable agreement on Jammu and Kashmir. All these strategic blunders led Pakistan to believe that it could get away by making another effort at grabbing Kashmir valley and forcing India to sue for peace. Fortunately for India, we had the Bharatiya Janata Party at the head of the government.[46]

The BJP's response to the Kargil War was thus a symbol of the party's resolve to deal decisively with Pakistani intransigence and defeat it 'by clearing each and every inch of the country'.[47]

However, the BJP-led government also represented its victory as a triumph of India's restraint in the face of Pakistani aggravation. In a terse warning to Pakistan, just after the cessation of hostilities in Kargil, Jaswant Singh said that the Indian government hoped that

> Pakistan would not be so unwise as to assume that India will not act in protecting its territorial integrity – land, sea, or air – simply because the Indian armed forces, under instructions from the government, acted with exemplary restraint during the Kargil confrontation.[48]

Such demonstrations of restraint were deemed necessary, based upon the objective of not wanting an escalation of the conflict to reach the stage at which the possibility of a nuclear conflict with Pakistan could invite US intervention into the India–Pakistan relationship specifically and into the South Asian region generally.[49] Any such possibility would compromise a long-held principle of Indian foreign policy because of the negative repercussions that it could have for India's territorial integrity. This conception of the twin imperialisms that could impact adversely Hindu India, on one hand

Muslim Pakistan's perennial challenge to Hindu India and on the other global Western imperialism – denoted by possible US intervention in India's regional policy – necessitated a course of action that stressed elements of both resolve and restraint in Indian foreign policy.

'Islamic terrorists' and 'illegal migration': India–Bangladesh relations in the BJP era

This section will examine Indian foreign policy in Bangladesh in the BJP era and attempt to make three points. The first is to show how Bangladesh came to be represented as a threat to the Indian state during this period. The second is to understand how this representation of Bangladesh as a specific kind of threat was dependent crucially upon this government's construction of Indian state identity. Third, it will plot how such representations of Bangladesh played a central role in informing Indian foreign policy towards Bangladesh during this period.

The Indian state played a crucial role in events that led to the formation of the state of Bangladesh. The close personal relationship between the leader of the Bangladeshi independence movement, Sheikh Mujibur Rehman and Indira Gandhi fostered further the close ties between the countries at the birth of Bangladesh. In fact from 1971 to 1975, Bangladesh became the largest single recipient of Indian aid.[50] If not more significant was the signing of the Twenty-Five Years of Friendship and Co-operation between the two countries on 19 May 1972. An important part of this agreement was that

> neither country would participate in any military alliance directed against the other, both would refrain from aggression against each other, neither would give assistance to any third party involved in an armed conflict against the other, and, in the event of an attack against the other, the parties would immediately enter into consultations in order to take measures to eliminate the threat.[51]

This treaty and the above excerpt were intended to frame the future of India–Bangladesh relations as close allies. However, the spirit, if not the letter, of the treaty began to unravel rapidly after 1975. The death of Sheikh Mujibur Rahman resulting from an army coup in that year led to a fundamental change domestically within Bangladesh and a gradual deterioration of the country's relationship with India.[52] From 1975 onwards, relations between the two became increasingly estranged with India being accused by the Bangladeshi government of supporting its domestic opponents operating from within Indian territory.[53] Despite the Indian state's vigorous and persistent denials, relations between the two countries continued to deteriorate during this period.

From the Indian point of view, one issue was a constant thorn in its relationship with Bangladesh: the problem of large-scale illegal migration from

Bangladesh into India across their shared, porous border.[54] Since the late 1970s, and especially in the 1990s, the Indian state had complained repeatedly about large-scale migration from Bangladesh into the Indian frontier states of West Bengal, Assam and Tripura.[55] In fact, as discussed in Chapter 4, the large influx of refugees into the Indian state of West Bengal, as a result of the civil war in Pakistan, was a critical factor in framing Mrs Gandhi's approach to Pakistan during that period. Moreover, in the state of Assam, this migration led to political agitation against the scale of such illegal migration, where there was genuine belief among the local Assamese population that they were being made a minority in their own state as a result of such large-scale migration from Bangladesh.[56] Indian authorities have claimed repeatedly that the Bangladeshi state has not done enough to stem the influx of such illegal migration into India, with the expected expressions of denial in response by Bangladeshi authorities.[57]

The issue of migration from Bangladesh was one of the main issues dominating bilateral relations between the two countries when the BJP-led government assumed political power in 1998. Even before assuming power, the BJP Party took an avid interest in the issue of migration into India from Bangladesh. It characterized the phenomenon of predominantly Muslim Bangladeshis being able to move illegally into India and remain there in ever-increasing numbers as a result of the Congress Party's strategy of winning Muslim electoral support in the border states concerned. For the BJP, the Congress Party was looking the other way when it came to dealing with illegal migration for fear of losing the support of the Muslim electorate who had settled illegally in India's border states. For example, Arun Shourie, later a minister in the BJP-led government's cabinet and key ideologue of the BJP, writing in 1992, dismissed previous Congress protestations that it was difficult to locate these 'illegal Bangladeshis' and how many of them there were. As he saw it,

> it is not that the Government, the ministers, the official machinery did not know the facts. The infiltrators could be seen in Delhi itself, in Assam etc. Tracts the size of some of our states could be seen as having been taken over by them. The politicians knew, as they were smuggling them on to electoral rolls and the rest. The Official machinery knew, as its personnel – for instance of the Border Security Force – had made a regular trade of letting the Bangladeshis sneak in. And they were reports galore documenting the avalanche.[58]

The issue of the Congress Party pandering to the perceived interests of the Muslim minority in India fed into the BJP's larger narrative of Muslim and minority 'appeasement' under the Congress governments of Nehru and Mrs Gandhi. More significantly, the implications of such large-scale migration for the religious demographics of the border states and the rest of India were not lost on BJP leaders, such as Shourie when he laments that

Serious religious and cultural dimensions are being increasingly felt in the states of West Bengal, Tripura and Bihar. It is observed that more and more Muslims immigrants are settling down in the border areas [...] the simmering communal tension in some of the border areas is one of the manifestations of the effects of large scale illegal migration of Bangladeshi nationals who have slowly displaced or dispossessed the local population, particularly those belonging to the Hindu community, in these areas.[59]

Therefore, before coming to power and leading a coalition government in 1998, the BJP had already lent an overtly religious complexion to the issue of 'illegal migration' from Bangladesh into India.[60] For the BJP, not only was illegal migration being supported by the Congress government for crude electoral support, it was also altering fundamentally the demographic of large parts of Hindu India via the predominantly Muslim character of its apparent avalanche.[61]

On coming to power in 1998, the BJP sought to deal with the issue of migration from Bangladesh by way of implementing various changes to the legal framework for dealing with illegal migration, some of these being set out in its 1998 election manifesto itself.[62] However, the distinctive approach of the BJP was to be noted in its linking of illegal migration into India to the presence of Al-Qaeda and Pakistan's ISI within Bangladesh.[63]

On 21 October 2002, a story in *Time* magazine, quoting eyewitnesses and 'senior Bangladeshi military sources', reported that on 21 December 2001 a group of 150 believed to be Al-Qaeda and Taliban fighters from Afghanistan had entered Bangladesh by boat.[64] This sparked a strong public denial from Bangladesh's foreign secretary, describing the story as 'a fiction and figment of wild imagination', based upon 'irresponsible journalism'.[65] Then, in a public address on 7 November 2002, India's deputy prime minister and home minister, L.K. Advani said that 'after the change in government in Bangladesh, there has been an increase in the activities of the Al-Qaeda and the ISI there'.[66] In addition to the Bangladeshi government's 'covert' support to these two organizations, he added that 'all insurgent groups of the Northeast are getting refuge there'.[67] In one statement, Advani had conflated all insurgent groups in India's Northeast province with the purported activities of Al-Qaeda and the ISI within Bangladesh. All three were perceived threats to India but, more significantly, Bangladesh was a refuge now not only for ethnic insurgent groups who carried out attacks and acts of terror within India, but it was home to particular types of terrorists, terrorists with Islamic orientations linked to Al-Qaeda and the ISI.

The link between illegal crossings along the Indo-Bangladesh border, ethnic insurgents and Islamic terrorists linked to Al-Qaeda and the ISI persisted in the BJP's official position in Bangladesh. In an official reply to the Bangladeshi government's 'concern' about Advani's comments, the Indian government reiterated Advani's point about the presence of such groups and that

A 'Hindu' foreign policy   111

India's concern has been conveyed from time to time to Government of Bangladesh including at the highest level about insurgent groups from the North Eastern States of India finding sanctuary in Bangladesh, undergoing training here and receiving assistance from elements inimical to India. We have also shared information regarding location of training camps and presence of specific militant groups and their leaders in Bangladesh.[68]

This representation of Bangladesh as a conduit for aiding illegal crossings across the border, providing refuge to insurgent groups and of recently being party to the ISI and Al-Qaeda in fanning domestic unrest in India was illustrated clearly in parliament by the external affairs minister, Yashwant Sinha in reply to a question about whether or not the Indian government was aware of the ISI and Al-Qaeda's presence in Bangladesh. In his opinion,

the Government have received periodic reports about various activities inimical to India's interest by agencies such as the ISI in Bangladesh. The Government have also received reports of alleged presence of Al-Qaeda activists in Bangladesh [...] Pakistan has established an elaborate infrastructure for the recruitment, indoctrination and training of terrorists on its territories under its control, to support its policy of sponsoring cross border terrorism in Jammu and Kashmir and other parts of India. Pakistan is also known to often misuse the territory of other countries for activities inimical to India's interest [...] The Government have shared its concern with Government of Bangladesh over the activities of ISI in Bangladesh.[69]

This was followed by the Indian Defence Minister, George Fernandes's public claim on 29 November 2002 that India had intelligence information and 'human evidence' to support its charge that the ISI and Al-Qaeda were using Bangladesh territory for anti-Indian activities.[70] It is significant that Fernandes made this allegation just a day after the Bangladeshi government had issued a press statement denying Yashwant Sinha's earlier allegation in the Indian Parliament. The important point here is not whether or not these assertions were accurate, or otherwise. As it was, there were articles like the one in *Time* that had speculated about the presence of Al-Qaeda and the ISI within Bangladesh as well.[71] The crucial point is how the BJP-led government linked cross-border movements, the ISI and Al-Qaeda in its approach to Bangladesh.

It has already been outlined how the BJP, before it came to power, had sought to represent the problem of illegal migration from Bangladesh by drawing attention to how India's Hindu population was being outnumbered and displaced by Muslim Bangladeshis, and how parties like the Congress had tolerated such illegal migration in an attempt to win the electoral support of these Muslim communities. After coming to power and in its foreign policy towards Bangladesh, the BJP added to this representation the spectre of the

ISI and Al-Qaeda aiding and training insurgent groups and fighting the Indian state through the tacit, if not open, approval of the Bangladeshi government. This representation of Hindu India being threatened by Muslim menace, embodied through the role that the ISI, Al-Qaeda and, to some extent, the Bangladesh government was playing, was unique to this government.

However, the BJP was not the only party who viewed the alleged activities of the ISI and Al-Qaeda in Bangladesh as a serious threat to Indian security. For example, during this period even the Left Front governments of the states of West Bengal and Tripura, who had traditionally been wary of the BJP's stand on the Muslim complexion of such illegal migration, had converging views with that of the BJP on the issue of the ISI and its role in fanning turmoil within India's border states. Stressing the threat of the ISI in the border states of India, the Chief Minister of Tripura, Manik Sarkar emphasized in February 2003 that the 'nasty design of ISI to destabilise India through these and other terrorist groups of the Northeast is public knowledge today'.[72]

However, what distinguished the BJP's approach to Bangladesh on this issue was its framing of it through the lens of a wider Muslim agenda, orchestrated mainly by Pakistan's ISI and wider, global Islamic forces, such as those represented by Al-Qaeda. Through the aiding and abetting of terrorist acts within India, this wider Muslim agenda against Hindu India aimed at destabilizing, and even dismembering the territorial frontiers of India. An important site of such representations was the manner and types of intelligence reports leaked to the press by Indian state and security apparatus from the time of Advani's statement in November 2002. For example, in reports leaked to a foreign newspaper by the Indian Home Ministry in early 2004, it was reported that the Indian government believed that the ISI, together with elements of Al-Qaeda, had been providing training for insurgent groups from India's Northeastern States in Bangladesh, with Bangladesh's knowledge and with the wider aim of converting 'Assam and some parts of its neighbouring states, including Tripura into a separate Islamic country'.[73] The establishment of particular madrassahs that would be used to incite terror and hatred against India would be part of the strategy, according to this report.

Versions of such 'leaks' also appeared in India's local press. An editorial in an Indian daily, *The Pioneer* – a periodical known to be relatively sympathetic to the BJP – revealed, based on information received from 'highly placed sources', that 'Bangladeshi Islamic fundamentalist organizations', and 'some Assam based Islamic rebel groups', under the direction of the ISI and Bangladesh's own security and intelligence services, were planning attacks in India and that 'their final aim is to carve out an independent Islamic state out of the Northeast'.[74] As was the case in the earlier report, newly constructed madrassahs on the Bangladesh side of the Indo-Bangla border were used to indoctrinate recruits for engagement in terrorist acts against India and to realize the formation of an Islamic state in the India's Northeast province.

This representation of the insurgency in India's Northeastern states, predominantly through an Islamic agenda, aided and abetted by Bangladesh, is a representation specific to the BJP-led government. As one of the senior members of the left-wing West Bengal state government pointed out, even though his state government agreed that the 'ISI was utilising some of the existing secessionist groups in the region to forward its own project of destabilising India, there was no Islamic terrorism as such' in India's Northeast.[75] This differs from the BJP-led government's representation of Bangladesh's role as a conduit for a new and even more insidious Muslim invasion of India's Northeast province.

The representation of Bangladesh as a specific type of threat to India was dependent crucially upon the manner in which Indian state identity had been constructed. By framing India as a majoritarian Hindu democracy, in which the Indian state reflected India's Hindu values, and in which Muslim imperialism threatened constantly to subjugate and humiliate Hindu India, it is clear to see how Bangladesh constituted a threat to India. Bangladesh's complicity in enabling the Muslim wave of illegal migrants across its border, especially those who had allied with regional and global Islamic forces, had severe demographic, cultural and security implications. This Muslim wave was therefore a threat to both the territorial integrity of India, as well as to the core identity of the Hindu Indian state.

In the view of this Indian government, Bangladesh was a hub of terrorism and this view is discernible in the public discourse of Indian leaders and in official parliamentary exchange, and in official and non-official counter-replies to Bangladesh's denials. It is especially interesting to note that the Indian state sought to represent this terrorist threat as specifically Muslim in nature, the aim of which was the formation of an Islamic state in India's Northeast region. When such representation of these border crossings is related to the Hindu nationalist imaginings of India's sacred territoriality, the link between Indian state identity and Indian foreign policy towards Bangladesh becomes much clearer.

Conclusion

The BJP-led government's foreign policy in both Pakistan and Bangladesh reveal the influence of the BJP's representation of Indian state identity. It viewed Pakistan's actions in Kargil and Bangladesh's role in border crossings through the prism of a perennial Muslim menace that strove constantly to subjugate and humiliate Hindu India. Such representations were made possible by its construction of India as a majoritarian Hindu state, embodying an ancient Hindu civilization. Specific actions on the part of Pakistan and Bangladesh could then be cast as evidence of persistent Muslim transgressions against Hindu India. Only by acknowledging its own Hindu character could the Indian state comprehend this Muslim threat visibly. Only then could Bharat defend itself appropriately and claim its rightful place amongst the great nation-states of the world.

Conclusion

The importance of the domestic realm in understanding how states formulate their foreign policy has been documented widely in the IR literature. Indian foreign policy has garnered broad research in this field. This study has sought to contribute to this body of literature by demonstrating how Indian foreign policy in South Asia has been impacted significantly by the manner in which different sets of Indian political elites come to acquire specific conceptions of 'Indian-ness' upon the basis of their contesting representations of Indian state identity.

The idea of India and India's foreign policy: the domestic identity politics framework

This study set out to answer two related questions. First, what implications have domestic identity politics had in the construction of the Indian state's conception of South Asia and India's role therein? Second, and related to the first question, how do these conceptions impact upon specific Indian foreign policy outcomes? It posits the hypothesis that domestic identity politics provides an important setting for understanding how Indian political elites conceptualize India's regional space and regional role in their formulation of Indian foreign policy. More specifically, it proposes that domestic identity politics provides a platform for political elites and their contestation over three central discourses associated with the idea of India itself – secularism, democracy and anti-imperialism. These contestations, it is argued, had a significant impact on Indian foreign policy in South Asia.

From Nehru to the BJP: Indian state identity and Indian foreign policy

The first two chapters considered the Nehru period, looking at how Nehru participated in the formulation and negotiation of the idea of India in the formative years of the Indian state. They then analysed how the three discourses of secularism, democracy and anti-imperialism had particular roots within the Indian nationalist movement and how they came to be defined as part of Indian state identity during this period. Nehru's immense influence, both institutionally as prime minister and external affairs minister, and as Gandhi's perceived deputy in the Indian nationalist movement, were critical in such an enterprise, imbuing Indian state identity with a specific character. His articulation of specific discourses related to secularism, democracy and anti-imperialism shaped the identity of the Indian state during this period but not without contestation from political elites from within and outside the Congress Party. The idea of India that Nehru negotiated within the context of such identity politics was one of a secular democracy, with the state a symbol of socio-economic change as well as protector of individual rights and liberties, ever mindful of its recent anti-colonial and anti-imperial roots.

During this period, the Indian state's role in South Asia was informed considerably by conceptions of its wider global role, which in turn was informed significantly by Nehru's framing of Indian state identity. However, despite Nehru's desire for the Indian state to play an important role within the global realm, South Asia occupied a relatively more crucial place within Indian foreign policy. In the case of its foreign policy towards Pakistan, within the specific case of the dispute over Kashmir, it was seen how the three different discourses of Indian state identity led to specific conceptions of India's regional space and role. However, these conceptions fed divergent interpretations of certain events relating to the Kashmir dispute and thus created various tensions in the formulation of Indian foreign policy. In the case of Indian foreign policy towards Nepal within the context of the 1950 Treaty of Friendship, India shifted from the imperative to frame its relations with Nepal upon the basis of 'reciprocity' to one in which it claimed a 'special position' within Nepal's foreign policy. Once again, the manner in which the Indian state perceived various events and actions, both in South Asia and beyond, through its conceptions of India's regional role contributed in large part to such a shift in Indian foreign policy.

In both cases, Indian foreign policy during the Nehru period demonstrated significant shifts in perceiving the role and motivations of 'external' involvement within South Asia, India's perceived regional space. As a result, by the mid-1950s, the Indian state increasingly viewed the possibility of any form of external involvement within South Asia as detrimental to Indian interests.

The demise of Nehru and the gradual ascendancy of Mrs Gandhi led to profound change within India. One of these changes was the re-construction of Indian state identity. By rearticulating Indian secularism through her political manoeuvres in the state of Jammu and Kashmir, she re-defined profoundly the discourse of secularism from one that posited secularism as the binary opposite of 'communal' politics. Instead, secularism came to represent the Indian state's manipulation of latent tensions and suspicions between different religious/ethnic communities for the purpose of consolidating political power. The representation of the Indian state as an independent arbiter of the competing demands of these communities, as was the case during the Nehru era, was no longer credible. Instead the Indian state under Mrs Gandhi increasingly became to be seen as wanting to play god.

Mrs Gandhi's implementation of the rupee devaluation, bank nationalization and her imposition of the Emergency, also changed fundamentally the democratic complexion of the Indian state. The discourse of democracy shifted from the earlier Nehruvian imperative of balancing the centralizing tendencies of the state with accommodating various levels of autonomy within the Congress party and within India. Instead, the discourse of Indian democracy shifted to one of appealing directly to the masses in the form of democratic populism. This meant that the Indian state's identity as a democratic institution came under increasing pressure with Mrs Gandhi's continual centralization of power within the prime minister's office.

Lastly, she sustained the Nehruvian mode of representing the Indian state's anti-imperial identity through a demonstration of India's determination to defend its territorial borders. Framing the discourse of anti-imperialism through a demonstration of the will and ability to defend India's territorial frontiers lent continuity to the manner in which the Indian state represented India as a symbol of anti-imperial ideals.

In terms of foreign policy, the Indian state under Mrs Gandhi persisted in a manner similar to the latter part of Nehru's tenure with the belief that without 'outside' meddling or intervention, the South Asian region would not be drawn into the machinations of Cold War politics. The possibility of the Cold War intruding into India's immediate region had for Mrs Gandhi, as it did for Nehru, very dangerous implications for the prospects of India's autonomy in protecting its territorial integrity. This imperative to prevent outside, especially great-power, influence into the region was the central driving force behind the need to codify bilateralism within the Simla Agreement. It was perceived that Pakistan was eager to offer itself as an ally to outside powers in order to counter its obsessive hatred of, and military inferiority to, India. The albeit reluctant agreement by Bhutto to bilateralize relations with India marked an important milestone in India's attempt to ensure that India's autonomy within South Asia was not curtailed. India – a state in which anti-imperialism was one of its existential attributes – had succeeded, to some extent, in making its main challenger, Pakistan, agree to end such external interventions in the region.

With regard to the Sri Lanka case, the core policy of ensuring that there was no extra-regional involvement in the conflict was impacted significantly by the Indian state's conception of its own regional space and its regional role therein. The Indian state's anti-imperial identity, informed as it was by the discourse on territoriality and protection of India's territorial space, linked the possible intrusion of super-power politics into South Asia to the spectre of Cold War bloc politics encroaching onto India's own territorial space. The Indian state's ideological position of non-alignment, stemming from its domestic conceptions of anti-imperialism made it integral that such bloc politics did not intrude into South Asia and then onto Indian territorial space.

The BJP era marked another important watershed in the history of independent India. The BJP, which led a coalition Indian government in this period, viewed itself, to a large extent, as the Congress Party's chief ideological challenger. Therefore, just as Nehru saw the idea of independent India as inseparable from his related discourse of secular India, similarly the BJP saw their idea of independent India as inseparable from the idea of Hindutva India. However, in contrast to the more exclusivist tone of the founding ideologues of Hindu nationalism, like Savarkar and Golwarkar of the RSS, the BJS and then the BJP has been consistent in its use of the term 'Bharatiya' instead of the term 'Hindu'. This was largely due to the fact that the BJP found itself as part of a coalition government and thus had to balance its own ideological goals with that of being the largest party within the central government.

In re-inventing the democratic identity of the Indian state, the BJP contested the discourse of Indian democracy framed during both the Indira Gandhi and Nehru periods in different ways. In relation to the Nehruvian discourse, the BJP framed its discourse of Indian democracy away from notions of individual liberties and minority rights to one of communal group rights and majoritarian interests. The Indira Gandhi era began the process of re-negotiating the discourse about Indian democracy by giving it a populist quality. The BJP carried on with such a re-representation of Indian democracy, framing its discourse on democracy in terms of majoritarian democracy, yet with one important difference. Mrs Gandhi negotiated the discourse of Indian democracy in order to concentrate political power at the level of the central state, with the result that Indian democracy came to be identified as the over-powering ability of the state to wield power in large spheres of Indian society. The BJP, however, utilized the discourse of majoritarian democracy not only to win and concentrate political power unto itself but more specifically to articulate a particular type of majoritarian democracy, intended in turn to re-invent the identity of the Indian state to reflect its seemingly 'Hindu' roots. Discourses of 'Hindu' democracy were meant to re-invent the idea of India by making the Indian state represent the BJP's notion of Indian-ness – the idea of India as *Bharat*.

The BJP also framed both the British and Muslim encounters in India's history as past instances of Hindu India's humiliation and subjugation. This reading of India's history through the prism of the humiliation and subjugation of Hindu India follows closely from Savarkar's reading of India as a Hindu nation and how both the Muslims and the British were 'foreigners' to such a representation of India during the colonial period. Leading on from this representation, the BJP brand of anti-imperialism exhibited a particular understanding and diagnosis of humiliation and a prognosis of redemption from such 'imperialisms'. In this narrative of loss and redemption, the subjugation of a once strong nation of Hindus is attributed first to the Muslims and the British and more recently to the Congress and its allied 'pseudo-secularists'.

With regard to its foreign policy towards Pakistan within the context of the Kargil War, the BJP represented its role in Kargil and India's resultant triumph as a victory for both the BJP's resolve and restraint. It meant to show how the BJP had not allowed Pakistani opportunism to be rewarded, a task in which previous Congress governments had failed terribly. Kargil was a symbol of the BJP's resolve to stand up to perennial Pakistani intransigence and defeat it. In terms of demonstrating 'resolve', as in the other two periods, conceptions of territorial integrity were linked to the discourse of anti-imperialism. More specifically, in the case of the BJP, such a discourse took on an implicitly 'Muslim' complexion, with Pakistan seen as the symbol such of Muslim intransigence. However, 'restraint' was also needed and this was based upon the Indian state's strategic reasoning, filtered through its perception of great-power intervention in its relationship with Pakistan and in South Asia more generally as manifestations of imperialism.

In the case of Indian foreign policy towards Bangladesh, and in the specific episode analysed in Chapter 6, members of the BJP-led government, through their public discourse, in official parliamentary exchange and in official and non-official counter-replies to Bangladesh's refutations, implicated the latter to be a hub and source of terrorism directed against India. More specifically, the BJP-led government sought to lend this ostensible terrorist threat a specifically 'Muslim' complexion, whose aim was the formation of an Islamic state in India's Northeast region. Such a representational exercise demonstrates how the BJP-led government sought to represent Indian state identity. When such conceptions of Indian state identity are related back to the Hindu nationalist imaginings of India's 'sacred' boundaries, which encompassed the South Asian region, the link between Indian state identity, conceptions of India's region space and role, and Indian foreign policy towards Bangladesh become clear. India, understood as a 'Hindu' state within its own regional space, therefore framed its foreign policy towards Bangladesh upon the basis of the latter representing a threat to India via its support of a specific Muslim form of terrorism.

Domestic identity politics and regional policy formulation: broader implications

Applying the domestic identity politics framework to understanding foreign policy has two broader implications beyond the specific subject examined in this study. These broader implications apply both to the case of Indian foreign policy after 2004 as well as to cases beyond India.

In the Indian case, 2005 marked a potentially unprecedented event in the history of Indian foreign affairs. In this year the US and Indian governments announced their joint intention to negotiate a civilian nuclear energy deal that would eventually allow India to import civilian nuclear technology as well as nuclear reactors and nuclear raw material required for civilian use of nuclear power. This was an unprecedented step as India was to become the first, and thus far the only, potential exception to strict global non-proliferation rules that have been in place since the signing of the Non-Proliferation Treaty (NPT) in 1968.[1] This triggered a heated debate within India about the potential benefits and pitfalls of such a deal, and more broadly, of such a seemingly intimate association with the US in India's foreign affairs. In 2008, this led to a near-collapse of the Congress Party-headed United Progressive Alliance (UPA) governing coalition, with the Left Front parties in the governing coalition pulling out of the government on the basis of their strong opposition to this nuclear agreement with the US.[2] An important aspect of this debate amongst Indian political elites centred on the perception of US intentions and the impact of this upon Indian foreign policy. This, I argue, was informed significantly by contesting representations of 'Indian-ness'. On one hand, the Congress Party saw the US's unprecedented historical move as a recognition of India's durable democratic credentials, as well as an acknowledgement of India's growing role within international politics. On the other hand, opponents of the agreement viewed the conditionalities attached to the agreement by the Bush administration as evidence of the US's efforts to impede India's nuclear weapon programme. More broadly, these political elites also viewed the agreement as a possible source of leverage that the US could utilize to pressure India in its foreign policy at the global level.[3] Such perceptions of US intentions are fed intimately by the enduring discourse of anti-imperialism and its link to Indian state identity. The analysis of such contesting discourses linked to 'Indian-ness' provides a more complex grasp of how domestic identity politics continues to impact Indian foreign policy to date.[4]

Beyond India, the domestic identity politics framework has a potentially important contribution to make to an understanding of how the domestic realm impacts foreign policy. This is especially the case in other postcolonial states. In important ways, this is largely because in most postcolonial states the ideational basis of statehood is still subject to intense contests between political elites. In fact, in many of these states, the acute struggle for political power is premised upon, amongst other factors, contests over the identity of the state. These domestic struggles over state identity will, in many ways, determine the nature of external 'threats' and the manner in which to respond to them. Tentatively stated, the link between domestic identity contestation, representations of state identity and formulating foreign policy therefore make postcolonial states ideal cases for the application of the domestic identity politics model.

Notes

Introduction

1 Nehru's speech in the Constituent Assembly, 8 November 1948. See Jawaharlal Nehru, *India's Foreign Policy – Selected Speeches, September 1946–April 1961* (New Delhi: Ministry of Information and Broadcasting, Government of India, 1971), p.17.
2 Ibid., p.21.
3 The Nehruvian and Hindu nationalist understandings of 'Indian' democracy will be addressed in greater depth in Chapter 1 and Chapter 5 respectively. For an introduction to Gandhian ideas of democracy, see Buddhadeva Bhattacharyya, *Evolution of the Political Philosophy of Gandhi* (Calcutta: Calcutta Book House, 1969); Thomas Pantham, 'Thinking With Mahatma Gandhi: Beyond Liberal Democracy', *Political Theory*, 11, 2 (1983) pp.165–88.
4 There are several surveys on how discourse analysis has been used recently within different academic disciplines but two excellent works are John Paul Gee, *An Introduction To Discourse Analysis – Theory and Method* (London and New York: Routledge, 1999) and Norman Fairclough, *Analysing Discourse – Textual Analysis For Social Science* (London and New York: Routledge, 2003).
5 For a fuller discussion of CDA, see Teun A. van Dijk, 'Critical Discourse Analysis', in Deborah Schiffrin *et al.* (ed.), *The Handbook Of Discourse Analysis* (Oxford and Malden, MA: Blackwell Pub, 2001), pp.353–5.
6 For further analysis of the differentiation between these two types of 'discourse analysis' projects, see Nelson Philips and Cynthia Hardy, *Discourse Analysis – Investigating Processes of Social Construction* (Thousand Oaks, London and New Delhi: Sage, 2002), pp.18–20.
7 Alexander Wendt, *Social Theory of International Politics* (Cambridge: Cambridge University Press, 1999), p.34.
8 David Campbell, *Writing Security: United States Foreign Policy and the Politics of Identity* (Manchester: Manchester University Press, 1992); Jutta Weldes, *Constructing National Interests: the United States and the Cuban Missile Crisis* (Minneapolis: University of Minnesota, 1999); Elizabeth Kier, 'Culture and French Military Doctrine Before World War II', in Peter Katzenstein (ed.), *The Culture of National Security* (New York: Columbia University Press, 1996); Alastair Ian Johnston, 'Cultural Realism and Strategy in Maoist China in Katzenstein' (ed.), *The Culture of National Security*; Janice Bially Mattern, 'The Power Politics of Identity', *European Journal of International Relations*, 7, 3 (2001); Patrick T. Jackson and Daniel Nexon, 'Constructivist-Realism or Realist-Constructivism', *International Studies Review*, 6, 2 (2004).

Notes 121

9 Weldes, *Constructing National Interests*, p.11. For a fuller discussion on how identity factors operate within such 'constraints' in the case of Europe's foreign policy, see Christopher Hill and William Wallace, 'Introduction: Actors and Actions', in Hill and Wallace (eds), *The Actors in Europe's Foreign Policy* (London and New York: Routledge, 1996), pp.8–10.
10 Ibid., pp.11–12.
11 Ibid., p.102.
12 Ibid., p.102.

1 Nehru and the invention of India

1 Judith Brown, *Nehru: A Political Life* (New Haven and London: Yale University Press, 2003), p.187.
2 Sunil Khilnani, *The Idea of India* (New York: Farrar, Straus and Giroux, 1997), p.8.
3 Donald Eugene Smith, *India As A Secular State* (Princeton, NJ: Princeton University Press, 1963); Prakash Chandra Upadhyaya, 'The Politics of Indian Secularism', *Modern Asian Studies*, 26, 4, (1992); Sumit Ganguly, 'The Crisis of Indian Secularism', *Journal of Democracy*, 144 (2003); Subramanian Swamy's, 'Redefining Secularism', *The Hindu*, 18 March 2004.
4 For a fuller exposition of Nehru's personal ideas on religion, nationalism and secularism, see M.N. Das's, *The Political Philosophy of Jawaharlal Nehru* (London: Allen & Unwin, 1961), pp.88–9.
5 This was Nehru's reply to a query about how to define secularism by a student at Oxford University in the mid-1950s. Taken from Asghar Ali Engineer's article, 'Nehru's Concept of Secularism', in *The Hindu* (Chennai), 1 April 1997.
6 As such India's British colonial administrators believed that India was not a political name but a geographical term and thus there was no such person as an 'Indian' but only people who were of different religions who happened to inhabit a place named 'India'. See Ainslie Embree, 'Indian Civilization and Regional Cultures: The Two Realities' in Paul Wallace (ed.), *Region and Nation in India* (New Delhi: Oxford and IBH, 1985), p.20.
7 See Nehru's autobiography, *The Discovery of India* (Delhi, Oxford and New York: Oxford University Press, 1994). His discussion on 'The Question of Minorities: The Moslem League – Mr M.A. Jinnah' is especially relevant. See pp.380–94.
8 For a detailed and incisive account of the ideas and processes that led to the demand for Pakistan, see Ayesha Jalal's authoritative book, *Jinnah: The Sole Spokesman* (Cambridge: Cambridge University Press, 1994).
9 Nehru, *The Discovery of India*, p.382.
10 Ibid., p.383.
11 It is estimated that about 12 million people became refugees as a result of migration and this figure is seen by many to be a modest estimate. See Tan Tai Yong and Ganesh Kudaisya, *The Aftermath of Partition in South Asia* (London and New York: Routledge, 2000), pp.2–28.
12 Ibid. See Chapter 2, 'The enigma of arrival: 14–15 August 1947 and the celebration of independence', pp.29–77.
13 Brecher, *Nehru: A Political Biography*, p.428.
14 Ibid., p.428. This observation is based on Brecher's personal interviews with individuals such as during this particular period. See also, Rajmohan Gandhi, *Patel: A Life* (Ahmedabad: Navjivan Publishing House, 1990). This biography of Patel explains that he suspected the loyalty of the majority of Muslims still in India after Partition and was of the view, shared by several others within Congress that several 'non-Muslim zones' should be created in India by forcing Indian Muslims to move to Pakistan, pp.431–3.
15 Quoted from Nehru's speech to Parliament, 19 August 1947, in J.S. Bright (ed.), *Before and After Independence: A Collection of the Most Important and Soul-Stirring*

122 Notes

      Speeches Delivered by Jawaharlal Nehru, Vols. 1 and 2. (New Delhi: Indian Printing Works, 1952), p.439.
16. Quoted from Nehru's letter to P. Subbarayan, dated 17 September 1952. Taken from S. Gopal (ed.), *Selected Works of Jawaharlal Nehru*, Second Series, Vol. 19 (New Dehli: Jawaharlal Nehru Memorial Fund, 1996), p.550. Subbaraya, was at this time the President of the Tamil Nadu Congress Committee.
17. A letter from Nehru to chief ministers, dated 2 May 1950. See Jawaharlal Nehru, *Letters to Chief Ministers, 1947–1964*, Vol. 2, G. Parthasarathi (ed.), (New Delhi: Jawaharlal Nehru Memorial Fund, 1985–9), pp.83–4.
18. Bright, *Before and After Independence*, pp.464–5.
19. In a public speech made in August 1945, Nehru saw the 'two-nation' theory as something representing a primitive stream of thought reminiscent of 'the Middle Ages', rather than fitting the present conditions of the time. Bright, *Before and After Independence*, p.85.
20. An often recounted episode of Nehru's very personal attempt to prevent attacks on Muslims in India in the early months after Partition is by a journalist who saw Nehru, in late August 1947, personally interpose himself between a group of Hindus who were about to attack a Muslim man on the streets of New Delhi even before the police had arrived on the scene. Nehru's risking his own safety to save a single Muslim individual seemed to have a profound impact throughout India, with many Muslims who had earlier intended to flee India apparently changing their minds on the basis of their belief that Nehru was sincere in protecting them and that their community could be safe in newly independent India. See Shashi Tharoor, *The Invention of India* (New Delhi: Penguin, 2003), pp.160–1.
21. Quoted from Sarvepalli Gopal's *Jawaharlal Nehru – A Biography*, Vol. 2 (London: Jonathan Cape, 1979), p.15.
22. Ibid., p.16. Rajendra Prasad, later to become the first President of India, and an acknowledged stalwart within the Congress Party, thought that Nehru's determination to protect Muslim minorities would be seen as, 'our action today is driving the people away from us'.
23. See Brown, *Nehru: A Political Life*, pp.194–5. See also B.N. Pandey's biography, *Nehru* (London and Basingstoke: Macmillan), pp.299–300.
24. Pandey, *Nehru*, p.302.
25. Nehru's letter to P. Tandon, dated 9 August 1951. See S. Gopal (ed.) *Selected Works of Jawaharlal Nehru*, Second Series, Vol. 16, pp.157–9.
26. Khilnani, *The Idea of India*, p.4.
27. *Oxford English Dictionary*, 2nd Edition, 1989 (http://dictionary.oed.com, last accessed 24 May 2004).
28. Das, *The Political Philosophy of Jawaharlal Nehru*, pp.95–8.
29. Ibid., pp.97–8.
30. Ibid., p.108.
31. Ibid., p.110.
32. For a fuller discussion, see Donald Eugene Smith, *India As a Secular State* (Princeton, NJ: Princeton University Press, 1963), pp.51–9.
33. See B.B. Misra, *The Indian Political Parties: An Historical Analysis of Political Behaviour Till 1947* (Delhi: Oxford University Press, 1976), pp.175–88; Stanley Wolpert, *Nehru: A Tryst With Destiny* (New York and Oxford: Oxford University Press, 1996), pp.108–11.
34. Brecher, *Nehru: A Political Biography*, p.215.
35. The franchise was not universal at this point. It was skewed in favour of the more affluent elite sections of the Indian population. See M.J. Akbar, *Nehru: The Making of India* (London and New York: Viking, 1998), p.260.
36. Brecher, *Nehru: A Political Biography*, pp.220 and 222.

37 Akbar, *Nehru: The Making of India*, p.260. Besides separate electorates for Muslims, the 1935 Act provided the reservation of one-third of the seats in the central legislature for Muslims, as well as reserving 33 per cent of seats in the same legislature for the unelected monarchs of the Indian princely states.
38 Congress won 711 out of the 1,585 seats in 11 provinces and obtained an overall majority in six provinces, whilst the Muslim League managed to win only 109 out of the 482 seats allocated to Muslims, obtaining only 4.82 per cent of the total Muslim votes. These figures have been taken from Tariq Ali's book, *The Nehrus and the Gandhis – An Indian Dynasty* (London: Pan Books, 1985), pp.58–60.
39 The elections of 1945, in which the Congress Party won majorities in eight of the 11 provinces and entered into a coalition with the non-communal Unionist Party in one province (the Punjab), established the party's claim to form the government of independent India in 1947.
40 The Constitution of India was formally inaugurated on 26 January 1950. It took almost three years of deliberation and drafting. It contains 395 articles (divided into 22 parts) and eight schedules. A full version of the Indian Constitution is provided by the Government of India, Ministry of Law and Justice on its website in *Constitution of India* (http://lawmin.nic.in/coi.htm, last accessed 14 May 2006).
41 Khilnani, *The Idea of India*, p.27.
42 Ibid., p.35.
43 Arend Lijphart, 'The Puzzle of Indian Democracy: A Consociational Interpretation', *The American Political Science Review*, 90, 2 (1996) p.261.
44 There were also separate personal laws for Christians and Parsis but given their relatively small communities, the Hindu and Muslim personal laws were the ones that pertained to the large majority of the Indian populace. See Smith, *India As a Secular State*, pp.84–6.
45 Ibid., p.280. In fact, the President of India, Rajendra Prasad, had threatened his resignation over Nehru's plans to reform Hindu personal law at this juncture.
46 See Taya Zinkin, 'Nehruism: India's Revolution Without Fear', *Pacific Affairs*, 28, 3 (1955) pp.229–30.
47 Smith, *India As a Secular State*, p.289.
48 Article 44 of the Indian Constitution (http://lawmin.nic.in/coi.htm, see section entitled, 'Article 1–242', last accessed 10 May 2005).
49 Nehru's letter to chief ministers, 4 October 1948, quoted in Brown, *Nehru: A Political Life*, p.224.
50 For a sympathetic discussion of Nehru's position on socialism and its utility for India, see B.R. Nanda, *Jawaharlal Nehru: Rebel and Statesman* (New Delhi: Oxford University Press, 1998), pp.185–93.
51 Nehru's personal letter to the finance minister, John Matthai, dated 13 September 1949, quoted from Gopal, *Jawaharlal Nehru – A Biography*, Vol. 2, p.98.
52 Patel's note for circulation among cabinet members, ibid. p.80. For a more detailed insight into Patel's views on socialism and private enterprise, see R. Gandhi, *Patel: A Life*, pp.490–1.
53 In some sense, their diverging views reflected how Nehru and Patel had different bases of support both within and beyond the Congress Party. See Benjamin Zachariah, *Nehru* (London and New York: Routledge, 2004), pp.102–17. See also Brecher, *Nehru*, pp.390–1.
54 Pandey, *Nehru*, p.357.
55 Both quotations are taken from Das, *The Political Philosophy of Jawaharlal Nehru*, p.165.
56 Brown, *Nehru*, pp.201–2; Brecher, *Nehru*, pp.455–7.
57 See Benjamin Zachariah, *Nehru*, pp.151–4. The eminent Indian political scientist, A. Appodorai, terms Nehru's efforts to blend a socialist, re-distributive ethos into the workings and the idea of democracy in India as an example of 'democratic

124 Notes

   socialism'. See A. Appodorai, *Indian Political Thinking: From Naoroji To Nehru* (Madras: Oxford University Press, 1971), pp.117–18.
58 Ibid., p.161.
59 Paul R. Brass, *The Politics of India Since Independence*, 2nd Edition (Cambridge, New York and Melbourne: Cambridge University Press, 1994), p.35.
60 Brown, *Nehru: A Political Life*, p.186.
61 For example, see the work by Sankaran Krishna, *Postcolonial Insecurities*.
62 This description of the status of the princely states is informed by Brecher's discussion of the subject. See Brecher, *Nehru: A Political Biography*, p.402. See also an authoritative account by V.P. Menon, *The Integration of the Indian States* (London and New York: Longman & Macmillan, 1956). V.P. Menon was the constitutional adviser to the Viceroy of India before Indian independence and later was made the inaugural Secretary of the States Ministry. He was considered to be a most trusted and close deputy of the home minister (and in this role also the minister of the states ministry) and deputy prime minister, Sardar Patel. Therefore, Menon was involved very closely in the negotiations about the accession of the princely states into the Indian Union.
63 Nehru, *The Discovery of India*, p.531.
64 For an in-depth discussion of the economic and administrative disruptions as a result of the territorial partition in 1947, in both the Punjab and Bengal, see Yong and Kudaisya, *The Aftermath of Partition in South Asia*, pp.141–63 and 204–20.
65 Nehru expressed these views in various public rallies in India between 17 July and 29 August 1945. See Bright, *Before and After Independence*, p.84.
66 For a more detailed discussion of this point see, George Tanham, *Indian Strategic Thought: An Interpretive Essay* (Santa Monica: RAND, 1992).
67 Brecher, *Nehru*, pp.353 and 403; Gopal, *Jawaharlal Nehru*, pp.171–7.
68 Although Patel is largely credited as 'India's strongman' who incorporated these states into the Indian Union, he and Nehru were of the same mind with regard to the importance of this incorporation. See, *Patel: A Life*, p.500–1; Menon, *The Integration of the Indian States*, pp.72–7.
69 For further details see H.V. Hodson, *The Great Divide* (London: Hutchison, 1969), pp.229–30.
70 For a copy of Nehru's letter to Mountbatten written on the 11 May 1947 in which he rejects the proposed British plan, see Jalal, *The Sole Spokesman*, p.272. See also, S. Gopal, *Jawaharlal Nehru: A Biography*, Vol. 1: 1889–1947 (Cambridge: Harvard University Press, 1976), pp.302–3.
71 S. Gopal, *Jawaharlal Nehru: A Biography*, Vol. 1, p.305.
72 See Articles 73 and 253 of the Indian Constitution (http://lawmin.nic.in/coi.htm, last accessed 10 May 2005).

2 Nehru and the birth of India's regional policy: the case of Pakistan and Nepal

 1 See Nehru's speech in Indian Constituent Assembly, 8 March 1949, in Jawaharlal Nehru, *India's Foreign Policy: Selected Speeches, September 1946–April 1961* (New Delhi: Ministry of Information and Broadcasting, Government of India, 1971), p.23.
 2 See A. Appodorai, *The Domestic Roots of India's Foreign Policy, 1947–1972* (Delhi: Oxford University Press, 1981), pp.80–1.
 3 See Nehru, *The Discovery of India*, pp.536–48. For an examination of Nehru's approach to the 1954 Afro-Asian Conference, see Sinderpal Singh, 'From Delhi to Bandung: Nehru, "Indian-ness" and "Pan-Asian-ness"', *South Asia: Journal of South Asian Studies*, 34, 1 (2011) pp.51–64.
 4 This was a term used by Winston Churchill to describe Nehru's vision of India's place in global affairs in a letter to the latter on 21 February 1955. See *Jawaharlal Nehru: A Biography – Volume 2*, p.283.

5 This point has not gone uncontested, although it remains the dominant, mainstream understanding of the origins of the Pakistan claim. For a defence of this dominant view against other contending views, see K.K. Aziz's *The Making of Pakistan: A Study in Nationalism* (Karachi: National Book Foundation, 1976), pp.54–6.
6 The use of the term 'Pakistan' was first coined by a Cambridge student, Rehmat Ali in about 1933. However, at that time this idea did not enjoy much support even within the Muslim League party. For a fuller discussion see Richard Symonds, *The Making of Pakistan* (Karachi: National Book Foundation, 1976), pp.56–7, 59.
7 These were the exact words of the Memorandum on States' Treaties and Paramountcy presented by the Cabinet Mission to His Highness the Chancellor of the Chamber of Princes on 12 May 1946. Quoted from Sisir Gupta's *Kashmir: A Study in India–Pakistan Relations* (New Delhi: Asia Publishing House, 1967), p.71. See also, Barbara N. Ramusack's *The Indian Princes and Their States* (Cambridge: Cambridge University Press, 2004), pp.271–4.
8 For a detailed exposition of this point of view, see Alastair Lamb, *Crisis in Kashmir* (London: Routledge & Kegan Paul, 1966), p.37.
9 See Jalal, *The Sole Spokesman*, pp.38–41.
10 See Prem Shankar Jha, *Kashmir 1947: Rival Versions of History* (New Delhi: Oxford University Press, 1996), p.112.
11 Most commentators believe that this was part of Hari Singh's plan to continue to stall and to hold out for independence, or at least to bargain with India and Pakistan to obtain the maximum amount of autonomy for his political position if and when he decided to join either state. See Gupta, *Kashmir*, pp.98–100.
12 Lamb defends the Pakistani version when he says that 'the Poonch rising was certainly not an act in which the Muslim League participated'. See Lamb, *Crisis in Kashmir*, p.38.
13 Nehru's statement to the Indian Constituent Assembly (Legislative), 25 November 1947. The Constituent Assembly was the Indian Parliament before it became a Constitutional Republic in 1950. Quoted from Jawaharlal Nehru, *India's Foreign Policy: Selected Speeches, September 1946–April 1961* (New Delhi: Government of India, 1971), p.446.
14 Michael Brecher's personal interview with Nehru as reported in the *National Herald*, 2 August 1956. Cited in Sarvepalli Gopal (ed.), *Jawaharlal Nehru – An Anthology* (Delhi: Oxford University Press, 1980), p.216.
15 Henderson to Acheson, 15 August 1949. See S. Gopal, *Selected Works of Jawaharlal Nehru*, Series Two, Vol. 12, pp.342–3.
16 Mountbatten was requested by Nehru to remain behind after independence to serve as India's first Governor General and to assist Nehru's new government in the mammoth task of handling the issue of the accession of the princely states into the Indian Union. Mountbatten stayed on as Governor General in India until 21 June 1948.
17 See Earl Mountbatten, *Time Only To Look Forward: Speeches of Rear Admiral the Earl Mountbatten of Burma* (London: Nicholas Kaye, 1949), p.269. Also quoted in Michael Brecher's *The Struggle for Kashmir* (Toronto: Ryerson Press, 1953), p.22.
18 Point made by Benjamin Zachariah, *Nehru* (London and New York: Routledge, 2004), p.178.
19 See Sumit Ganguly, *The Crisis In Kashmir: Portents of War, Hopes of Peace* (Cambridge: Cambridge University Press and The Woodrow Wilson Centre Press), p.11. Brecher notes also India's legal claim for the state as a result of the signing of the Instrument of Accession (*The Struggle for Kashmir*, p.38). Alistair Lamb has raised questions about whether or not the Instrument of Accession was actually signed by Hari Singh. However, his view remains controversial and is not supported by the majority of scholars writing on the Kashmir issue. See Alastair

Lamb, *Kashmir: A Disputed Legacy, 1846–1990* (Karachi: Oxford University Press, 1992).
20 Quoted from Dhirendra Sharma (ed.), *India's Commitment of Kashmir (Political Analysis with Documents)* (New Delhi: Philosophy and Social Action Publication, 1994), p.35.
21 Brecher, *The Struggle for Kashmir*, p.40.
22 In a series of interviews conducted between 1964 and 1966 with Michael Brecher, Krishna Menon a close confidante of Nehru and India's chief representative at the UN from 1952–62 notes, with hindsight, that Nehru's initial decision to bring the matter to the UN for adjudication was 'a tactical error but in our idealism we thought that the United Nations would set it right'. See, Michael Brecher, *India and World Politics: Krishna Menon's View of the World* (London: Oxford University Press, 1968), p.195.
23 See the text of Nehru's speech to the United Nations General Assembly, Paris, 3 November 1948 in Nehru, *India's Foreign Policy*, pp.162–7.
24 Nehru's letter to Sheikh Abdullah, 12 December 1947. See Sarvepalli Gopal, *Selected Works of Jawaharlal Nehru*, Series Two, Vol. 4 (Delhi: Jawaharlal Nehru Memorial Fund, 1994), pp.368–9.
25 Nehru's message broadcast by the United Nations Radio network from Lake Success, New York, 5 May 1950. See Nehru, *India's Foreign Policy*, pp.167–8.
26 Sankaran Krishna, *Postcolonial Insecurities*, p.22.
27 Document No. S/1100, paragraph 75, dated 9 November 1948. See United Nations, *Documents on the United Nations Commission on India and Pakistan (UNCIP)* (www.un.org/english, last accessed 25 July 2006). For a detailed inspection of the issues surrounding the resolution, see Girilal Jain's, 'India, Pakistan and Kashmir', in B.R. Nanda (ed.) *Indian Foreign Policy: The Nehru Years* (Delhi: Vikas Publishing House, 1976), pp.52–9.
28 For the various details of the Indian and Pakistani positions, see Gupta, *Kashmir*, pp.155–64, 181–98.
29 See S.M. Burke's *Mainsprings of Indian and Pakistani Foreign Policies* (Minneapolis, MN: University of Minnesota Press, 1974), p.141.
30 Ibid., p.153.
31 Nehru was empathic in informing the US government that such provision of arms to Pakistan would make the latter even more likely to use force to settle its disputes with India. See Nehru's note to the Indian foreign secretary authorizing communication to the United States ambassador, 4 April 1957. See S. Gopal, *Nehru: A Biography*, Vol. 3, p.50.
32 This is a quotation from Nehru's speech during a debate on foreign affairs in the Lok Sabha, 29 September 1954. See Nehru, *India's Foreign Policy*, p.89. The Manila Treaty was the treaty that gave birth to SEATO.
33 Krishna Menon describes how by this stage Nehru was convinced that within the UN 'Kashmir was a Cold War issue; its part of the desire to forge a ring around the Soviet Union, part of the policy of what is called "containment"'. See Brecher, *India and World Politics*, pp.195–6.
34 Jha, *Kashmir 1947*, p.208.
35 This is from an interview published in *The Journal of the Indo-Japanese Association* (July–November 1957), cited in Gopal (ed.), *Jawaharlal Nehru*, p.225.
36 In fact, so dependent was Sikkim's position that Indira Gandhi eventually incorporated it into the Indian state in 1974 at the request of the popularly elected representatives of Sikkim. As for Bhutan, its 1949 Treaty with India entrenched the Indian state's right to conduct Bhutan's foreign policy. For a fuller discussion of the legal-constitutional position of Bhutan and Sikkim at the time of India's independence in 1947, see Pradyumna P. Karan and William M. Jenkins, *The Himalayan*

Kingdoms: Bhutan, Sikkim and Nepal (London and Toronto: D. Van Nostrand, 1963), pp.51–5 for Bhutan and pp.74–8 for Sikkim.
37 Quoted from Asad Husain's *British India's Relations With the Kingdom of Nepal, 1857–1947: A Diplomatic History of Nepal* (London: Allen & Unwin, 1970), p.39.
38 Ibid., p.64.
39 Karan and Jenkins, *The Himalayan Kingdoms*, p.88.
40 The treaty comprises ten articles. They are quoted from the transcripts of the original documents provided by the Indian Ministry of External Affairs (MEA), *Treaty of Friendship* on its official website. (http://www.mea.gov.in/, last accessed 10 January 2005). See also Avtar Singh Bhasin (ed.), *Documents on Nepal's Relations With India and China, 1949–1966* (Bombay and New Delhi: Academic Books, 1970), pp.31–3.
41 Ibid.
42 Ibid. The Treaty of Trade and Commerce was signed between the countries at the same time but its implications do not impact sufficiently upon the analysis at hand to warrant a detailed discussion of it. However one notable aspect of this treaty was that it allowed 'in favour of the Government of Nepal full and unrestricted right of commercial transit of all goods and manufactures through the territory and ports of India', a condition which was vital for Nepal's land-locked economy (http://www.mea.gov.in/, last accessed 15 November 2012).
43 Sarvepalli Gopal, *Jawaharlal Nehru: A Biography – Volume 2, 1947–1956* (London: Jonathan Cape, 1979), p.68.
44 See George Tanham, *Indian Strategic Thought: An Interpretive Essay* (Santa Monica: RAND, 1992), pp.19–24.
45 This is taken from a speech made in Parliament, 6 December 1950. See Jawaharlal Nehru, *Indian Foreign Policy*, p.435.
46 This was codified in a treaty signed between India and China in 1954. See Gopal, *Nehru: A Biography – Volume 2*, pp.256–8.
47 See Tanham, *Indian Strategic Thought*, p.28.
48 Gopal, *Nehru: A Biography – Volume 2*, p.258.
49 See Warner Levi, 'Government and Politics in Nepal: II', *Far Eastern Survey*, (14 January 1953) p.5; for a wider study of Rana rule within Nepal and the challenges to it, see Adrian Sever, *Nepal Under The Ranas* (Delhi: Oxford and IBH Publishing, 1993).
50 A speech in the Lok Sabha, 6 December 1950. See A.S. Bhasin (ed.), *Documents on Nepal's Relations With India and China, 1949–1966*, p.24.
51 Jayaprakash Narayan's letter to Nehru, 17 November, 1950, quoted from Gopal, *Jawaharlal Nehru: A Biography – Volume 2*, p.69.
52 B.P. Koirala was the Nepali Congress representative and leader who went to Delhi to seek Nehru's support for military action. This excerpt is quoted from Nehru's reply to Narayanan, 20 November 1950, taken from Gopal, *Jawaharlal Nehru: A Biography – Volume 2*, p.69.
53 See T. Louise Brown, *The Challenge To Democracy In Nepal: A Political History* (London and New York: Routledge, 1996), p.25; Sumit Ganguly and Brian Shoup, 'Nepal: Between Dictatorship and Anarchy', *Journal Of Democracy*, 16, 4 (2005) p.131.
54 L. Brown, *The Challenge To Democracy in Nepal*, pp.26–7.
55 See Gopal, *Nehru: A Biography – Volume 2*, pp.263–4.
56 Press conference in New Delhi, 11 June 1951, quoted from S. Gopal, *Selected Works of Jawaharlal Nehru, 2nd Series*, Vol. 16, p.488.
57 Ibid., p.488.
58 Nehru's letter to B.K Gokhale, Indian Ambassador to Nepal, 1952–5. This letter dated 6 July 1954, quoted from S. Gopal, *Selected Works of Jawaharlal Nehru, 2nd Series*, Vol. 26, pp.490–2.

59 A.S. Bhasin (ed.), *Documents on Nepal's Relations With India and China, 1949–1966*, p.27.
60 Minutes from Nehru's conversation with Zhou En-Lai, 20 October 1954, Peking, China, quoted from S. Gopal, *Selected Works of Jawaharlal Nehru*, 2nd Series, Vol. 27, p.20.
61 Ibid., p.31.The above conversation, including quotes, is from minutes of Nehru's conversation with Zhou, 21 October, Peking.
62 Ibid., p.196. Nehru's draft memoir to the Nepalese government, 8 May 1954.
63 Ibid., p.196. See also T.N. Kaul's account of the exchange. Kaul, at that time, was the Joint Secretary of the Ministry of External Affairs (MEA) and responsible for the Eastern and Northern Divisions within the MEA. See T.N. Kaul, *A Diplomat's Diary (1947–1999): The Tantalizing Triangle – China, India and USA* (New Delhi: Macmillan, 2000), pp.56–7.
64 S. Gopal, *Selected Works of Jawaharlal Nehru*, 2nd Series, Vol. 27, p.196; Kaul, *A Diplomat's Diary*, p.57.
65 Ibid., p.197. Nehru's note to T.N. Kaul and R.K. Nehru, 17 November 1954. The two paragraphs to which Nehru refers made reference to both countries respecting each other's territorial integrity and sovereignty and to come to each other's aid in the case of an act of aggression by a third country against the other. These two paragraphs were not dissimilar from the understanding contained within the 1950 treaty.
66 Ibid., p.74. Both the question and Nehru's reply were from a press conference held in New Delhi, 13 November 1954.
67 S. Gopal, *Jawaharlal Nehru: A Biography – Volume 3* (London: Jonathan Cape, 1984), p.34.
68 Ibid., p.35.
69 Ibid., p.134.
70 Ibid., p.134. Nehru's note to B.P. Koirala, Prime Minister of Nepal, dated 31 March 1960.

3 'The Empress of India': Indira Gandhi and the idea of India

1 See Yogendra K. Malik and Dhirendra K. Vajpeyi's chapter, 'India: The Years of Indira Gandhi', in Yogendra K. Malik and Dhirendra K. Vajpeyi (eds), *India: The Years of Indira Gandhi* (Leiden, New York, Copenhagen and Cologne: E.J. Brill, 1988), p.1.
2 This phrase was used by the Indian journalist Kuldip Nayar, incidentally a one-time fervent critic of Indira Gandhi. See Kuldip Nayar, *India After Nehru* (New Delhi: Vikas Publications), p.208.
3 *Economist*, quoted in Katherine Frank, *Indira: The Life of Indira Nehru Gandhi* (London: HarperCollins Publishers, 2001), p.342.
4 Malik and Vajpeyi, *India: The Years of Indira Gandhi*, p.1; Brass, *The Politics of India Since Independence*, pp.32–3.
5 This was the Constitutional (44th Amendment) Act. See 'Constitution of India', on the website of the Government of India, Ministry of Law and Justice (Legislative Department) (http://indiacode.nic.in/coiweb/amend/amend44.htm, last accessed 16 June 2006). See B.S. Raghavan, 'Who is Secular', *Business Line*, 3 May 2002.
6 In a personal letter to the then chief minister of Mysore Mrs Gandhi said that 'the decision of the Mysore Government to take out a procession of Mother India during the Dussehra festivities [...] has made me wonder whether you should support anything that suggests revivalism'. Quoted from Zareer Masani, *Indira Gandhi: A Biography* (London: Hamish Hamilton, 1975), p.279.
7 For example, see Victoria Schoefield, *Kashmir In Conflict: India, Pakistan And The Unending War* (London and New York: I.B. Taurus, 2003), pp.143–88; S. Ganguly,

The Crisis In Kashmir: Portents of War, Hopes of Peace, pp.58–91; Sten Widmalm, *Kashmir In Comparative Perspective: Democracy and Violent Separatism In India* (London: RoutledgeCurzon, 2002), pp.61–92; S.Widmalm, 'The Rise and Fall of Democracy in Jammu and Kashmir', *Asian Survey*, 37, 11 (1997) pp.1006–9; Christopher Snedden, 'Would a Plebiscite Have Resolved the Kashmir Dispute?', *South Asia: Journal of South Asian Studies*, 28, 1 (2005) pp.68–9.

8 Brass, *The Politics of India Since Independence*, p.219; Schoefield, *Kashmir In Conflict*, pp.293–5.

9 The multi-volume encyclopaedia was entitled *The Children's Encyclopaedia* and was sold widely in Britain during the early part of the twentieth century. See Arthur Mee, *The Children's Encyclopaedia*, various volumes (London: Educational Book Company, 1908).

10 Mrs Gandhi's determination to get rid of Farooq as chief minister is ably described in Pranay Gupte's *Mother India: A Political Biography of Indira Gandhi* (New York and Ontario: Macmillian, 1992), pp.389–90.

11 Frank, *Indira*, p.468.

12 See Tavleen Singh, *Kashmir: A Tragedy of Errors* (New Delhi: Penguin, 1996), pp.30–4.

13 See Inder Malhotra, *Indira Gandhi: A Personal and Political Biography* (Boston, MA: Northeastern University Press, 1991), p.278.

14 P.N. Dhar was personal adviser and then head of the prime minister's personal secretariat under Mrs Gandhi from 1973–9, and one of her closest advisers during this period. He recounts that when he met Mrs Gandhi in an informal capacity in April 1984, she complained bitterly about Farooq and that he needed to be toppled from power in Jammu and Kashmir sooner rather than later. See P.N. Dhar, *Indira Gandhi, the 'Emergency' and Indian Democracy* (New Delhi: Oxford University Press, 2001), p.367.

15 B.K. Nehru, cousin of Indira Gandhi and seen by many as the quintessential apolitical civil servant, was Governor of Jammu and Kashmir until he was removed in early 1984 after he refused to be involved in the unconstitutional removal of Farooq's government. In his biography, he relates that in cases where bribes were paid to defecting MPs, 'the standard rate was two thousand lakh rupees per bought defector'. See B.K. Nehru, *Nice Guys Finish Second* (Delhi: Viking Penguin, 1997), p.627. For a discussion about the ways in which defectors were offered cabinet positions in the new government, see Gupte, *Mother India*, p.391.

16 Frank, *Indira*, p.486. For Farooq's version of events, see Farooq Abdullah, *My Dismissal* (New Delhi: Vikas Publishing, 1985).

17 Gupte, *Mother India*, p.391.

18 See Sumit Ganguly, 'The Crisis of Secularism', *Journal of Democracy*, 14, 4 (2003) pp.14–16. For a critique of efforts to apply the secularism ideal to the Indian case, see Ashis Nandy, 'The Politics of Secularism and the Recovery of Religious Toleration', in Rajeev Bhargava (ed.), *Secularism and Its Critics* (New Delhi: Oxford University Press, 1999).

19 For examples of such works, see Pupul Jayakar, *Indira Gandhi: An Intimate Biography* (New York: Pantheon Books, 1992); Uma Vasudev, *Two Faces of Indira Gandhi* (Delhi: Vikas Publications, 1977); Dorothy Norman (ed.), *Indira Gandhi: Letters to an American Friend, 1950–1984* (New York: Harcourt Jovanovich, 1985); Blerna S. Steinberg, 'Indira Gandhi: The Relationship Between Personality Profile and Leadership Style', *Political Psychology*, 26, 5 (2005); William H. Hampton and Virgina Schroeder, *The Two-Edged Sword: A Study of Paranoia Personality In Action* (Santa Fe, NM: Sunstone Press, 1990), pp.92–4, 140.

20 For the political economy explanation, see Lloyd Rudolph and Susanne Rudolph, *In Pursuit of Lakshmi: The Political Economy of the Indian State* (Chicago and

London: Chicago University Press, 1986). For the manner in which de-institutionalism was critical to the fraying of democracy during Mrs Gandhi's first term in office, see Rajni Kothari, *Democratic Polity and Social Change in India* (Bombay: Allied Publishers, 1976). To understand how an expanding electorate and regional politics within India began to increasingly assert themselves, see Paul Brass 'Pluralism, Regionalism and Decentralizing Tendencies in Contemporary Indian Politics' in A.J. Wilson and Dennis Dalton (eds) *The States of South Asia: Problems of National Integration* (London: C. Hurst, 1982).

21 See Michelguglielmo Torri, 'Factional Politics and Economic Policy: The Case of India's Bank Nationalization', *Asian Survey*, 15, 12 (1975) p.1077.
22 Frank, *Indira*, p.290.
23 Masani, *Indira Gandhi*, pp.146–7.
24 See Francine Frankel, *India's Political Economy: 1947–77* (Princeton, NJ: Princeton University Press, 1978), pp.295–7.
25 Masani, *Indira Gandhi*, p.156; Frank, *Indira*, p.296.
26 This is the claim made by Inder Malhotra, one of Mrs Gandhi's biographers, who had a certain degree of exclusive access to Mrs Gandhi at this time due to his position as a close family friend of Mrs Gandhi and especially her late husband, Feroze. See Inder Malhotra, *Indira Gandhi*, p.20.
27 See also Mary C. Carras, *Indira Gandhi in The Crucible of Leadership: A Political Biography* (Boston, MA: Beacon Press, 1979), pp.153–4.
28 See Krishan Bhatia, *A Biography of Prime Minister Gandhi* (New York: Praeger Publishers, 1974), p.202.
29 Frankel, *India's Political Economy*, p.299.
30 For more details on the radio address, see Bhatia, *A Biography of Prime Minister Gandhi*, p.204.
31 Stanley Kochanek notes how from the end of Nehru's era, the 'passing of the old nationalist leadership eroded the effective power of the high command, and power in the Congress became decentralized'. In this case, 'High command' refers to the apex leadership of the Congress Party. See Stanley Kochanek, 'Mrs Gandhi's Pyramid: The New Congress', in Henry Hart (ed.), *Indira Gandhi's India* (Boulder, CO: Westview Press, 1976), p.110.
32 As discussed in Chapter 1, on the issue of the Indian state protecting Muslim minorities in the immediate aftermath of the Partition, as well as in his opposition to Tandon as president of the Congress Party, Nehru was relatively isolated from members of his cabinet and senior members of his party.
33 Mrs Gandhi announced the measure nationally on All India Radio on 20 July 1969. For a transcript of the announcement, see Indira Gandhi, *Selected Speeches and Writings of Indira Gandhi* (New Delhi: Ministry of Information and Broadcasting, 1971), p.133.
34 Congress lost 95 seats, won only 282 seats out of 520 seats and had a slim overall majority of 44 seats. At the state level, Congress lost its majorities in the state legislatures of seven states. See Robert Hardgrave Jr., 'The Congress in India: Crisis and Split', *Asian Survey*, 10, 3 (1970) p.256.
35 See Pupul Jayakar's *Indira Gandhi*, pp.153–4. See also, Michelguglielmo Torri, 'Factional Politics and Economic Policy: The Case of India's Bank Nationalization', *Asian Survey*, 15, 12, pp.1077–96.
36 Torri, 'Factional Politics and Economic Policy', p.1089.
37 Frank, *Indira*, p.315, fn.57.
38 Jayakar, *Indira Gandhi*, p.154. Based upon a personal interview with Indira Gandhi.
39 Mrs Gandhi's faction of the Congress Party came to be known as the Congress-R (Requisitioned, or Ruling), as opposed to the other part of the split Congress Party, which came to be known as the Congress-O (Organization).

40 Masani, *Indira Gandhi*, p.211.
41 For a detailed discussion of these events, see Norman D. Palmer, 'India in 1975: Democracy in Eclipse', *Asian Survey*, 16, 2 (1976), pp.95–9.
42 For a fuller discussion of the details leading to the Allahabad High Court decision, see Dom Moraes, *Mrs Gandhi* (London: Jonathan Cape, 1980), pp.202–18. See also Mary C. Carras, *Indira Gandhi in The Crucible of Leadership*, pp.170–7.
43 For a discussion of the legal aspects of the Emergency, see Imtiaz Omar, *Emergency Powers and the Courts in India and Pakistan* (The Hague: Kluwer Law International, 2002), pp.31–8.
44 Moraes, for one, argues that Mrs Gandhi's decision to declare the Emergency had deeper roots than simply a crude desire to hold on to power. See Moraes, *Mrs Gandhi*, p.220. For the various ways in which the Emergency was interpreted, see Emma Tarlo, *Unsettling Memories: Narratives of the Emergency in Delhi* (London: Hurst & Company, 2003).
45 Jayakar, *Indira Gandhi*, p.209.
46 Moraes, *Mrs Gandhi*, p.220. For a discussion of Mrs Gandhi's economic policies during the Emergency, see Atul Kohli, *Democracy and Discontent: India's Growing Crisis of Governability* (Cambridge: Cambridge University Press, 1990), pp.307–20.
47 See Frank, *Indira*, p.390.
48 For a fuller elaboration of this argument, see Brass, *The Politics of India Since Independence*, p.35. See also Kuldeep Mathur, 'The State and the Use of Coercive Power in India', *Asian Survey*, 32, 4, (1992); For the link between use of state coercion and the Congress Party's inability to bring significant economic growth and to deal successfully with its various separatist groups, see Raju G.C. Thomas, *Democracy, Security, and Development in India* (New York: St.Martin's Press, 1996).
49 Brass, *The Politics of India Since Independence*, p.40.
50 For a discussion of the differences in state-centre relations between the Nehru and Mrs Gandhi periods, see Sumitra Kumar Jain, *Party Politics and Centre-State Relations In India* (New Delhi: Abhinav Publications, 1994), pp.39–66.
51 For a more detailed discussion about the ways in which President's Rule has been used since the start of the Mrs Gandhi period, see Harbir Singh Kathuria, *President's Rule In India, 1967–1989* (Delhi: Uppal Publishing, 1990). For a discussion about state chief ministers and their relationship to the central government during this period, see Bhagwan D. Dua, 'Federalism or Patrimonialism: The Making and Unmaking of Chief Ministers in India', *Asian Survey*, 25, 8 (1985).
52 For example, see Robert W. Bradnock, *India's Foreign Policy Since 1971* (London: Pinter Publishers, 1990); Richard Sission and Leo E. Rose, *War and Secession: Pakistan, India and the Creation of Bangladesh* (Berkeley: University of California Press, 1990).
53 For a Pakistani perspective along these lines, see Qutubuddin Aziz, *Blood and Tears* (Karachi: United Press of Pakistan, 1974).
54 For a revisionist account of the war that portrays Indian intervention as based upon the need to reaffirm the class dominance of Indian state elites within India and the region, see Imtiaz Ahmed 'The Superpowers Strategy in the Third World: The 1971 South Asian Crisis', in Emajuddin Ahmed (ed.), *The Foreign Policy of Bangladesh: A Small State's Imperative* (Dhaka: University Press Ltd, 1984).
55 The scale of terror and killing is well described in Ali, *The Nehrus and The Gandhis*, pp.172–3. For a detailed account of the different stages of the civil war and subsequent Indian intervention, see Subrata Roy Chowdhary, *The Genesis of Bangladesh* (New York: Asia Publishing House, 1972).
56 In all, 9 million refugees entered Indian soil during this period. This figure is taken from R.K. Murthy's, *The Cult of the Individual: A Study of Indira Gandhi* (New Delhi: Sterling Publishers, 1977), p.67. Mrs Gandhi compared the number of refugees who had come into India from East Pakistan to the 'population of some of

the countries of Europe, such as Austria and Belgium'. This quotation is an excerpt from her speech to the National Press Club, Washington, 5 November 1971. See Indira Gandhi, *India: The Speeches and Reminiscences of Indira Gandhi, Prime Minister of India* (London: Hodder and Stoughton, 1975), p.163.
57 It cost the Indian Government US$3 million a day to feed and house the incoming refugees. See Moraes, *Mrs Gandhi*, p.187.
58 Ibid., p.190. These were the words of the military commander in charge of East Pakistan, General Amir Abdullah Khan Niazi.
59 Some members of parliament taunted Indira for 'begging' other nations and not acting to preserve the territorial dignity of India. J.P. Narayan, an ardent follower of Mohandas Gandhi, a contemporary of Nehru and by now a respected elder statesman, was annoyed with Mrs Gandhi for snubbing his advice to declare war on Pakistan immediately. See Jayakar, *Indira Gandhi*, pp.168–70.
60 See Masani, *Indira Gandhi*, pp.245–7.
61 Frank, *Indira*, p.336. This private exchange was related to Frank by T.N. Kaul, then Indian Foreign Secretary, who was party to Mrs Gandhi's discussion with Richard Nixon during her visit to Washington in November 1971.
62 Jayakar, *Indira Gandhi*, p.173.
63 Chadda, *Ethnicity, Security and Separatism in India*, p.87.
64 Ibid., p.87.
65 For further detail on the sequence of events, see Gupte, *Mother India*, pp.409–11. For a Pakistani military perspective, see Siddiq Salik, *Witness To Surrender* (Karachi: Oxford University Press, 1978), pp.130–205.
66 Jayakar, *Indira Gandhi*, p.179.
67 Durga, the Goddess of War, is worshipped widely in India. According to Hindu religious belief, Durga restored the gods to their rightful place by fighting alone against demons. Parallels with the representation of Mrs Gandhi's victory are noticeable. See Masani, *Indira Gandhi*, p.250.

4 A 'new' phase in Indian foreign policy: the case of Pakistan and Sri Lanka

1 Although Yahya Khan had promised to hand over political power to the political parties on the basis of the 1970 general elections, it is not clear whether or not he would have readily done so if not for the fact that, within Pakistan, he was associated firmly with the country's humiliating defeat, whereas Bhutto was seen to be Pakistan's – especially West Pakistan's – saviour. See Rafi Raza, *Zulkifar Ali Bhutto and Pakistan, 1967–1977* (Karachi: Oxford University Press, 1997), pp.136–7. Incidentally, Raza was a close associate of Bhutto and, with the latter, was one of the founding members of the Bhutto-led Pakistan's People Party (PPP). He was later a member of cabinet in Bhutto's government.
2 See S.M. Burke, *Mainsprings of Indian and Pakistani Foreign Policies* (Minneapolis, MN: University of Minnesota Press, 1974), pp.216–17.
3 Ibid., p.215.
4 See T.N. Kaul, *A Diplomat's Diary (1947–1999): The Tantalising Triangle – China, India and USA* (New Delhi: Macmillan, 2000), pp.116–17. Kaul was India's foreign secretary during the time of the Summit. See also Masani, *Indira Gandhi*, p.252.
5 In fact, press reports had already announced prematurely the failure of the summit. Ibid., p.253. The text of the document signed at Simla can be found in Kaul, *A Diplomat's Diary*, pp.221–3.
6 See J.N. Dixit's *India–Pakistan In War and Peace* (London: Routledge, 2002), p.470.
7 See Sumit Ganguly's *The Crisis in Kashmir: Portents of War, Hopes of Peace* (Cambridge: Cambridge University Press and The Woodrow Wilson Centre Press, 1997), pp.166–8.

8 Dixit, *India–Pakistan In War and Peace*, p.472.
9 Ibid., p.230.
10 P.N. Dhar relates how he, as personal adviser to Indira during the Simla negotiations, was one of those who took this line and advised Indira accordingly. See P.N. Dhar *Indira Gandhi, the 'Emergency' and Indian Democracy*, pp.206–8.
11 Masani, *Indira Gandhi*, pp.252–3. See also Dixit, *India–Pakistan In War and Peace*, p.229.
12 Henry Kissinger, *White House Years* (London: Weidenfeld & Nicolson, 1979), p.848.
13 Lawrence Ziring, 'Pakistan and India: Politics, Personality and Foreign Policy', *Asian Survey*, 18, 7 (1978) pp.709–11; M.S. Rajan, 'Bangladesh and After', *Pacific Affairs*, 45, 2 (1972), pp.131–205; Geoffrey Warner, 'Review Article – Nixon, Kissinger and the Breakup of Pakistan, 1971', *International Affairs*, 81, 5 (2005) pp.1105–7.
14 Even senior Indian civil servants of this period admit to the Indian military's role, directed by Indira, in this regard. See Dixit, *India–Pakistan in War and Peace*, pp.180, 207–8.
15 As one biographer notes, Indira's victory in 1971 meant that 'she had given India what neither Nehru nor Shastri had been able to deliver, a decisive military victory'. See Masani, *Indira Gandhi*, p.249.
16 This is a translation of a speech delivered in Hindi by Indira at a public rally in Calcutta, 3 December 1971. See Indira Gandhi, *India and Bangladesh: Selected Speeches and Statements, March to December 1971* (New Delhi: Orient Longman, 1972), p.123.
17 Bhutto stalled in his agreement to recognise Bangladesh before consenting officially in February 1974. See Dixit, *India–Pakistan in War and Peace*, p.231.
18 For example, Sheikh Abdullah, in coming out of the political exile imposed upon him, proclaimed a few weeks after the Simla Agreement in Srinagar that the events related to the formation of Bangladesh had demonstrated that the Kashmiris had made the right choice in not joining theocratic Pakistan. See Sheikh Abdullah, *Flames of the Chinar* (New Delhi: Penguin Books, 1993), p.128.
19 Indira's address to the National Press Club, Washington, 5 November 1971, quoted from Indira Gandhi, *India: The Speeches and Reminiscences of Indira Gandhi* (London: Hodder & Stoughton, 1975), pp.164–5.
20 Dixit's personal insights as one of the senior Indian civil servants privy to the events of this period are invaluable. On receiving news that the Pakistani military had launched air strikes on Indian airfields, one of Indira's closest aides is reported to have said to her that 'the fool has done exactly what one had expected'. The aide was referring to General Yahya Khan, Pakistan's military ruler. See the subsection entitled, 'Exactly What One Had Expected' in Dixit's *India–Pakistan In War and Peace*, pp.209–11.
21 These were Indira's words to Dom Moraes when he asked her how she had approached the Bangladesh crisis. See Moraes, *Mrs Gandhi*, p.88.
22 The following account of the attitudes and actions of the states in the UN are taken from Dixit, *India–Pakistan In War and Peace*, pp.212–16.
23 Ibid., pp.216–17.
24 Sources are sparse for what transpired between Indira and Bhutto at the Simla Summit. On the Indian side, they consist of the recollections of three individuals who were involved in the official Indian negotiation team. These are D.P. Dhar, T.N. Kaul and P.N. Haskar. Of the three, Haskar does not provide any details in his two memoirs, while Kaul's recollections, though significant, are limited to events just before the two leaders agreed to the terms of the historic Simla Agreement. Only Dhar's memoirs chronicle the details of what transpired between the two leaders at Simla. These are supplemented by the recollections of Haskar in a personal interview given to Katherine Frank and available in her biography of

Indira. The Pakistani sources have either been silent on the details of the Simla discussions, they or have accepted implicitly Dhar's narrative of events. For the Indian perspective, see P.N. Dhar, *Indira Gandhi, the 'Emergency' and Indian Democracy* and T.N Kaul, *A Diplomat's Diary*. For a Pakistani perspective that accepts implicitly the Indian representation of events and, specifically, Dhar's rendition of the exchange between Indira and Bhutto, see Rafi Raza, *Zulkifar Ali Bhutto and Pakistan, 1967–1977*, p.216. As mentioned earlier in this chapter, Raza was one of Bhutto's close confidantes and he was later a cabinet minister in Bhutto's government. During the time of the Simla Summit, he was Bhutto's personal assistant.

25 This argument is made by K.P. Misra in 'Trilateralism in South Asia', *Asian Survey*, 14, 7 (1974) pp.628, 631–2.

26 See US Department of State Memorandum prepared for the Secretary of State, Henry Kissinger in which it is noted that 'Bhutto has been a hard liner on India', and that 'the events in East Pakistan will push him even further in this direction'. Cited in Roedad Khan (compiled and selected), *The American Papers: Secret and Confidential India–Pakistan–Bangladesh Documents, 1965–1973* (Karachi: Oxford University Press, 2000), p.749. On an inter-personal level, Bhutto once responded to Indira's characterisation of him as 'unbalanced' with the reply that 'she was a mediocre woman with mediocre intelligence. There's nothing great about her'. Both remarks were made in interviews to the journalist, Oriana Fallaci, *Interview With History* (Boston: Houghton Mifflin, 1976), pp.188 and 190.

27 Ibid., p.753.

28 Dhar relates how Indira stated that 'she was sympathetic to his concerns and she would hate to appear to be dictating terms to a defeated adversary' in light of his need to maintain his relatively recent position as democratically leader of Pakistan. See P.N. Dhar, *Indira Gandhi, the 'Emergency' and Indian Democracy*, p.193.

29 See Husain Haqqani, 'Pakistan's Endgame in Kashmir', *India Review*, 2, 3 (2003) pp.41–2.

30 Haskar claims this was Indira's justification in not pushing Bhutto too far on the permanent division of Kashmir. See Frank, *Indira*, p.345. Several authors writing on the Simla Summit take this line as well. See for example, Lawrence Ziring, 'Pakistan and India: Politics, Personality and Foreign Policy', p.712. See also, Victoria Schofield, 'Kashmir – Today, Tomorrow?', *Asian Affairs*, 28, 3 (1997) p.318.

31 Bhutto won 81 of West Pakistan's 138 seats in the December 1970 election in Pakistan as the leader of the Pakistan Peoples' Party. He also did so – did what in the campaign promise to promote 'Islamic Socialism' and to redistribute land and national wealth more equitably. See Chowdhary, *The Genesis of Bangladesh*, p.8.

32 Kaul, *A Diplomat's Diary*, p.117.

33 Burke, *Mainsprings of Indian and Pakistani Foreign Policies*, p.209.

34 Ibid., p.209.

35 An excerpt from the minutes of President Nixon's private meeting with the Senior Review Group on Pakistan, 11 August 1971, cited in Khan, *The American Papers*, p.659.

36 This point is made clearly by a leading scholar of Indian foreign policy, Surjit Mansingh in *India's Search for Power – Indira Gandhi's Foreign Policy, 1966–1982* (London, California and New Delhi: Sage Publications, 1984), p.143.

37 Ibid., p.147.

38 In the words of a US RAND Corporation analyst, 'while respectful and expressing sympathy for the anti-imperialist intent of the Soviet proposal, Prime Minister Gandhi has persistently rebuffed Soviet entreaties for endorsement and most major Indian political figures have rejected the Soviet proposal as incompatible with India's traditional policy of non-alignment'. Cited in Arnold L. Horelick, 'The

Soviet Union's Asian Collective Security Proposal: A Club in Search of Members', *Pacific Affairs*, 47, 3 (1974), pp.269–85.
39 P.N. Dhar relates how in a conversation with S.K. Singh, Foreign Secretary under the Rao government and, in 1971, a senior official within the MEA, the latter revealed that there was a strong feeling within the government and the MEA that Pakistan was trying to involve the US in the 1971 war in order to 'undermine India's autonomy to protect its own territorial integrity'. See Dhar, *Indira Gandhi*, p.209.
40 On this count, the Indian administration was correct. In an US Department of State memorandum, it is noted how General Yahya Khan, in September 1971, was searching actively for 'outside' assurances of military intervention in the event of an India–Pakistan military conflict – the US, China and Iran being the targets of such explicit overtures. See Khan, *The American Papers*, pp.679–80.
41 This was the term of reference during the colonial and postcolonial period until it was changed on 22 May 1972 with the adoption of a new constitution. For a full list of the constitutional amendments, see the official website of the Government of Sri Lanka, *Constitution of Sri Lanka* (http://www.priu.gov.lk/Cons/1978Constitution/ConstitutionalReforms.htm, last accessed 17 March 2005).
42 For an in-depth understanding of Sri Lanka's status during colonial rule, see S.A. Pakeman's *Ceylon* (London: Ernest Benn, 1964), pp.50–8.
43 For details, see A. Jeyaratnam Wilson, *Politics in Sri Lanka, 1947–1973* (London and Basingstoke: Macmillan Press, 1974), pp.275–6.
44 This is of course a broad generalization. For example, the Tamil-speaking Muslims see themselves as neither Tamil nor Singhalese but as a distinct ethnic and religious community. See Jonathan Spencer's 'Introduction: The Power of the Past', in Jonathan Spencer (ed.), *Sri Lanka: History and the Roots of Conflict* (London and New York: Routledge, 1990), p.8.
45 This is a rather broad simplification. In fact, both the Sri Lankan government and the Tamil parties have been in fierce disagreement over whether, besides the Northern area, the eastern area of the island was part of the 'traditional' Tamil homeland. See Wilson, *Politics in Sri Lanka*, pp.164–5.
46 The passing of legislation to make Singhala the national language of administration, the 'Singhala-only' policy, came about during the administration of S.W.R.D. Bandaranaike who won elections in 1956. See K.M. De Silva, *A History of Sri Lanka* (London: Hurst & Company; Berkeley and Los Angeles: University of California Press, 1981), pp.513–14. See also, S.D. Muni, *Pangs of Proximity – India and Sri Lanka's Ethnic Crisis* (New Delhi, California and London: Sage Publications, 1993), p.43.
47 For a fuller discussion of the various Tamil groups and their orientations, see C. Joshua Thomas, *Sri Lanka's Turmoil and the Indian Government: A Study of Ethnic Conflict* (New Delhi: Omsons Publications, 1995), pp.53–4.
48 Ibid., pp.56–7.
49 Ibid., pp.57–8.
50 See K.M. De Silva, *Regional Powers and Small State Security – India and Sri Lanka* (New Delhi: Vikas Publishing; Baltimore: Woodrow Wilson Centre Press, 1996), p.99.
51 Thomas, *Sri Lanka's Turmoil and the Indian Government*, pp.63–4.
52 Ibid., p.67.
53 Quoted in P. Vankateshwar Rao, 'Ethnic Conflict in Sri Lanka: India's Role and Perception', *Asian Survey*, 28, 4 (1988) p.420.
54 Ibid., pp.423–4; David Carment, 'The International Dimensions of Ethnic Conflict: Concepts, Indicators and Theory', *Journal of Peace Research*, 30, 2 (1993) p.139; P.S. Suryanarayana, *The Peace Trap: An Indo-Lanka Political Crisis* (New Delhi: Affiliated East-West Press, 1988).

136 Notes

55 This quotation is taken from the biography of Indira by Pranay Gupte. See Gupte, *Mother India*, p.530.
56 See Muni, *Pangs of Proximity*, p.71.
57 See Suryanarayana, *The Peace Trap*, pp.56–65.
58 For example, see Robert W. Bradnock, *India's Foreign Policy Since 1971* (London: Pinter Publishers & The Royal Institute of International Affairs, 1990), pp.59–83; Imtiaz Ahmed, 'Regional Hegemony in South Asia: The Indian State and Sri Lankan Tamil's War of Liberation', in Emajuddin Ahmed and Abul Kalam (eds), *Bangladesh, South Asia and the World* (Dhaka: Academic Press, 1992), pp.76–101.
59 See Chapter 3 for a good example of the manner in which Indira sought to exploit the sentiments of both the Hindu and Muslim communities in Jammu and Kashmir in the 1983 state elections.
60 See A. Jeyaratnam Wilson, *The Break-up of Sri Lanka*, p.203.
61 K.M. De Silva, *Regional Powers and Small State Security*, p.25.
62 In fact, these Israeli personnel were from the Israeli internal security agency, Sin Beth and operated through an Israeli 'interest section' in the American embassy in Sri Lanka. Also, it was believed within the Indian administration that the Israeli government was providing arms and ammunition to the Sri Lankan government in its fight against Tamil militant groups via unmarked Hercules aircrafts. See Thomas, *Sri Lanka's Turmoil and the Indian Government*, p.68.
63 Muni, *Pangs of Proximity*, p.53.
64 Ibid., pp.54–5.
65 Thomas, *Sri Lanka's Turmoil and The Indian Government*, p.68.
66 Cited in Inder Malhotra, *Indira Gandhi*, p.286.
67 The IPKF withdrew unconditionally from Sri Lanka in March 1991 during the V.P. Singh government. See Chadda, *Ethnicity, Security and Separatism in India*, p.173.
68 This phrase taken from K.M. De Silva, *Regional Powers and Small State Security*, p.100.
69 The role of RAW in training and supporting Tamil militant groups, especially the LTTE, is now public knowledge. See S.D. Muni's *Pangs of Proximity*, p.72.
70 On the Sri Lankan side, the evidence comes from K.M. De Silva, whose interviews with senior Sri Lankan politicians of the time have led him to claim that it was believed that the US envoy, Vernon Walters, informed the Sri Lankan President in a personal and confidential conversation that the US believed 'that there was a very real prospect of an Indian invasion'. This conversation supposedly took place shortly before Indira's death. See De Silva, *Regional Powers and Small State Security*, p.142. A slightly different account is given by one of Indira's biographers, Pranay Gupte, who claims that in a personal conversation Indira made an offer to the Sri Lankan President '[to send] Indian troops to put down the insurgency if requested' by the Sri Lankan President. See Gupte, *Mother India*, p.536.
71 For a discussion about how Indian political elites saw such developments in Sri Lanka, see Bhabhani Sen Gupta, 'The Indian Doctrine', *India Today*, 31 August 1983. For a perspective of a retired senior Indian military officer, see Jasjit Singh, 'The US Transmitters in Sri Lanka', *Times of India* (New Delhi), 6 March 1985.
72 See J.N. Dixit, *Assignment to Colombo* (Delhi: Konark Publishers, 1998). Subsequently to become India's High Commissioner to Sri Lanka in 1985, Dixit was involved intimately in Indian negotiations with Sri Lanka at this time. Dixit recalls that the approach of the Sri Lankan government was disturbing to him and other Indians officials involved in the Sri Lankan issue because it seemed that Sri Lanka was bent on 'getting outside powers involved right on India's doorstep', p.90.

73 See Chadda, *Ethnicity, Security and Separatism in India*, pp.173–4; De Silva, *Regional Powers and Small State Security*, p.119.
74 Muni, *Pangs of Proximity*, p.73.
75 Ibid., p.73.
76 Wilson, *The Break-Up of Sri Lanka*, p.211.
77 For a fuller discussion of the debate concerning this phrase, see Devin T. Hagerty, 'India's Regional Security Doctrine', *Asian Survey*, 31, 4 (1991) pp.351–63.
78 This doctrine has also been described as India's 'Monroe Doctrine', the 'Indian doctrine' and the 'Rajiv Doctrine'. See James Holmes and Toshi Yoshihara, 'India's "Monroe" Doctrine and Asia's Maritime Future', *Strategic Analysis*, 32, 6 (2008) pp.997–1011.

5 The BJP era and the construction of Indian identity

1 See Thomas Blom Hansen, *The Saffron Wave: Democracy and Hindu Nationalism in Modern India* (Princeton: Princeton University Press, 1999), p.3.
2 Although the BJP formed the central government after the 1996 elections for a mere fortnight before it lost the political support of smaller political allies.
3 In fact, the BJP's predecessor, the Bharatiya Jana Sangh merged with other parties to form the Janata Party, which formed the central government after the defeat of Congress (I) in the 1977 elections. Atal Bihari Vajpayee, later to lead the BJP party and become prime minister in 1998, was the external affairs minister in this government. The Janata Party soon fractured under the weight of infighting for the top leadership position and was defeated in the 1980 elections that led to the return of Mrs Gandhi's Congress (I) Party. The Bharatiya Jana Sangh will be discussed in further detail in the next section of this chapter.
4 For an introduction to the 'Sangh Parivar', see Ram Puniyani, *Contours of Hindu Rashtra: Hindutva, Sangh Parivar and Contemporary Politics* (Delhi: Kalpaz, 2006).
5 See V.D. Savarkar, *Hindutva: Who Is a Hindu?* (New Delhi: Hindi Sahitya Sadan, 2003). This is a reproduction of his 1923 work. Savarkar would later become the president of the Hindu nationalist organisation, the Hindu Mahasabha from 1937–42.
6 See Sumit Sarkar, 'Inclusive Democracy and its Enemies', *Interventions: International Journal of Postcolonial Studies*, 7, 3 (2005) p.307; Ishtiaq Ahmed, 'The 1947 Partition of India: A Paradigm for Pathological Politics in India and Pakistan', *Asian Ethnicity*, 3, 1 (2003) p.17.
7 Savarkar, *Hindutva: Who Is a Hindu?*, pp.84 and 92. The phrase *Sanskriti* in this context is derived from the phrase 'Sanskrit', which is the regarded as 'the sacred and classical language of the Hindus'. See John T. Platts, *A Dictionary of Urdu, Classical Hindi and English*, p.684 (http://dsal.uchicago.edu/dictionaries/platts/, last accessed 8 March 2007).
8 Ibid., p.39. 'Bharat' is the official Sanskrit term for India. See South Asian Journalist Association, *South Asian Journalist Association Handbook* (http://www.saja.org/stylebook.html#B, last accessed 8 March 2007). The word 'Santani' translates as 'lineage, race, descent, family'. See Platts, *Dictionary of Urdu, Classical Hindi and English*, p.680.
9 Ibid., Preface (page not numbered).
10 See Note 8.
11 Rashtriya Swayamsevak Sangh translates Rashtriya Swayamsevak Sangh into 'Association of National Volunteers'. See Christopher Jaffrelot, *Hindu Nationalist Politics: 1925 to The 1990s* (New Delhi: Penguin Books, 1999), p.33.
12 For a study of the events leading to the formation of the RSS and its early core beliefs, see Smita Narula, 'Overlooked Danger: The Security and Rights

Implications of Hindu Nationalism in India', *Harvard Human Rights Journal*, 16 (2003) pp.42–6.
13. M.S. Golwalkar, *We, Or Our Nationhood Defined* (Nagpur: Bharat Prakashan, 1947), pp.55–6.
14. See Craig Baxter, *The Jana Sangh – A Biography Of An Indian Political Party* (Philadelphia: University of Pennsylvania Press, 1969), p.37. See also, Jaffrelot, *Hindu Nationalist Politics*, pp.114–15.
15. Jaffrelot, *Hindu Nationalist Politics*, pp.64–75.
16. For an analysis of the RSS expectations concerning the formation of a new party for the purposes of engaging in democratic elections, see K.R. Kalkani, *Principles For a New Party* (Delhi: Vijay Pustak Bhandar, 1951).
17. Quoted from a part of Mookerjee's speech to mark the official founding of the BJS on 21 October 1951 in New Delhi. Cited in Baxter, *The Jana Sangh*, p.72.
18. Ibid., p.312.
19. Chetan Bhatt, *Hindu Nationalism: Origins, Ideologies and Modern Myths* (Oxford and New York: Berg, 2001), p.154.
20. See Jyotirinda Das Gupta, 'The Janata Phase: Reorganization and Redirection in Indian Politics', *Asian Survey*, 19, 4 (1979) p.392.
21. For a detailed examination of the composition of BJP members belonging to the RSS over time, see Parvathy Appaiah, *Hindutva: Ideology and Politics* (New Delhi: Deep & Deep Publications, 2003), pp.155–7.
22. As discussed in the Nehru chapter, the alleged right wing of the Congress Party, associated with individuals such as Deputy Prime Minister Sardar Patel, were critical of Nehru's brand of secularism and shared some of the sentiments of the Hindu nationalist voices immediately after independence.
23. Appaiah, *Hindutva*, p.165.
24. See Pratap Chandra Swain, *Bharatiya Janata Party: Profile and Performance* (New Delhi: A.P.H Publishing Corporation, 2001), p.92.
25. Ibid., p.92.
26. Ibid., p.93.
27. Ayodha and the Ram temple will be discussed later in this section. This was part of Advani's speech to the BJP's national executive meeting, quoted in Appaiah, *Hindutva*, p.6.
28. Peter Van der Deer, quoted in Appaiah, *Hindutva*, p.166.
29. See Richard Fox, 'Hindu Nationalism In The Making, Or the Rise of the "Hindian"', in Richard Fox (ed.), *National Ideologies and the Production of National Cultures*, American Ethnological Society, Monograph Series, No. 2, (Washington: American Anthropological Association, 1990), pp.63–81.
30. For a detailed study of how Ram and the popular epic, the *Ramayana* have played a central role in the BJP's representation of the Babri mosque's place in ancient Indian history, see Bharat Wariavwalla, 'Religion and Nationalism in India: *Ram the God of the Hindu Nation*', *The Round Table*, 89, 357 (2000) pp.593–606.
31. For details on the episodes leading to the demolition and the BJP's role in it, see Peter Van Der Deer, *Religious Nationalism: Hindus and Muslims In India* (Berkeley, Los Angeles and London: University of California Press, 1994), pp.5–7. Also see Gerald James Larson, *India's Agony Over Religion* (Albany: SUNY Press, 1995), pp.266–77; Sarvepalli Gopal (ed.), *Anatomy of a Confrontation: The Babri Masjid-Ram Janmabhumi Issue* (New Delhi: Viking, 1991). In September 2010, the Allahabad High Court ruled that the disputed land at Ayodha to be divided amongst the three key litigants. For details of the ruling see, 'Ram born at Ayodha site, idols to stay: HC', *India Today*, 30 September 2011.
32. 'Mandir' translates into 'Hindu temple', 'Janmasthan' as 'birthplace', (the reference here to Ram's birthplace) and 'Bharat Mata' as 'Mother India'. Quoted from Bhatt, *Hindu Nationalism*, p.174.

33 For a discussion of the legal genealogy of the Hindu Code bill, see Gauri Kulkarni, 'Uniform Civil Code', *Legal Service of India* (http://www.legalserviceindia.com/articles/ucc.htm, last accessed 7 July 2005). For the socio-political implications of the Hindu Code Bill, see Christophe Jaffrelot, 'Nehru and The Hindu Code Bill', *Debating India*, 18 August 2003.
34 The BJP party member who introduced the bill was Bhagwan Shankar Rawat. For details of the debate on this bill between different members and its consequent rejection in the Lok Sabha, see the Lok Sabha website, *Lok Sabha Debates* (http://parliamentofindia.nic.in/ls/lsdeb/ls11/ses4/2302059701.htm, last accessed 11 May 2005).
35 Shri L.K. Advani, in *The Illustrated Weekly of India*, 6 March 1993.
36 For a discussion about how the 'special status' of the state has been eroded over time, see A.G. Noorani, 'Article 370: Law and Politics', *Frontline*, 7, 19 (16–29 September 2000). For a legal perspective on Article 370, see Paras Diwan, 'Kashmir and the Indian Union: The Legal Position', *The International and Comparative Law Quarterly*, 2, 3 (1953).
37 In fact, the BJS founder and leader, S.P. Mookerjee later tried to enter Jammu and Kashmir in May 1963 as part of the party's ongoing agitation against Article 370. See Chetan Bhatt, *Hindu Nationalism*, p.161; Jaffrelot, *Hindu Nationalist Politics*, pp.129–30.
38 See Venkitesh Ramakrishan, 'All For Survival', *Frontline* (Chennai), 15, 8 (11–24 April 1998). Also see 'Article 370 To Stay, Says Advani' in *Times of India* (Mumbai), 27 April 2000.
39 Ashutosh Varshney, 'Contested Meanings: India's National Identity, Hindu Nationalism and the Politics of Anxiety', *Daedalus*, 122, 3 (1993) pp.227–34.
40 For a discussion about the links between secularism and democracy within the context of Hindu nationalist thoughts, see Rajeev Bhargava, 'Liberal, Secular Democracy and Explanations of Hindu Nationalism', *Commonwealth and Comparative Politics*, 40, 3 (2002) pp.72–96.
41 Quoted in Y. Malik and V.B. Singh, *Hindu Nationalists In India* (Boulder, CO: Westview, 1996), p.41.
42 Bhargava, 'Liberal, Secular Democracy and Explanations of Hindu Nationalism', pp.82–94.
43 For the practical implications of this argument, see Narula, 'Overlooked Danger: The Security and Rights Implications of Hindu Nationalism in India', pp.56–60.
44 For a critical look at the BJP and the role of other Hindu nationalist groups in the Gujarat violence, see N. Jamal Ansari, 'Reflection of Gujarat Genocide', *Mainstream* (New Delhi), XI, 19 (2002); Sumanta Banerjee, 'Gujarat Carnage and a Cynical Democracy', *Economic and Political Weekly*, 37, 18 (2002). For a pro-BJP and Hindu nationalist view see, Krishen Kak, 'Conspiracy of Silence', *The Pioneer* (New Delhi), 11 January 2003; Editorial, 'Secularists to Blame', *The Free Press Journal* (Mumbai), 2 March 2002.
45 A detailed narrative of the events leading to and during the Gujarat communal violence are contained in the public report delivered to the government by an independent fact finding mission. See Karmal Mitral Chenoy, S.P. Chukla, K.S. Subramaniam and Achin Vanaik, *Gujarat Carnage 2002*, 10 April 2002 (www.sacw.net/Gujarat2002/GujCarnage.html, last accessed 25 June 2006).
46 Ibid.
47 Ibid.
48 Ibid.
49 'Newton Modi Has a Lot to Answer', *Times of India* (New Delhi), 2 March 2002.
50 'Modi Puts State Money Where Biased Mouth Is', *Indian Express* (Ahmedabad), 5 March 2002.
51 S. Sethuraman, 'NDA Survival No Mark of Stability', *Business Line* (Chennai) 9 May 2002.

52 'BJP Rules Out Modi's Resignation', *Rediff.com*, 12 September 2003 (www.in.rediff.com/news/2003/sep/12bset3.htm, last accessed 6 June 2006).
53 Narula, 'Overlooked Danger: The Security and Rights Implications of Hindu Nationalism in India', pp.46–7.
54 The International General Secretary of the VHP, who played a decisive role in both the violence in Gujarat and later the political mobilization of votes for the BJP state elections victory, is quoted to have said that the successful strategy of the Hindu right in Gujarat could be applied successfully throughout India with the result that a 'Hindu Rashtra [state] can be expected in the next two years'. See 'Hindu Rashtra in Two Years' Time: Togadia', *Rediff.com*, 15 December 2002 (www.rediff.com/election/2002/dec/15guj13.htm, last accessed 11 July 2006).
55 For a study of how the Indira Gandhi period was in some senses a precursor to the BJP's era in terms of its construction of populist electoral strategies, see Sumantra Bose 'Hindu Nationalism and the Crisis of the Indian State', in Sugata Bose and Ayesha Jalal (ed.), *Nationalism, Democracy and Development: State and Politics in India* (New Delhi: Oxford University Press, 1999), pp.117–21.
56 For a fuller discussion of the differences between Gandhi's and Savarkar's ideas of the idea of India, see, Hansen, *The Saffron Wave*, pp.67–79.
57 Appaiah, *Hindutva*, p.163.
58 Swain, *Bharatiya Janata Party*, p.94.
59 See the BJP official website for full details of its constitution and its basic philosophy of 'Integral Humanism', *Bharatiya Janata Party* (http://www.bjp.org/philo.htm last accessed 19 July 2005).
60 Stuart Corbridge and John Harris, *Reinventing India: Liberalization, Hindu Nationalism and Popular Democracy* (Cambridge: Polity Press; Malden: Blackwell Publishers, 2000), p.189.
61 For a Hindu nationalist reading of Indian history within the context of anti-imperialism, see K.N. Panikkar, *Outsider as Enemy: The Politics of Rewriting History in India*, (Pennsylvania: University of Pennsylvania, Center for the Advanced Study of India Working Paper, November 2000), pp.3, 5–6.
62 Corbridge and Harris, *Reinventing India*, p.190.
63 Hansen, *The Saffron Wave*, p.11.
64 Runa Das, 'Postcolonial (In)securities, the BJP and the Politics of Hindutva: Broadening the Security Paradigm between the Realist and Anti-Nuclear/Peace Groups in India', *Third World Quarterly*, 24, No. 1 (2003) p.90.

6 A 'Hindu' foreign policy: dealing with Pakistan and Bangladesh

1 See Seeram Chaulia, 'BJP, India's Foreign Policy and the "Realist Alternative" to the Nehruvian Tradition', *International Politics*, 39, 2 (June 2002) p.220.
2 Chetan Bhatt, *Hindu Nationalism*, p.94.
3 See Tapan Raychaudhuri, 'Shadows of the Swastika: Historical Perspectives on the Politics of Hindu Communalism', *Modern Asian Studies*, 34, 2 (2000) p.264.
4 See Jaswant's Singh's *Defending India* (New York: St. Martin's Press, 1999), p.xiv.
5 As a sign of the centrality of the Kargil episode in the view of the BJP party, it inaugurated an intricate set of commemoration rituals for all party members, including lighting up party buildings, in July 2006, six years after the Kargil conflict. It was part of its celebration of the sixth anniversary of India's 'triumph' in the Kargil War and termed *Vijay Divas* ('Vijay' refers to 'Operation Vijay', the name given to India's military operation during the Kargil War and 'Divas' translates into 'anniversary'). Its centrality was also evident from the fact that it was celebrated as part of the BJP's *Rajat Jayanti* ('Silver Jubilee') celebrations. See the publication by the Bharatiya Janata Party, *Kargil Day – 26 July: Vijay Divas* (http://www.bjp.org/, last accessed 15 August 2006).

Notes 141

6 For a specific discussion about India's response to the December 2001 bombing of its parliament, see Rahul Roy-Chaudhury, 'India's Response To Terrorism After 13 December 2001', *Conflict, Security and Development*, 3, 2 (2003).
7 Points of view differ on the nature of the conflict, as well as the combatants themselves. The original official Pakistani position was that it was Kashmiri freedom fighters and not Pakistani regular soldiers that first occupied the icy heights in the Kargil sector. For a semi-official account from the Pakistani perspective, see Shireen Mazari's *The Kargil Conflict 1999 – Separating Fact From Fiction* (Islamabad: Institute of Strategic Studies, 2003). Within India itself, the conflict has been variously described as 'skirmishes', 'intrusions', or 'limited military operations'. See the transcript of a press conference hosted by the then external affairs minister, Jaswant Singh, on 23 September 1999 in New York, where he refers to the Kargil conflict as a 'war like situation'. See the official website of the Ministry of External Affairs (MEA), Government of India (http://meaindia.nic.in/, last accessed 23 March 2006). Others observers in India see the conflict as akin to a state of conventional war. See J.N. Dixit, *India–Pakistan in War and Peace* (London and New York: Routledge, 2002), p.35.
8 Jaswant Singh reflects this view within the BJP leadership when he represents Kargil as the 'betrayal' of the Lahore process. Author interview, 6 December 2011.
9 As one observer notes, 'in political and dominant media mythology, Kargil was seen as the betrayal of Lahore'. See Subarno Chattarji, 'Media Representations of the Kargil War and the Gujarat Riots', in Shuddhabrata Sengupta *et al.* (eds), *Sarai Reader: Crisis/Media* (New Delhi: Sarai Publications, 2004), p.115. Also see US Congressman Gene Ackerman, describing Pakistan's alleged actions in Kargil as the 'the betrayal of the Lahore Declaration'. See 'Ackerman Challenges Pakistan to Reverse "The Betrayal" of Lahore Declaration', 21 July 1999, *Rediff On The Net* (http://www.rediff.com, last accessed 18 January 2006).
10 See A.B. Vajpayee's interview with Amir Taheri, *Interview of Prime Minister of India, Shri Atal Bihari Vajpayee with Asharq Alawsat's Amir Taheri: Part I and Part II*, MEA, Government of India (http://meaindia.nic.in/interview/2002/08/27i01.htm, last accessed 25 May 2006).
11 In the midst of the Kargil conflict, External Affairs Minister Jaswant Singh is quoted to have said publicly that 'it is a pity that on Lahore Declaration, even before the ink on it was dry, Pakistan chose to violate its spirit and its letter'. This was in reply to a question at a press conference in New Delhi, 12 June 1999. The full transcript is available at the website of the Embassy of India, Washington DC (http://www.indianembassy.org/new/Kargil/JSingh_June_12_1999.html). Also significantly, the BJP website carries a news article, written in 2004, from an Indian daily which makes the point that Nawaz Shariff was aware that planning for Kargil was underway even before Vajpayee reached Lahore in February 1999, thus validating the view within the party and its leadership about the two events overlapping each other. See 'General: Kargil Was On Before Vajpayee's Lahore Visit', *Indian Express* (Mumbai), 14 July 2004.
12 See Chidanand Rajghatta, 'US welcomes move on bus diplomacy', *Indian Express*, (Mumbai), 23 February 1999.
13 In fact, the editor of one of the leading Indian dailies seemingly first mooted the idea of a bus service between the two cities. For details see, Sevanti Ninan, 'Spotlight Summit', *Hindu* (Chennai), 15 July 2001.
14 See Sukumar Muralidharan, 'A not-so-smooth ride', *Frontline* (Chennai), 16, 5, 27 February–12 March 1999.
15 For the full text of the Lahore Declaration, see the Indian Ministry of External Affairs website. See 'Lahore Declaration', MEA, Government of India (http://mea.gov.in/jk/lah-decl.htm).

16 Ibid. For a fuller discussion of the nuclear weapons issue within the context of the Lahore Declaration, see Dinshaw Mistry, 'Diplomacy, Sanctions and the U.S. Non-proliferation Dialogue with India and Pakistan', *Asian Survey*, 39, 5 (1999) p.768.
17 Mistry, 'Diplomacy, Sanctions and the U.S. Non-proliferation Dialogue with India and Pakistan', pp.759–60, 768. Although the author concedes that the pressure for talks between the two states came from the US administration, he believes that the nuclear confidence-building measures agreed between India and Pakistan was a result of a bilateral effort and not direct US diplomacy.
18 'Lahore Declaration', MEA, Government of India.
19 Ibid.
20 See S. Chandrasekharan, 'Kargil and Nuclear Deterrence', *South Asian Analysis Group Papers*, 7 August 1999 (http://www.saag.org/papers/paper71.html, last accessed 21 January 2006).
21 This press release was issued in New Delhi, 5 July 2005, Embassy of India, Washington DC (http://www.indianembassy.org/pic/PR_1999/July_1999/PR_July_ 05_1999.html, last accessed 5 May 2006). For the contents of the US–Pakistan Joint Statement, see 'Nawaz, Clinton Agree On Pullout by Mujahideen', *Dawn Wire Service* (Karachi), 28, 5, 10 July 1999.
22 Lok Sabha Debates, *Session IV*, 26 February 1999 (http://parliamentofindia.nic.in/ ls/lsdeb/ls12/ses4/04260299.htm, last accessed 13 May 2006).
23 Interview conducted 1 June, 1999 (interviewer not stated). See the Indian embassy website (http://www.indianembassy.org/new/NewDelhiPressFile/Jaswant_Singh_June_ 01_1999.htm, last accessed 11 July 2006).
24 There are various claims about when the actual intrusion actually took place. One claim from retired senior Indian army generals involved in the Kargil conflict is that the intrusion took place as early as June 1998. Author interview with Retired-Brigadier Devinder Singh, 8 December 2011.
25 Figures taken from '1999 Kargil Conflict', *Global Security.Org* (http://www.glo balsecurity.org/military/world/war/kargil-99.htm, last accessed 2 June 2006).
26 See J.N. Dixit, *Makers of Indian Foreign Policy: From Raja Ram Mohun Roy to Yashwant Sinha* (New Delhi: Harper Collins, 2004), p.261. For a confirmation of this point by Strobe Talbott, the US Deputy Secretary of State during the Clinton administration, see his, *Engaging India: Diplomacy, Democracy and the Bomb* (Washington, DC: Brookings Institution Press, 2004), pp.164–9.
27 See the official website of the Ministry of Defence, India for an example of an official declaration of victory, 'Kargil War: A Glorious Victory for India' (http:// mod.nic.in/samachar/17/html/ch8.htm, last accessed 21 July 2006).
28 As discussed earlier in this chapter, the semi-official Pakistani view is contained within Shireen Mazari's account, *The Kargil Conflict 1999*. For an Indian military view from the highest level, see V.P. Malik, 'Kargil: Where Defence Met Diplomacy', *Indian Express* (Mumbai), 25 July 2002. General Malik was the Indian Chief of Army Staff during the Kargil conflict. Strobe Talbott summed up the American administration's view of Pakistani intentions and actions in Kargil in *Engaging India*. Talbott was US Deputy Secretary of State during the Clinton administration. Another important US view can be found in Bruce Riedel's *American Diplomacy and the 1999 Kargil Summit at Blair House*, Policy Paper, Centre for the Advanced Study of India (University of Pennsylvania: Philadelphia, 2002). Riedel was a former Senior Director for Near East and South Asian Affairs at the US National Security Council.
29 See the editorial, 'Kargil: Success and Complications', *Frontline*, 16, 15, (17–30 July 1999). Even Mazari, writing from a mainly pro-Pakistani perspective, does not deny the broad aims of the Pakistani strategy but instead criticizes the lack of anticipation shown by certain parts of the Pakistani establishment regarding the

scale and intensity of the Indian response. See Mazari, *The Kargil Conflict 1999*, pp.44–52.
30 One view is that the army top brass assumed initially that the intrusion was going to be very localised and small-scale and that this explained why Indian forces were held at a disadvantage when the scale of the intrusion turned out to be much larger than first assumed. Author interview with Retired-Brigadier Devinder Singh, 8 December 2011.
31 See an analysis of the Kargil Committee stated tasks in Praveen Swami, 'A Probe and Its Prospects', *Frontline* (Chennai), 16, 17, (14–27 August 1999).
32 For the full report, as well as an executive summary of the report, see the website of the Rajya Sabha, India's upper house of parliament, *Kargil Committee Report* (www.rajyasabha.nic.in/25indi1.htm, last accessed 22 November 2005).
33 Ibid., Chapter II.
34 Ibid., Chapter III.
35 Ibid., Chapter I.
36 Ibid., Chapter II.
37 Ibid., 'Executive Summary'.
38 In fact, there were was widespread criticism from both opposition parties and a large body of impartial observers, academicians, retired servicemen, foreign policy and intelligence experts that the committee was staffed by people too close to the government for it to serve effectively in an impartial capacity. See Vinod Sharma, 'Kargil Enquiry An Eyewash Say Opposition And Experts', *Hindustan Times* (New Delhi), 26 July 1999. See also, Praveen Swami, 'A Probe and Its Prospects', *Frontline*.
39 K. Subrahmanyam, Chairperson of the Kargil Review Committee, in an interview in 2001 warned that Musharraf 'has gone on to say that low-intensity conflict with India will continue even if the Kashmir issue were resolved'. See the interview with Siddarth Srivastava, 'India Suffering From Guilt Complex', *The Times of India* (New Delhi), 31 May 2001. See also General Malik's assessment of Pakistan's strategy of avoiding conventional war by threatening to use nuclear weapons in G. Desai, 'Limited War Can Erupt Anytime: Gen. Malik', *Times of India*, (New Delhi) 7 January 2000.
40 *Kargil Committee Report*. For a reiteration of this point made by the committee, see BJP, *Kargil Day – 26 July*, pp.16–17.
41 *Kargil Committee Report*. For a fuller prognosis, see Praveen Swami, 'A Committee and Some Questions: A First-person Account with Regard to the Kargil Review Committee and its Implications', *Frontline* (Chennai), 17, 2, 22 January–4 February 2000. Swami was one of several individuals summoned by the committee to give evidence in light of his reports in the early phase of the Kargil conflict on the involvement of regular Pakistani military elements in the intrusion and how he obtained such information.
42 See 'BJP Chief Wants Capture of Azad Kashmir', *The News*, (Lahore), 4 July 1999.
43 Govindarcharya is quoted in R. Upadhyaya, 'The Kargil Crisis: Political Dimensions', *South Asian Analysis Group*, 18 June 1999 (http://www.saag.org/papers/paper68.html, last accessed 12 June 2006).
44 *Panchjanya*, 20 June 1999, quoted in M.V. Ramana, 'A Nuclear Wedge', *Frontline* (Chennai), 18, 25, 8–21 December 2001. 'Bheema' and 'Durga' are figures from Hindu religious texts.
45 See the comments by L.K. Advani, 'India For Treating Kargil As Limited War: Advani', *Hindustan Times* (New Delhi), 20 June 1999.
46 BJP, *Kargil Day – 26 July*, p.2. According to Jaswant Singh, unlike earlier India–Pakistan conflicts, India managed to win wide international support for its position, as well as recover lost territory from Pakistan. Author interview, 6 December 2011.

47 BJP, 'Foreword', *Kargil Day – 26 July*.
48 See C. Raja Mohan, 'Jaswant Cautions Pakistan', *Hindu* (Chennai), 12 August 1999.
49 In the words of Jaswant Singh, the Kargil War was a 'victory of restraint' for India because it achieved the objective to contain the conflict and thus deny any role for the international community, especially the US, in the conflict. Author interview, 6 December 2011.
50 In fact, in 1975 Indian aid to Bangladesh totalled approximately Rs299.88 crore, compared to India's total aid to Nepal and Bhutan since the 1950s, which totalled approximately Rs305.32 crore. See Vernon M. Hewitt, *The International Politics of South Asia* (Manchester and New York: Manchester University Press, 1992), p.34.
51 See S.S. Bhindra, *Indo-Bangladesh Relations* (New Delhi: Deep and Deep, 1982), p.20.
52 See Yasmeen Murshed and Nazim Kamran Choudhury, 'Bangladesh's Second Chance', *Journal of Democracy*, 8, 1 (1992), p.75. For a detailed discussion of the changing place and politics of 'Islamism' within Bangladeshi politics since the early 1980s see Ali Riaz, '"God Willing": The Politics and Ideology of Islamism in Bangladesh', *Comparative Studies of South Asia, Africa and the Middle East*, 23, 1 and 2 (2003).
53 Hewitt, 'The International Politics of South Asia', p.36. For a more detailed exposition of the changing nature of domestic politics and identity in Bangladesh during this period of transition and beyond, see Ahmed Saifuddin, *The Roles of Religion and National Identity in Bangladesh* (Finland: Abo Akademi University Press, 2000), pp.175–209.
54 The dispute over the sharing of water resources has also been a feature of India–Bangladesh relations but it is not discussed here, as it is a mainly bilateral 'issue' from the Bangladesh point of view, rather than for India. For a discussion of how the dispute between the two states over water sharing was inherited by Bangladesh from its earlier incarnation as part of the Pakistani state, see Wayne Wilcox, 'A Decade of Ayub', *Asian Survey*, 9, 2 (1969) p.90.
55 In fact, in 1992 the Indian government engaged in a short-lived and largely ineffective policy of sending 'illegal Bangladeshis' back to Bangladesh but this was largely ineffective because it was deemed to be extremely difficult to identify who these 'illegal Bangladeshis' were. For a more detailed and critical assessment of this issue by one of India's former foreign secretaries, see Muchkund Dubey, 'Inept Handling of a Sensitive Issue', *Hindu*, 9 December 1992.
56 Such migration into Assam predates even Indian independence, with one noted authority on the subject placing immigration into Assam between 1901 and 1971 at about 7.4 million out of a total population of about 15 million in 1971. See Wyron Weiner, *Sons of the Soil: Migration and Ethnic Conflict in India* (Princeton, NJ: Princeton University Press, 1978). Also see Weiner's 'The Political Demography of Assam's Anti-Immigration Movement', *Population and Development Review*, 9, 2 (1983) p.283. For specific details of how this migration has fuelled political turmoil in the state of Assam, see Sanjib Baruah, 'Immigration, Ethnic Conflict and Political Turmoil – Assam, 1979–85', *Asian Survey*, 26, 11 (1986).
57 For example, the then Indian foreign secretary, J.N. Dixit relates that in May 1992, in a personal meeting between Indian Prime Minister Narashima Rao and the Bangladesh Prime Minister, Khaleda Zia, the latter denied flatly any claims that there was large-scale illegal migration from Bangladesh into India. See J.N. Dixit, *My South Block Years: Memoirs of a Foreign Secretary* (New Delhi: UBS Publishers, 1997), p.158.
58 See Arun Shourie, *A Secular Agenda* (New Delhi: HarperCollins, 1997), pp.269–70.
59 Ibid., p.270.
60 Arun Shourie was not the only voice lending a 'communal' edge to discussions about the illegal migration of Bangladeshis into India. For example, in 1992 the

Notes   145

president of the West Bengal state chapter of the BJP, argued that there was a need to differentiate between Hindu and Muslim Bangladeshis who entered India illegally upon the basis that the former were probably experiencing religious persecution in Bangladesh and thus were mainly refugees, whilst the latter were predominantly economic migrants. See Tapan Sikdar, 'How West Bengal Congress is Providing Fillip to Muslim Infiltrators', *BJP Today*, 1–10 September 1992.

61 For another example of the view that illegal Bangladeshi migration represented a 'Muslim invasion' of 'Hindu' India, see the work of the BJP ideologue, Rai Baljit, *Demographic Aggression Against India* (Chandigarh: B.S. Publications, 1993).

62 See a copy of the BJP's 1998 election manifesto on its official website, *Bharatiya Janata Party* (http://www.bjp.org/manifes/chap8.htm, last accessed 14 January 2006).

63 ISI is the abbreviation for Pakistan's Inter-Service Intelligence Agency. It is considered to be one of the most influential and powerful institutions in Pakistan's military establishment, with allegedly influential roles both within and beyond the Pakistani state. For a fuller discussion see Sean P. Winchell, 'Pakistan's ISI: The Invisible Government', *International Journal of Intelligence and Counter Intelligence*, 16, 3 (2003) pp.374–88.

64 Alex Perry, 'Deadly Cargo', *Time*, 21 October 2002.

65 A press briefing by the Bangladesh Foreign Secretary Shamsher Mobin Chowdhury, Dhaka, 16 October 2002, quoted in Avtar Singh Bhasin, *India–Bangladesh Relations: Documents, 1971–2002*, Vol. 1. (New Delhi: Geetika Publishers, 2003), p.572.

66 In October 2001, the BNP (Bangladesh National Party)-led alliance won in the general election and formed the first centre-right coalition government in the history of the country, with two 'Islamist' parties as part of the ruling alliance. For further detail, see Ali Riaz '"God Willing": The Politics and Ideology of Islam in Bangladesh', pp.301–2.

67 Advani's remarks were made after inaugurating the Fifty-first All India Police Games in the state of Haryana. See, 'Al-Qaeda, ISI Activities on the Rise in Bangladesh: Advani', *The Hindu* (New Delhi), 8 November 2002.

68 A press release from the Indian High Commission in Dhaka, 10 November 2002, Dhaka. A.S. Bhasin, *India–Bangladesh Relations*, p.575.

69 A.S. Bhasin, *India–Bangladesh Relations*, p.588. Also see, 'Dhaka ISI Nerve Centre: Sinha', *The Tribune* (Chandigarh), 28 November 2002.

70 See 'George Rubbishes Dhaka's Claim', *The Tribune* (Chandigarh), 30 November 2002.

71 Sections of the Indian press were also carrying reported links between Al-Qaeda, the ISI and insurgent groups in India's Northeastern States. For example, see 'Arrested ISI Spymaster Was on Way to Guwahati', *Sentinel* (Guwahati), 12 January 2000; 'Axom Xumaise Al Qaida' ('Assam Targeted by Al-Qaeda'), *Dainik Khabar* (Guwahati), 22 August 2002; 'ISI Agent in Assam Rifle Held', *Hindustan Times* (New Delhi), 13 July 2002. 'Guwahati' is a city on the border of India and Bangladesh in the Northeastern States and its district of Dirpur is the capital of the state of Assam. 'NE' is an abbreviation for the Northeastern States of India and 'Assam Rifle' is a regiment that is part of the Indian army.

72 The terrorists groups that Sarkar was referring to were the NLFT (National Liberation Front of Tripura) and ATTF (All-Tripura Tiger Force). Part of a speech made by Manik Sarkar at a conference of chief ministers on internal security, 7 February 2003, New Delhi. See Manini Chatterjee, 'When it Comes to ISI, Red is Like Saffron', *Indian Express* (New Delhi), 13 February 2003.

73 See Sultan Shahin, 'India Frets Over Pakistan–Bangladesh Nexus', *Asia Times* (Hong Kong), 6 March 2004. Shahin claims that the above information was based upon his 'sources in India's Ministry of Home Affairs'. The phenomenon of 'media leaks' by sections of the Indian government to the press after Advani's comments in November 2002 is something that the Bangladeshi High Commissioner in India,

Tufail K. Haider thinks is significant with regard to the Indian government's approach to the specific issue of alleged ISI and Al-Qaeda involvement in training insurgent groups from India within Bangladesh's territory. See his interview with S. Sudarshan in *Outlook* (New Delhi), 23 December 2002.
74 Surajit Talukdar and Swapan Kumar Paul, 'High Security on Indo-Bangla Border', *The Pioneer* (New Delhi), 6 November 2003.
75 Comment by CPI(M) – Communist Party of India (Marxist) – politburo member Prakash Karat at conference of chief ministers on internal security, 7 February 2003, New Delhi. See Manini Chatterjee, 'When it Comes to ISI, Red is Like Saffron'.

Conclusion

1 For an overview of the NPT and its various interpretations, see Daniel H. Joyner, *Interpreting the Nuclear Non-Proliferation Treaty* (New York: Oxford University Press, 2011).
2 For more details, see Vandana Bhatia, 'The US–India Nuclear Agreement: Revisiting the Debate', *Strategic Analysis*, 36, 4 (2012) pp.612–23.
3 Sitaram Yechury, the spokesperson for the Communist Party of India (Marxist), declared publicly that as a result of the US–India nuclear deal, 'the US is planning to launch an attack on Iran, and India will be forced to join ranks with the US as a strategic ally'. See 'India possible US ally for attacking Iran: Yechury', *The Hindu*, 21 July 2008 (http://www.hindu.com/thehindu/holnus/002200807211656.htm, last accessed 15 October 2010).
4 For a study of how 'masculinist' and Orientalist nuclear discourses are implicated in the debate about the US–India nuclear deal, see Runa Das, 'The United States-India Nuclear Relations after 9/11: Alternative Discourses', *Asian Journal of Political Science*, 20, 1 (2012) pp.86–107.

Bibliography

Abdullah, Farooq, *My Dismissal*. New Delhi: Vikas Publishing, 1985.
Abdullah, Sheikh, *Flames of the Chinar*, New Delhi: Penguin Books, 1993.
Acharya, Amitav, *Constructing a Security Community in Southeast Asia: ASEAN and the Problem of Regional Order*, London: Routledge, 2001.
Adler, Emmanuel, 'Europe's New Security Order: A Pluralistic Security Community', in Beverly Crawford (ed.), *The Future of European Security*, Berkeley, CA: University of California Press, 1992.
Advani, L.K., *The Illustrated Weekly of India*, 6 March 1993, 13–15.
Ahmed, Imtiaz, 'Kautilya's Concept of Diplomacy, *Journal of the Asiatic Society of Bangladesh*, XXIX, 1984, 65–88.
——'The Superpowers Strategy in the Third World: The 1971 South Asian Crisis', in Emajuddin Ahmed (ed.), *Foreign Policy of Bangladesh: A Small State's Imperative*, Dhaka: University Press Limited, 1984.
——'Regional Hegemony in South Asia: The Indian State and Sri Lankan Tamils' War of Liberation', in Emajuddin Ahmed and Abul Kalam (eds), Bangladesh, South Asia and the World, Dhaka: Academic Press, 1992.
——*State and Foreign Policy: India's Role in South Asia*, New Delhi: Vikas Publishing, 1993.
Ahmed, Ishtiaq, 'The 1947 Partition of India: A Paradigm for Pathological Politics in India and Pakistan', *Asian Ethnicity*, 3, 2003, 9–28.
Akbar, M.J., *Nehru: The Making of India*, London and New York: Viking, 1998.
Ali, Tariq, *The Nehrus and the Gandhis: An Indian Dynasty*, London: Pan Books, 1985.
Andersen, Walter K., 'India in 1982: Domestic Challenges and foreign Policy Successes', *Asian Survey*, 23, 1983, 111–22.
Ansari, N. Jamal, 'Reflection of Gujarat Genocide', *Mainstream*, Xl, 2002, 21–3.
Appaiah, Parvathy, *Hindutva: Ideology and Politics*, New Delhi: Deep & Deep Publications, 2003.
Appodorai, A., *Indian Political Thinking: from Naoroji to Nehru*, Madras: Oxford University Press, 1971.
——*The Domestic Roots of India's Foreign Policy, 1947–1972*, Delhi: Oxford University Press, 1981.
Ayoob, Mohammed, 'Security in the Third World: The Worm About to Turn?', *International Affairs*, 60, 1983–4, 41–51.
——'The Third World in the System of States: Acute Schizophrenia or Growing Pains?', *International Studies Quarterly*, 33, 1989, 67–79.
——'The Security Problematic of the Third World', *World Politics*, 43, 1991, 257–83.

Bibliography

——*The Third World Security Predicament: State-Making, Regional Conflict and the International System*, Boulder, CO: Lynne Rienner, 1995.

——'Subaltern Realism: International Relations Theory Meets the Third World', in Stephanie G. Neuman (ed.), *International Relations Theory and the Third World*, New York: St. Martin's Press, 1998.

Aziz, K.K., *The Making of Pakistan: A Study in Nationalism*, Karachi: National Book Foundation, 1976.

Aziz, Qutubuddin, *Blood and Tears*, Karachi: United Press of Pakistan, 1974.

Bandyopadhyaya, Jayantanuja, *The Making of India's Foreign Policy: Determinants, Institutions, Processes and Personalities*, New Delhi: Allied Publishers, 1970.

Banerjee, Sumanta, 'Gujarat Carnage and a Cynical Democracy', *Economic and Political Weekly*, 37, 2002, 37–41.

Barnett, Michael 'Sovereignty, Nationalism and Regional Order in the Arab States System', *International Organization*, 49, 1995, 479–510.

——*Dialogues in Arab Politics: Negotiations in Regional Order*, New York: Columbia University Press, 1998.

——'Radical Chic? Subaltern Realism: A Rejoinder', *International Studies Review*, 4, 2002, 49–62.

——'The Israeli Identity and the Peace Process', in Shibley Telhami and Michael Barnett (eds), *Identity and Foreign Policy In The Middle East*, New York: Cornell University Press, 2002.

Baruah, Sanjib, 'Immigration, Ethnic Conflict and Political Turmoil – Assam, 1979–85', *Asian Survey*, 26, 1986, 1184–206.

Baxter, Craig, *The Jana Sangh – A Biography of An Indian Political Party*, Philadelphia: University of Pennsylvania Press, 1969.

Bharatiya Janata Party, *Kargil Day*. Online. Available at http://www.bjp.org (accessed 3 June 2010).

——*1998 Election Manifesto*. Online. Available at http://www.bjp.org (accessed 11 June 2010).

——*Integral Humanism*. Online. Available at http://www.bjp.org (accessed 11 June 2010).

Bhargava, Rajeev, 'Liberal, Secular Democracy and Explanations of Hindu Nationalism', *Commonwealth and Comparative Politics*, 40, 2002, 72–96.

Bhasin, Avtar Singh (ed.), *India–Bangladesh Relations: Documents, 1971–2002*, Vol. 1, New Delhi: Geetika Publishers, 2003.

Bhasin, Avtar Singh (ed.), *Documents on Nepal's Relations With India and China, 1949–1966*, Bombay and New Delhi: Academic Books, 1970.

Bhatia, Krishan, *A Biography of Prime Minister Gandhi*, New York: Praeger Publishers, 1974.

Bhatia, Vandana, 'The US–India Nuclear Agreement: Revisiting the Debate', *Strategic Analysis*, 36, 2012, 612–23.

Bhatt, Chetan, *Hindu Nationalism: Origins, Ideologies and Modern Myths*, Oxford and New York: Berg, 2001.

Bhattacharyya, Buddhadeva, *Evolution of the Political Philosophy of Gandhi*, Calcutta: Calcutta Book House, 1969.

Bhindra, S.S., *Indo-Bangladesh Relations*, New Delhi: Deep and Deep Publishers, 1982.

Boesche, Roger, 'Kautilya's Arthasastra on War and Diplomacy in Ancient India', *The Journal of Military History*, 67, 2003, 9–37.

Bose, Sumantra, 'Hindu Nationalism and the Crisis of the Indian State', in Sugata Bose and Ayesha Jalal (eds), *Nationalism, Democracy and Development: State and Politics in India*, New Delhi: Oxford University Press, 1999.

Bradnock, Robert W., *India's Foreign Policy Since 1971*, London: Pinter Publishers and The Royal Institute of International Affairs, 1990.

Brass, Paul R., 'Pluralism, Regionalism and Decentralizing Tendencies in Contemporary Indian Politics', in A.J. Wilson and Dennis Dalton (eds), *The States of South Asia: Problems of National Integration*, London: C. Hurst, 1982.

——*The Politics of India Since Independence*, 2nd Edition, Cambridge, New York and Melbourne: Cambridge University Press, 1994.

Brecher, Michael, *The Struggle for Kashmir*, Toronto: Ryerson Press, 1953.

——*Nehru: A Political Biography*, London: Oxford University Press, 1959.

——*India and World Politics: Krishna Menon's View of the World*, London: Oxford University Press, 1968.

Bright, J.S. (ed.), *Before and After Independence: A Collection of the Most Important and Soul-stirring speeches delivered by Jawaharlal Nehru*, vols. 1 and 2, New Dehli: Indian Printing Works, 1952.

Brown, Judith, *Nehru: A Political Life*, New Haven and London: Yale University Press, 2003.

Brown, T. Louise, *The Challenge To Democracy In Nepal: A Political History*, London and New York: Routledge, 1996.

Burke S.M., *Mainsprings of Indian and Pakistani Foreign Policies*, Minneapolis, MN: University of Minnesota Press, 1974.

Buultjens, Ralph, 'The Ethics of Excess and Indian Intervention in South Asia', *Ethics and International Affairs*, 3, 1989, 89–106.

Buzan, Barry, *People, States and Fear: An Agenda for International Security Studies in the Post-Cold War Era*, Boulder, CO: Lynne Rienner, 1990.

——and Gowher Rizhi, *South Asian Insecurity and the Great Powers*, London: Macmillian, 1986.

——and Ole Weaver, *Regions and Powers – The Structure of International Security*, Cambridge: Cambridge University Press, 2003.

Campbell, David, *Writing Security: United States Foreign Policy and the Politics of Identity*, Manchester: Manchester University Press, 1992.

Carment, David, 'The International Dimensions of Ethnic Conflict: Concepts, Indicators and Theory', *Journal of Peace Research*, 30, 1993, 137–50.

Carras, Mary C., *Indira Gandhi in the Crucible of Leadership: A Political Biography*, Boston, MA: Beacon Press, 1979.

Chadda, Maya, *Ethnicity, Security and Separatism in India*, New York: Columbia University Press, 1997.

Chandrasekharan, S., 'Kargil and Nuclear Deterrence', *South Asian Analysis Group Papers*, 7 August 1999. Online. Available at http://www.saag.org/papers/paper71.html (accessed 12 August 2010).

Chattarji, Subarno, 'Media Representations of the Kargil War and the Gujarat Riots', *Sarai Reader: Crisis/Media*, in Monica Narula, Shuddhabrata Sengupta and Ravi Sundaram (eds), New Delhi: Sarai Publications, 2004.

Chatterjee, Manini, 'When it Comes to ISI, Red is Like Saffron', *Indian Express* (New Delhi), 13 February 2003. Online. Available at http://www.indianexpress.com/ (accessed 21 July 2010).

Chaulia, Seeram, 'BJP, India's Foreign Policy and the "Realist Alternative" to the Nehruvian Tradition', *International Politics*, 39, 2002, 215–34.

Bibliography

Chenoy, Karmal Mitral, S.P. Chukla, K.S. Subramaniam and Achin Vanaik, *Gujarat Carnage 2002*, 10 April 2002. Online. Available at http://www.indianexpress.com/ (accessed 8 November 2009).

Chowdhary, Subrata Roy, *The Genesis of Bangladesh*, New York: Asia Publishing House, 1972.

Cohen, Stephen P., 'Book Review', *Journal of Asian Studies*, 32, 1972, 191–2.

Corbridge, Stuart and John Harris, *Reinventing India: Liberalization, Hindu Nationalism and Popular Democracy*, Cambridge: Polity Press; Malden: Blackwell Publishers, 2000.

Crenshaw, Martha, 'Book Review', *The Journal of Asian Studies*, 57, 1998, 1191–2.

Das, M.N., *The Political Philosophy of Jawaharlal Nehru*, London: Allen & Unwin, 1961.

Das, Runa, 'Postcolonial (In)securities, the BJP and the Politics of Hindutva: Broadening the Security Paradigm between the Realist and Anti-nuclear/Peace Groups in India', *Third World Quarterly*, 24, 2003, 77–96.

——'The United States-India Nuclear Relations after 9/11: Alternative Discourses', *Asian Journal of Political Science*, 20, 2012, 86–107.

De Silva, K.M., *A History of Sri Lanka*, London: Hurst & Company; Berkeley and Los Angeles: University of California Press, 1981.

——*Regional Powers and Small State Security–India and Sri Lanka*, New Delhi: Vikas Publishing; Baltimore: Woodrow Wilson Centre Press, 1996.

Desai, G., 'Limited War Can Erupt Anytime: Gen. Malik', *Times of India* (New Delhi), 7 January 2000. Online. Available at http://timesofindia.indiatimes.com (accessed 10 January 2011).

Deutsch, Karl, Sidney A. Burrell, Robert A. Kann and J. Maurice Lee (eds), *Political Community and the North Atlantic Area*, Princeton, NJ: Princeton University Press, 1957.

Devotta, Neil, 'Is India Over-extended? When Domestic Disorder Precludes Regional Intervention', *Contemporary South Asia*, 12, 2003, 365–80.

Dhar, P.N., *Indira Gandhi, the 'Emergency' and Indian Democracy*, New Delhi: Oxford University Press, 2001.

Diez, Thomas, 'Speaking "Europe": The Politics of Integration Discourse', in Thomas Christiansen, Knud Erik Jorgensen and Antje Wiener (eds), *The Social Construction of Europe*, London: Sage, 2001.

van Dijk, Teun A. 'Critical Discourse Analysis', in Deborah Schiffrin, Deborah Tannen and Heidi E. Hamilton (eds), *The Handbook of Discourse Analysis*, Oxford and Malden, MA: Blackwell Publishers, 2001.

Diwan, Paras, 'Kashmir and the Indian Union: The Legal Position', *The International and Comparative Law Quarterly*, 2, 1953, 333–53.

Dixit, J.N., *My South Block Years: Memoirs of a Foreign Secretary*, New Delhi: UBS Publishers, 1997.

——*Assignment to Colombo*, Delhi: Konark Publishers, 1998.

——*India–Pakistan In War and Peace*, London: Routledge, 2002.

——*Makers of Indian Foreign Policy: From Raja Ram Mohun Roy to Yashwant Sinha*, New Delhi: Harper Collins, 2004.

Dua, Bhagwan D., 'Federalism or Patrimonialism: The Making and Unmaking of Chief Ministers in India', *Asian Survey*, 25, 1985, 793–804.

Dubey, Muchkund, 'Inept Handling of a Sensitive Issue', *The Hindu* (Chennai), 9 December 1992. Online. Available at http://www.thehindu.com (accessed 10 December 2010).

Embree, Ainslie, 'Indian Civilization and Regional Cultures: The Two Realities', in Paul Wallace (ed.), *Region and Nation in India*, New Delhi: Oxford University Press and IBH, 1985.

Engineer, Asghar Ali, 'Nehru's Concept of Secularism', *The Hindu* (Chennai), 1 April 1997. Online. Available at http://www.thehindu.com (accessed 4 November 2010).

Fairclough, Norman, *Analysing Discourse – Textual Analysis for Social Science*, London and New York: Routledge, 2003.

Falk, Richard and Saul H. Mendlovitz (eds), *Regional Politics and World Order*, San Francisco: W.H. Freeman, 1973.

Fallaci, Oriana, *Interview With History*, Boston: Houghton Mifflin, 1976.

Fontera, Richard M., 'Anti-colonialism as a Basic Indian Foreign Policy', *The Western Political Quarterly*, 13, 1960, 421–32.

Fox, Richard, 'Hindu Nationalism in the Making, or the Rise of the "Hindian"', in Richard Fox (ed.), *National Ideologies and the Production of National Cultures*, American Ethnological Society, Monograph Series, No. 2, Washington: American Anthropological Association, 1990.

Frank, Katherine, *Indira: The Life of Indira Nehru Gandhi*, London: Harper Collins Publishers, 2001.

Frankel, Francine, *India's Political Economy: 1947–77*, Princeton, NJ: Princeton University Press, 1978.

Gandhi, Indira, *Selected Speeches and Writings of Indira Gandhi*, New Delhi: Ministry of Information and Broadcasting, 1971.

——*India and Bangladesh: Selected Speeches and Statements, March to December 1971*, New Delhi: Orient Longman, 1972.

——*India: The Speeches and Reminiscences of Indira Gandhi, Prime Minister of India*, London: Hodder and Stoughton, 1975.

Gandhi, Rajmohan, *Patel: A Life*, Ahmedabad: Navjivan Publishing House, 1990.

Ganguly, Sumit, *The Crisis In Kashmir: Portents of War, Hopes of Peace*, Cambridge: Cambridge University Press and Woodrow Wilson Centre Press, 1997.

——'The Crisis of Indian Secularism', *Journal of Democracy*, 14, 2003, 11–25.

——and Brian Shoup, 'Nepal: Between Dictatorship and Anarchy', *Journal of Democracy*, 16, 2005, 129–43.

Gee, John Paul, *An Introduction to Discourse Analysis: Theory and Method*, London and New York: Routledge, 1999.

Ghose, Bisakha, 'Book Review', *International Affairs*, 74, 1998, 243–5.

Golwalkar, M.S., *We, or Our Nationhood Defined*, Nagpur: Bharat Prakashan, 1947.

Gopal, Sarvepalli (ed.), *Jawaharlal Nehru: A Biography*, Vol. 2, London: Jonathan Cape, 1979.

——*Jawaharlal Nehru: An Anthology*, Delhi: Oxford University Press, 1980.

——*Jawaharlal Nehru: A Biography*, Vol. 3, London: Jonathan Cape, 1984.

——*Anatomy of a Confrontation: The Babri Masjid-Ram Janmabhumi Issue*, New Delhi: Viking, 1991.

——*Selected Works of Jawaharlal Nehru*, Second Series, New Dehli: Jawaharlal Nehru Memorial Fund, 1996.

Government of India, *Report of the Kargil Review Committee*. Online. Available at http://rsdebate.nic.in/handle/123456789/110129 (accessed 26 August 2010).

——*Lok Sabha Debates*. Online. Available at http://164.100.47.132/LssNew/Debates/debatearchive.aspx (accessed 22 September 2010).

Bibliography

Government of Sri Lanka, *Constitution of the Democratic Socialist Republic of Sri Lanka*. Online. Available at http://www.priu.gov.lk/Cons/1978Constitution/CONTENTS.html (accessed 15 July 2010).

Gowen, Herbert H., 'The Indian Machiavelli, or Political Theory in India Two Thousand Years Ago', *Political Science Quarterly*, 44, 1929, 173–92.

Gupta, Bhabani Sen, 'India and Disarmament', in B.R. Nanda (ed.), *Indian Foreign Policy: The Nehru Years*, Delhi, Bombay, Bangalore and Kanpur: Vikas Publishing, 1976.

——'The Indian Doctrine', *India Today*, 31 August, 1983, 20.

Gupta, Jyotirinda Das, 'The Janata Phase: Reorganization and Redirection in Indian Politics', *Asian Survey*, 19, 1979, 390–403.

Gupta, Karunakar, *India in World Politics: A Period of Transition*, Calcutta: Scientific Book Agency, 1969.

Gupta, Sisir, *Kashmir: A Study in India–Pakistan Relations*, New Dehli: Asia Publishing House, 1967.

Gupte, Pranay, *Mother India: A Political Biography of Indira Gandhi*, New York and Ontario: Macmillian, 1992.

Hagerty, David T., 'India's Regional Security Doctrine', *Asian Survey*, 31, 1991, 351–63.

——'South Asia's Big Bangs: Causes, Consequences and Prospects', *Australian Journal of International Affairs*, 53, 1999, 19–29.

Hall, Rodney Bruce, *National Collective Identity: Social Constructs and International Systems*, New York: Columbia University Press, 1999.

Hampton, William H. and Virgina Schroeder, *The Two-Edged Sword: A Study of Paranoia Personality in Action*, Sante Fe, NM: Sunstone Press, 1990.

Hansen, Thomas Blom, *The Saffron Wave: Democracy and Hindu Nationalism in Modern India*, Princeton: Princeton University Press, 1999.

Haqqani, Husain, 'Pakistan's Endgame in Kashmir', *India Review*, 2, 2003, 34–54.

Hardgrave Jr., Robert, 'The Congress in India: Crisis and Split', *Asian Survey*, 10, 1970, 256–62.

Hewitt, Vernon M., *The International Politics of South Asia*, Manchester and New York: Manchester University Press, 1992.

Hill, Christopher and William Wallace, 'Introduction: Actors and Actions', in Christopher Hill and William Wallace (eds), *The Actors in Europe's Foreign Policy*, London and New York: Routledge, 1996.

Hodson, H.V., *The Great Divide*, London: Hutchison, 1969.

Holmes, James and Toshi Yoshihara, 'India's "Monroe" Doctrine and Asia's Maritime Future', *Strategic Analysis*, 32, 6, 2008, pp.997–1011.

Hurrell, Andrew, 'Regionalism in Theoretical Perspective', in Andrew Hurrell and Louise Fawcett (eds), *Regionalism in World Politics: Regional Organization and World Order*, Oxford: Oxford University Press, 1995.

Husain, Asad, *British India's Relations With the Kingdom of Nepal, 1857–1947: A Diplomatic History of Nepal*, London: Allen and Unwin, 1970.

Jackson, Patrick T. and Daniel Nexon, 'Constructivist-realism or Realist-constructivism', *International Studies Review*, 6, 2004, 337–41.

Jaffrelot, Christophe, *Hindu Nationalist Politics: 1925 to the 1990s*, New Delhi: Penguin Books, 1999.

——'Nehru and the Hindu Code Bill', *Outlook*, 8 August 2003. Online. Available at http://www.outlookindia.com/article.aspx?221000 (accessed 6 December 2010).

Jain, Girilal, 'India, Pakistan and Kashmir', in B.R. Nanda (ed.), *Indian Foreign Policy: The Nehru Years*, Dehli: Vikas Publishing House, 1976.

Jain, Sumitra Kumar, *Party Politics and Centre-State Relations in India*, New Delhi: Abhinav Publications, 1994.
Jalal, Ayesha, *Jinnah: The Sole Spokesman*, Cambridge: Cambridge University Press, 1994.
Jayakar, Pupul, *Indira Gandhi: An Intimate Biography*, New York: Pantheon Books, 1992.
Jayasuria, K., 'Singapore: The Politics of Regional Definition', *Pacific Review*, 7, 1994, 411–20.
Jha, Prem Shankar, 'Kashmir 1947: Rival Versions of History', New Delhi: Oxford University Press, 1996.
Job, Brian, 'The Insecurity Dilemma: National, Regime and State Securities in the Third World', in Brian Job (ed.), *The Insecurity Dilemma: National Security of Third World States*, Boulder, CO: Lynne Rienner, 1992.
Johnston, Alastair Ian, 'Cultural Realism and Strategy in Maoist China', in Peter Katzenstein (ed.), *The Culture of National Security*, New York: Columbia University Press, 1996.
Joyner, Daniel H., *Interpreting the Nuclear Non-Proliferation Treaty*, New York: Oxford University Press, 2011.
Kak, Krishen, 'Conspiracy of Silence', *The Pioneer* (New Delhi), 11 January 2003. Online. Available at http://www.dailypioneer.com (accessed 14 February 2011).
Kalkani, K.R., *Principles For a New Party*, Delhi: Vijay Pustak Bhandar, 1951.
Kapur, Ashok, 'Indian Security and Defence Policies Under Indira Gandhi', *Journal of Asian and African Studies*, 22, 1987, 176–93.
——'The Indian Subcontinent: The Contemporary Structure of Power and the Development of Power Relations', *Asian Survey*, 28, 1988, 693–710.
Karan, Pradyumna P. and William M. Jenkins, *The Himalayan Kingdoms: Bhutan, Sikkim and Nepal*, London and Toronto: D. Van Nostrand, 1963.
Kathuria, Harbir Singh, *President's Rule In India, 1967–1989*, Delhi: Uppal Publishing, 1990.
Kaul, T.N., *A Diplomat's Diary (1947–1999): The Tantalizing Triangle – China, India and USA*, New Delhi: Macmillian, 2000.
Khan, Roedad, *The American Papers: Secret and Confidential India–Pakistan–Bangladesh Documents, 1965–1973*, Karachi: Oxford University Press, 2000.
Khilnani, Sunil, *The Idea of India*, New York: Farrar, Straus and Giroux, 1997.
Kier, Elizabeth, 'Culture and French Military Doctrine before World War II', in Peter Katzenstein (ed.), *The Culture of National Security*, Columbia: Columbia University Press, 1996.
Kissinger, Henry, *White House Years*, London: Weidenfeld and Nicolson, 1979.
Kochanek, Stanley, 'Mrs Gandhi's Pyramid: The New Congress', in Henry Hart (ed.) *Indira Gandhi's India*, Boulder, CO: Westview Press, 1976.
Kohli, Atul, *Democracy and Discontent: India's Growing Crisis of Governability*, Cambridge: Cambridge University Press, 1990.
Kothari, Rajni, *Democratic Polity and Social Change in India*, Bombay: Allied Publishers, 1976.
Krishna, Sankaran, *Postcolonial Insecurities: India, Sri Lanka and the Question of Nationhood*, Minneapolis, MN and London: University of Minnesota Press, 1999.
Kulkarni, Gauri, 'Uniform Civil Code', *Legal Service of India*. Online. Available at http://www.legalserviceindia.com/articles/ucc.htm (accessed 23 July 2010).
Lamb, Alastair, *Crisis in Kashmir*, London: Routledge & Kegan Paul, 1966.
——*Kashmir: A Disputed Legacy: 1846–1990*, Karachi: Oxford University Press, 1992.

Lapid, Yosef and Friedrich Kratochwil (eds), *The Return of Culture and Identity in IR Theory*, London: Lynne Rienner, 1996.
Larson, Gerald James, *India's Agony over Religion*, Albany: SUNY Press, 1995.
Levi, Warner, 'Government and Politics in Nepal: II', *Far Eastern Survey*, 22, 1953, 5–10.
Lijphart, Arend, 'The Puzzle of Indian Democracy: A Consociational Interpretation', *The American Political Science Review*, 90, 1996, 258–68.
Lynch, Marc, 'Jordan's Identity and Interests', in S. Telhami and M. Barnett (eds), *Identity and Foreign Policy in the Middle East*, New York: Cornell University Press, 2002.
McSweeney, Bill, *Security, Identity and Interests: A Sociology of International Relations*, Cambridge: Cambridge University Press, 1999.
Malhotra, Inder, *Indira Gandhi: A Personal and Political Biography*, Boston, MA: Northeastern University Press, 1991.
Malik, V.P., 'Kargil: Where Defence Met Diplomacy', *Indian Express* (Mumbai), 25 July 2002. Online. Available at http://www.indianexpress.com (accessed 18 April 2010).
Malik, Yogendra K. and Dhirendra K. Vajpeyi (eds), *India: The Years of Indira Gandhi*, Leiden, New York, Copenhagen and Cologne: E.J. Brill, 1988.
——and V.B. Singh, *Hindu Nationalists In India*, Boulder, CO: Westview Press, 1996.
Mansingh, Surjit, *India's Search for Power – Indira Gandhi's Foreign Policy, 1966–1982*, London, California and New Delhi: Sage Publications, 1984.
Masani, Zareer, *Indira Gandhi: A Biography*, London: Hamish Hamilton, 1975.
Mathur, Kuldeep, 'The State and the Use of Coercive Power in India', *Asian Survey*, 32, 1992, 337–49.
Mattern, Janice Bially, 'The Power Politics of Identity', *European Journal of International Relations*, 7, 2001, 349–98.
Mazari, Shireen, *The Kargil Conflict 1999: Separating Fact from Fiction*, Islamabad: Institute of Strategic Studies, 2003.
Mee, Arthur, *The Children's Encyclopaedia*, London: Educational Book Company, 1908.
Menon, V.P., *The Integration of the Indian States*, London and New York: Longman & Macmillan, 1956.
Ministry of Defence, Government of India, *Kargil War: A Glorious Victory for India*. Online. Available at http://mod.nic.in/samachar/17/html/ch8.htm (accessed 8 March 2010).
Ministry of External Affairs, Government of India, *1950 Treaty of Friendship*. Online. Available at http://www.mea.gov.in/bilateral-documents.htm?dtl/6295/Treaty+of+Peace+and+Friendship (accessed 21 August 2010).
——*Lahore Declaration February, 1999*. Online. Available at http://mea.gov.in/in-focus-article.htm?18997/Lahore+Declaration+February+1999 (accessed 11 February 2011).
Ministry of Law and Justice, Government of India, *The Constitution of India*. Online. Available at http://lawmin.nic.in/coi/coiason29july08.pdf (accessed 24 October 2010).
Misra, B.B., *The Indian Political Parties: An Historical Analysis of Political Behaviour till 1947*, Delhi: Oxford University Press, 1976.
Misra, K.P., 'Trilateralism in South Asia', *Asian Survey*, 14, 1974, 627–36.
Mistry, Dinshaw, 'Diplomacy, Sanctions and the U.S. Non-proliferation Dialogue with India and Pakistan', *Asian Survey*, 39, 1999, 753–71.
Mohan, C. Raja, 'Jaswant Cautions Pakistan', *The Hindu* (Chennai) 12 August 1999. Online. Available at http://www.thehindu.com (accessed 12 September 2010).
Moraes, Dom, *Mrs Gandhi*, London: Jonathan Cape, 1980.

Mountbatten, Earl, *Time Only To Look Forward: Speeches of Rear Admiral the Earl Mountbatten of Burma*, London: Nicholas Kaye, 1949.
Muni, S.D., *Pangs of Proximity: India and Sri Lanka's Ethnic Crisis*, New Delhi, California and London: Sage Publications, 1993.
Muralidharan, Sukumar, 'A Not-so-Smooth Ride', *Frontline* (Chennai), 16, 5, 27 February–12 March 1999. Online. Available at http://www.frontlineonnet.com/fl1605/16050130.htm (accessed 23 September 2010).
Murshed, Yasmeen and Nazim Kamran Choudhury, 'Bangladesh's Second Chance', *Journal of Democracy*, 8, 1997, 70–82.
Murthy, R.K., *The Cult of the Individual: A Study of Indira Gandhi*, New Delhi: Sterling Publishers, 1977.
Nanda, B.R., *Jawaharlal Nehru: Rebel and Statesman*, New Delhi: Oxford University Press, 1998.
Nandy, Ashis, 'The Politics of Secularism and the Recovery of Religious Toleration', in Rajeev Bhargava (ed.), *Secularism and Its Critics*, New Delhi: Oxford University Press, 1999.
Narula, Smita, 'Overlooked Danger: The Security and Rights Implications of Hindu Nationalism in India', *Harvard Human Rights Journal*, 16, 2003, 41–68.
Nayar, Kuldip, *India after Nehru*, New Delhi: Vikas Publications, 1975.
Nehru, B.K., *Nice Guys Finish Second*, New Delhi: Viking, 1997.
Nehru, Jawaharlal, *India's Foreign Policy: Selected Speeches, September 1946–April 1961*, New Delhi: Ministry of Information and Broadcasting, Government of India, 1971.
——*Letters to Chief Ministers, 1947–1964*, Vol. 2, New Delhi: Jawaharlal Nehru Memorial Fund, 1985–9.
——*The Discovery of India*, Delhi, Oxford and New York: Oxford University Press, 1994.
Neumann, Iver, 'A Region-building Approach to Northern Europe', *Review of International Studies*, 20, 1994.
——*Russia and the Idea of Europe: A Study in Identity and International Relations*, London and New York, Routledge, 1995.
——*Uses of the Other: The 'East' in European Identity Formation*, Manchester: Manchester University Press, 1999.
Ninan, Sevanti, 'Spotlight Summit', *The Hindu* (Chennai), 15 July 2001. Online. Available at http://www.thehindu.com (accessed 6 September 2010).
Noorani, A.G., 'Article 370: Law and Politics', *Frontline*, 7, 19, 16–29 September 2000. Online. Available at http://www.frontlineonnet.com/fl1719/17190890.htm (accessed 17 June 2010).
Norman, Dorothy (ed.), *Indira Gandhi: Letters to an American Friend, 1950–1984*, New York: Harcourt Jovanovich, 1985.
Nye, Joseph (ed.), *International Regionalism*, Boston, MA: Little, Brown, 1968.
Omar, Imtiaz, *Emergency Powers and the Courts in India and Pakistan*, Hague: Kluwer Law International, 2002.
Oxford English Dictionary, 2nd Edition, 1989. Online. Available at http://dictionary.oed.com (accessed 11 March 2008).
Pakeman, S.A., *Ceylon*, London: Ernest Benn, 1964.
Palmer, Norman D., 'India in 1975: Democracy in Eclipse', *Asian Survey*, 16, 1976, 95–110.
Pandey, B.N., *Nehru*, London and Basingstoke, Macmilian, 1976.

Panikkar, K.N., *Outsider as Enemy: The Politics of Rewriting History in India*, Pennsylvania: University of Pennsylvania, Center for the Advanced Study of India Working Paper, November 2000.

Pantham, Thomas, 'Thinking with Mahatma Gandhi: Beyond Liberal Democracy', *Political Theory*, 11, 1983, 165–88.

Perry, Alex, 'Deadly Cargo', *Time*, 21 October 2002.

Philips, Nelson and Cynthia Hardy, *Discourse Analysis: Investigating Processes of Social Construction*, Thousand Oaks, London and New Delhi: Sage Publications, 2002.

Platts, John T., *A Dictionary of Urdu, Classical Hindi and English*. Online. Available at http://dsal.uchicago.edu/dictionaries/platts/ (accessed 21 November 2009).

Puniyani, Ram, *Contours of Hindu Rashtra: Hindutva, Sangh Parivar and Contemporary Politics*, Delhi: Kalpaz, 2006.

Raghavan, B.S., 'Who is Secular', *Business Line*, 3 May, 2002. Online. Available at http://www.thehindubusinessline.com (accessed 2 April 2010).

Rai Baljit, *Demographic Aggression against India*, Chandigarh: B.S. Publications, 1993.

Rajan, M.S., 'Bangladesh and After', *Pacific Affairs*, 45, 1972, 191–205.

Rajghatta, Chidanand, 'US Welcomes Move on Bus Diplomacy', *Indian Express*, (Mumbai), 23 February 1999. Online. Available at http://www.indianexpress.com (accessed 17 June 2010).

Ramakrishan, Venkitesh, 'All for Survival', *Frontline* (Chennai), 15, 11–24 April 1998. Online. Available at http://www.frontlineonnet.com/fl1508/15080230.htm.(accessed 25 June 2010).

Ramana, M.V., 'A Nuclear Wedge', *Frontline* (Chennai), 18, 8–21 December 2001. Online. Available at http://www.frontlineonnet.com/fl1825/18250840.htm (accessed 4 September 2010).

Ramusack, Barbara N., *The Indian Princes and Their States*, Cambridge: Cambridge University Press, 2004.

Rana, A.P., *The Imperatives of Nonalignment: A Conceptual Study of India's Foreign Policy Strategy in the Nehru Period*, Delhi: Macmillian, 1976.

Rao, P. Vankateshwar, 'Ethnic Conflict in Sri Lanka: India's Role and Perception', *Asian Survey*, 28, 1988, 419–36.

Raychaudhuri, Tapan, 'Shadows of the Swastika: Historical Perspectives on the Politics of Hindu Communalism', *Modern Asian Studies*, 34, 2000, 259–79.

Raza, Rafi, *Zulkifar Ali Bhutto and Pakistan, 1967–1977*, Karachi: Oxford University Press, 1997.

Reid, Anthony, 'A Saucer Model of Southeast Asian Identity', *Southeast Asian Journal of Social Science*, 27, 1999, 7–23.

Riaz, Ali, '"God Willing": The Politics and Ideology of Islamism in Bangladesh', *Comparative Studies of South Asia, Africa and the Middle East*, 23, 2003, 301–20.

Riedel, Bruce, *American Diplomacy and the 1999 Kargil Summit at Blair House*, Policy Paper, Centre for the Advanced Study of India, Philadelphia, PA: University of Pennsylvania, 2002.

Roy-Chaudhury, Rahul, 'India's Response to Terrorism after 13 December 2001', *Conflict, Security and Development*, 3, 2003, 277–85.

Rudolph, Lloyd and Susanne Rudolph, *In Pursuit of Lakshmi: The Political Economy of the Indian State*, Chicago and London: Chicago University Press, 1986.

Sahni, Varun, 'The Protean Polis and Strategic Surprises: Do Changes Within India Affect South Asian Strategic Stability?', *Contemporary South Asia*, 14, 2005, 219–31.

Saifuddin, Ahmed, *The Roles of Religion and National Identity in Bangladesh*, Finland: Abo Akademi University Press, 2000.
Salik, Siddiq, *Witness to Surrender*, Karachi: Oxford University Press, 1978.
Sarkar, Sumit, 'Inclusive Democracy and Its Enemies', *Interventions: International Journal of Postcolonial Studies*, 7, 2005, 304–9.
Savarkar, V.D., *Hindutva: Who Is a Hindu?*, New Delhi: Hindi Sahitya Sadan, 2003.
Schaffer, Howard and Teresita Shaffer, 'Better Neighbours? India and South Asian Regional Politics', *SAIS Review*, 18, 1998, 109–21.
Schoefield, Victoria, *Kashmir in Conflict: India, Pakistan and the Unending War*, London and New York: I.B. Taurus, 2003.
——'Kashmir – Today, Tomorrow?', *Asian Affairs*, 28, 1997, 315–24.
Sethuraman, S., 'NDA Survival No Mark of Stability', *Business Line* (Chennai) 9 May 2002. Online. Available at http://www.thehindubusinessline.com (accessed 15 July 2010).
Sever, Adrian, *Nepal Under The Ranas*, Delhi: Oxford and IBH Publishing, 1993.
Sharma, Dhirendra, *India's Commitment to Kashmir (Political Analysis with Documents)*, New Delhi: Philosophy and Social Action Publication, 1994.
Sharma, Vinod, 'Kargile Enquiry an Eyewash Say Opposition and Experts', *Hindustan Times* (New Delhi), 26 July 1999. Online. Available at http://www.hin dustantimes.com (accessed 17 March 2010).
Shourie, Arun, *A Secular Agenda*, New Delhi: HarperCollins, 1997.
Sikdar, Tapan, 'How West Bengal Congress is Providing Fillip to Muslim Infiltrators', *BJP Today*, September 1–10, 1992.
Singh, Jasjit, 'The US Transmitters in Sri Lanka', *Times of India* (New Delhi), 6 March 1985. Online. Available at http://timesofindia.indiatimes.com (accessed 29 June 2010).
Singh, Jaswant, *Defending India*, New York: St. Martin's Press, 1999.
Singh, Sinderpal, 'Border Crossings and "Islamic Terrorists": Representing Bangladesh in Indian Foreign Policy During the BJP Era', *India Review*, 8, 2009, 144–62.
——'From Delhi to Bandung: Nehru, Indian-ness and "Pan-Asian-ness"', *South Asia: Journal of South Asian Studies*, 34, 2011, 51–64.
Singh, Tavleen, *Kashmir: A Tragedy of Terrors*, New Delhi: Penguin, 1996.
Sission, Richard and Leo E. Rose, *War and Secession: Pakistan, India and the Creation of Bangladesh*, Berkeley: University of California Press, 1990.
Smith, Donald Eugene, *India as a Secular State*, Princeton, NJ: Princeton University Press, 1963.
Smith, Steve, 'Wendt's World', *Review of International Studies*, 26, 2000, 151–63.
Snedden, Christopher, 'Would a Plebiscite have Resolved the Kashmir Dispute?', *South Asia: Journal of South Asian Studies*, 28, 2005, 64–86.
South Asian Journalist Association, *South Asian Journalist Association Handbook*, Online. Available at http://www.saja.org/stylebook.html#B (accessed 15 June 2010).
Spencer, Jonathan, 'Introduction: The Power of the Past', in Jonathan Spencer (ed.), *Sri Lanka: History and the Roots of Conflict*, London and New York: Routledge, 1990.
Srivastava, Siddarth, 'India Suffering from Guilt Complex', *The Times of India* (New Delhi), 31 May 2001. Online. Available at http://timesofindia.indiatimes.com (accessed 15 June 2010).
Steinberg, Blerna S., 'Indira Gandhi: The Relationship between Personality Profile and Leadership Style', *Political Psychology*, 26, 2005, 755–90.
Sudarshan, S., 'Advani's Reaction is Still Untenable', *Outlook* (New Delhi) 23 December 2002. Online. Available at http://119.82.71.51/article.aspx?218408 (accessed 11 August 2010).

Bibliography

Sultan Shahin, 'India Frets over Pakistan–Bangladesh Nexus', *Asia Times* (Hong Kong), 6 March 2004. Online. Available at http://www.atimes.com/atimes/South_Asia/FC06Df02.html (accessed 6 January 2011).

Suryanarayana, P.S., *The Peace Trap: An Indo-Lanka Political Crisis*, New Delhi: Affiliated East-West Press, 1988.

Swain, Pratap Chandra, *Bharatiya Janata Party: Profile and Performance*, New Delhi: A.P.H Publishing Corporation, 2001.

Swami, Praveen, 'A Probe and Its Prospects', *Frontline* (Chennai), 16, 14–27 August 1999.

—— 'A Committee and Some Questions: A First-person Account with Regard to the Kargil Review Committee and its implications', *Frontline* (Chennai), 17, 22 January–4 February 2000.

Swamy, Subramanian, 'Redefining Secularism', *The Hindu*, 18 March 2004. Online. Available at http://www.thehindu.com (accessed 13 June 2010).

Symonds, Richard, *The Making of Pakistan*, Karachi: National Book Foundation, 1976.

Talbott, Strobe, *Engaging India: Diplomacy, Democracy and the Bomb*, Washington, DC: Brookings Institution Press, 2004.

Talukdar, Surajit and Swapan Kumar Paul, 'High Security on Indo-Bangla Border', *The Pioneer* (New Delhi), 6 November 2003. Online. Available at http://www.dailypioneer.com (accessed 11 March 2010).

Tanham, George, *Indian Strategic Thought: An Interpretive Essay*, Santa Monica: RAND, 1992.

Tarlo, Emma, *Unsettling Memories: Narratives of the Emergency in Delhi*, London: Hurst & Company, 2003.

Thapar, Romila, 'The Mauryan Empire in Early India', *Historical Research*, 79, 2006, 287–305.

Tharoor, Shashi, *The Invention of India*, New Delhi: Penguin, 2003.

Thomas, C. Joshua, *Sri Lanka's Turmoil and the Indian Government: A Study of Ethnic Conflict*, New Delhi: Omsons Publications, 1995.

Thomas, Raju G.C., *Democracy, Security, and Development in India*, New York: St. Martin's Press, 1996.

Tilly, Charles, 'International Communities, Secure or Otherwise', Emanuel Adler and Michael Barnett (eds), *Security Communities*, Cambridge: Cambridge University Press, 1998.

Torri, Michelguglielmo, 'Factional Politics and Economic Policy: The Case of India's Bank Nationalization', *Asian Survey*, 15, 1975, 1077–96.

United Nations, *Documents on the United Nations Commission on India and Pakistan (UNCIP)*. Online. Available at http://www.un.org/english (accessed 25 July 2009).

Upadhyaya, Prakash Chandra, 'The Politics of Indian Secularism', *Modern Asian Studies*, 26, 1992, 815–53.

Upadhyaya, R., 'The Kargil Crisis: Political Dimensions', *South Asian Analysis Group*, 18 June 1999. Online. Available at http://www.saag.org/papers/paper68.html (accessed 12 June 2010).

Van Der Deer, Peter, *Religious Nationalism: Hindus and Muslims in India*, Berkeley, Los Angeles and London: University of California Press, 1994.

Varshney, Ashutosh, 'Contested Meanings: India's National Identity, Hindu Nationalism and the Politics of Anxiety', *Daedalus*, 122, 1993, 227–61.

Vasudev, Uma, *Two Faces of Indira Gandhi*, Delhi: Vikas Publications, 1977.

Wariavwalla, Bharat, 'India in 1988: Drift, Disarray or Pattern?', *Asian Survey*, 29, 2, 1989, 189–98.
——'Religion and Nationalism in India: *Ram* the God of the Hindu Nation', *The Round Table*, 89, 2000, 593–606.
Warner, Geoffrey, 'Review Article – Nixon, Kissinger and the Breakup of Pakistan, 1971', *International Affairs*, 81, 2005, 1097–118.
Weaver, Ole, 'Three Competing "Europes": French, German, Russian', *International Affairs*, 66, 1990, 477–94.
Weiner, Wyron, *Sons of the Soil: Migration and Ethnic Conflict in India*, Princeton, NJ: Princeton University Press, 1978.
——'The Political Demography of Assam's Anti-immigration Movement', *Population and Development Review*, 9, 1983, 279–92.
Weldes, Jutta, *Constructing National Interests: The United States and the Cuban Missile Crisis*, Minneapolis, MN and London: University of Minnesota Press, 1999.
Wendt, Alexander, 'The Agent–Structure Problem in International Relations Theory', *International Organization*, 41, 1987, 353–70.
——'Collective Identity Formation and the International State', *American Political Science Review*, 88, 1994, 384–96.
——*Social Theory of International Politics*, Cambridge: Cambridge University Press, 1999.
——'Anarchy is What States Make of It: The Social Construction of Power Politics', *International Organization*, 46, 1999, 391–425.
——'The State as Person in International Theory', *Review of International Studies*, 30, 2004, 289–316.
Wesley, Michael, 'The Politics of Exclusion: Australia, Turkey and Definitions of Regionalism', *Pacific Review*, 10, 1997, 523–55.
White, Mark J., 'New Scholarship on the Cuban Missile Crisis', *Diplomatic History*, 26, 2002, 147–53.
Widmalm, Sten, 'The Rise and Fall of Democracy in Jammu and Kashmir', *Asian Survey*, 37, 1997, 1005–30.
——*Kashmir In Comparative Perspective: Democracy and Violent Separatism in India*, London: Routledge-Curzon, 2002.
Wilcox, Wayne, 'A Decade of Ayub', *Asian Survey*, 9, 1969, 87–93.
Wilson, A. Jeyaratnam, *Politics in Sri Lanka, 1947–1973*, London and Basingstoke: Macmillan Press, 1974.
Winchell, Sean P., 'Pakistan's ISI: The Invisible Government', *International Journal of Intelligence and CounterIntelligence*, 16, 2003, 374–88.
Wolpert, Stanley, *Nehru: A Tryst With Destiny*, New York and Oxford: Oxford University Press, 1996.
Yong, Tan Tai and Ganesh Kudaisya, *The Aftermath of Partition in South Asia*, London and New York: Routledge, 2000.
Zachariah, Benjamin, *Nehru*, London and New York: Routledge, 2004.
Zehfuss, Maja, *Constructivism in International Relations: The Politics of Reality*, Cambridge: Cambridge University Press, 2002.
Zinkin, Taya, 'Nehruism: India's Revolution without Fear', *Pacific Affairs*, 28, 1955, 221–34.
Ziring, Lawrence, 'Pakistan and India: Politics, Personality and Foreign Policy', *Asian Survey*, 18, 1978, 706–30.

Bibliography

Newspaper articles

'Ackerman Challenges Pakistan to Reverse "The Betrayal" of Lahore Declaration', 21 July 1999, *Rediff On The Net*. Online. Available at http://www.rediff (accessed 22 November 2009).

'Al-Qaeda, ISI Activities on the Rise in Bangladesh: Advani', *The Hindu* (New Delhi), 8 November 2002. Online. Available at http://www.thehindu.com (accessed 16 June 2010).

'Arrested ISI Spymaster was on Way to Guwahati', *The Sentinel* (Guwahati), 12 January 2000. Online. Available at http://www.sentinelassam.com (accessed 28 August 2009).

'Article 370 to Stay, Says Advani', *The Times of India* (Mumbai), 27 April 2000. Online. Available at http://timesofindia.indiatimes.com (accessed 4 February 2009).

'Axom Xumaise Al Qaida' ('Assam Targeted by Al-Qaeda'), *Dainik Khabar* (Guwahati), 22 August 2002. Online. Available at http://dainikkhabar.com (accessed 12 August 2009).

'BJP Chief wants Capture of Azad Kashmir' *The News* (Lahore), 4 July 1999. Online. Available at http://www.thenews.com.pk/TodaysPrint.aspx?ID=5 (accessed 14 April 2009).

'BJP Rules out Modi's Resignation', *Rediff On The Net*. Online. Available at http://www.rediff (accessed 2 May 2009).

'Dhaka ISI Nerve Centre: Sinha', *The Tribune* (Chandigarh), 28 November 2002. Online. Available at http://www.tribuneindia.com (accessed 18 March 2009).

'General: Kargil was on Before Vajpayee's Lahore Visit', *The Indian Express* (Mumbai), 14 July 2004. Online. Available at http://www.indianexpress.com (accessed 2 March 2009).

'George Rubbishes Dhaka's Claim', *The Tribune* (Chandigarh), 30 November 2002. Online. Available at http://www.tribuneindia.com (accessed 11 March 2009).

'Hindu Rashtra in Two Years Time: Togadia', *Rediff On The Net*. Online. Available at http://www.rediff (accessed 4 May 2009).

'India for Treating Kargil as Limited War: Advani', *Hindustan Times* (New Delhi), 20 June 1999. Online. Available at http://www.hindustantimes.com (accessed 25 June 2009).

'India Possible US Ally for Attacking Iran: Yechury', *The Hindu* (Chennai), 21 July 2008. Online. Available at http://www.thehindu.com (accessed 13 June 2009).

'ISI Agent in Assam Rifles Held', *Hindustan Times* (New Delhi), 13 July 2002. Online. Available at http://www.hindustantimes.com (accessed 14 June 2009).

'Kargil: Success and Complications', *Frontline*, 16, 17–30 July 1999. Online. Available at http://www.frontlineonnet.com/fl&1615/16150110;.htm (accessed 17 August 2009).

'Modi Puts State Money Where Biased Mouth Is', *Indian Express* (Ahmedabad), 5 March 2002. Online. Available at http://www.indianexpress.com (accessed 5 March 2009).

'Nawaz, Clinton Agree on Pullout by Mujahideen', *Dawn Wire Service* (Karachi), 28, 5, 10 July 1999. Online. Available at http://archives.dawn.com/fixed/subs/dwssub.htm (accessed 28 March 2009).

'Newton Modi has a Lot to Answer', *Times of India* (New Delhi), 2 March 2002. Online. Available at http://timesofindia.indiatimes.com (accessed 12 February 2009).

'Secularists to Blame', *The Free Press Journal* (Mumbai), 2 March 2002. Online. Available at http://freepressjournal.in (accessed 12 March 2009).

'1999 Kargil Conflict', *Global Security.Org*. Online. Available at http://www.globalsecurity.org/military/world/war/kargil-99.htm (accessed 18 January 2009).

Index

Abdullah, Farooq 50–2, 129
Abdullah, Sheikh 30, 34, 50, 126, 133
Acheson, Dean 32, 125
Advani: on democracy 94; on the Hindu Code Bill 92; on *Hindutva* 90; on the ISI in Bangladesh 110, 112
All-India Muslim League 13–14, 19, 29, 51, 123, 125

Bangladesh: as East Pakistan 61–3; illegal migration from 11, 108–12, 144; role of ISI 110–13, 145–6, 149, 157; as a United Nations issue 70–2
Bharatiya Jana Sangh 85–6, 88–9, 91–2, 117, 138–9
Bharatiya Janata Party: and Article 370 91–2, 139; and Assam 109, 112; attitude towards Pakistan 99–113, 118, 137, 140–3, 145; and bilateralism with Pakistan 102–3, 116; and the concept of *Bharat* 86–7, 90–1, 97, 113, 117, 137–8; on the concept of *Hindutva* 86, 89–91, 93, 95, 97, 117, 137–8, 140; on democracy 93–6, 98, 113–17, 120–1, 123, 127, 129–31, 133–4, 137, 139; and the discourse of anti-imperialism 96–8, 114–17, 119, 140; and the Gujarat riots 94–5, 139–41; and the Hindu Code Bill 91–2, 138–9; and Hindu nationalism 117, 137–40; and India's Northeast States 110, 112–13 ,118; on Jammu and Kashmir 92, 100–5, 107, 111, 115, 129, 136, 139; and the Kargil War 100, 102–5, 107, 118, 141; and minority appeasement 52, 89, 91–2, 109; and Muslim personal law 91–2; on the notion of national humiliation 97, 117; notions of betrayal 100–1, 106; on nuclear war and nuclear weapons 101–2, 104–5, 107, 141; position of Christians 88, 90; position on temple at Ayodha 90–1, 94, 138; on 'pseudo-secularism' 52, 89, 92, 98, 117; and its relationship with the *Rashtriya Swayamsevak Sangh* (RSS) 87–91, 93, 97, 106–7, 117, 137–8; on the role of the ISI 110–13, 145–6; on socialism 97, 123–4; territorial integrity 106–7, 113, 135
Bhutto, Zulfikar Ali: and Bangladesh 66, 70, 132–4; bilateralism with India 116; and Jammu and Kashmir 67–9; and the Simla Agreement 66–9, 73–6
Brass, Paul 60, 130
Brown, Judith 12, 121

China: and East Pakistan 71, 74–5, 135; and Nepal 28, 40–1, 43–6, 127–8; and Tibet 40, 45–6
Clinton, Bill 104, 142

Desai, Morarji 56–7
Dixit, J.N. 72, 133, 136, 141–2, 144

Fernandes, George 111
Foucault 4

Gandhi, Indira Nehru: and addressing Tamil sentiments 76–9, 81, 84; and bank nationalization 48, 54–7, 64, 116, 130; and the Congress (I) 50–2, 85, 137; and democratic populism 7, 54, 57–8, 60, 64–5, 73–4, 84, 116; and discourses of anti-imperialism 61–4, 74, 80, 82, 84, 116, 119; and the Emergency 7, 48, 53, 59–61, 64, 70, 88, 93, 116, 129, 131; and the *Garibi*

162   Index

Hatao campaign 56; as goddess *Durga* 64,132; and the Indira Doctrine 80, 83; and the Indo-Soviet Treaty of Peace, Friendship and Co-operation 74; and notions of India's territorial integrity 61, 63–4, 75–6, 116, 135; and rupee devaluation 54–5, 64, 116; and the Simla Agreement 3–4, 7, 10, 65–76, 80, 102, 116, 133–4; and the Soviet Union's Asian Collective Security proposal 75, 135; and the United States 55, 62–3, 71–5, 81–2, 90, 134–6; and the 1983 Jammu and Kashmir state elections 48–52, 115, 129

Gandhi, M.K. 6, 88, 96

Gandhi, Rajiv: and the Indian Peacekeeping Force (IPKF) 76, 79, 81, 83, 136; and the 'Rajiv Doctrine' 78

Golwarkar, M.S. 91, 117

Hindu Mahasabha 9, 90, 137

illegal migration 11, 108–12, 144

India: and the discourse of democracy 2–4, 7, 10, 17–23, 26, 29, 32–3, 40–2, 47–8, 53–61, 65, 69–73, 84–5, 93–6, 98, 113–17, 120–1, 123, 127, 129–31, 133–4, 137, 139–40, 142, 144; and the East Pakistan issue 61–3, 66, 69–72, 74–5, 80, 83, 131–2, 134; and the Emergency 7, 48, 53, 59–61, 64, 70, 88, 93, 116, 129, 131, 133; and great-power politics 36–7, 42–4, 74, 116, 118; and the role of socialism 3, 19, 22–3, 97, 123–24; and its territorial borders 1, 24, 40, 61–3, 80, 82–4, 116; and the United States 35–6, 42, 46, 62, 68, 75, 78, 120, 146

Indian National Congress: and Congress Working Committees 16, 55; and democratic populism 7, 54, 57–8, 60, 64–5, 73–4, 84, 116; and the formation of Congress (I) 50–2; in the Indian Constituent Assembly, 14, 18, 31, 120, 124–5

Jammu and Kashmir National Conference Party 30, 50–2

Janata Party 88–9, 137–8, 140

Jinnah, Muhammad Ali 29, 121

Kamaraj, K. 54–7

Kargil Review Committee 104–5, 143

Kargil War: as a 'limted war' 107, 141; and nuclear weapons 101–2, 104–5, 107, 141–3; role of intellgence agencies 106

Kaul, T.N. 45, 73, 128, 132–3

Khilnani Sunil 12, 17, 20, 121–3

Kissinger, Henry 68, 133–4

Liberation Tigers of Tamil Eelam (LTTE) 77–8, 136

Modi, Narendra 95, 139

Mountbatten, Earl Louis 33–4, 124–5

Narayan, J.P. 41, 59, 132

National Democratic Alliance (NDA) 85, 93, 139

Nehru, B.K. 129

Nehru, Jawarharlal: and the Afro-Asian states 29, 34, 39, 124; and approach towards China 40, 42–6, 127–8; and the Cold War 29, 34–6, 44, 116, 126; and democracy in India 2–4, 7, 17–23, 26, 29, 32–3, 40–2, 47, 120, 123; and the drafting of India's constitution 1, 13–14, 19–23, 26; and the Hindu Code Bill 20, 91, 138–9; and the 'Light of Asia' 29; and minorities in India 13, 16, 20–1, 26, 53, 121–2; and notions of anti-imperialism 4, 25–6, 34–6, 39–41, 44, 47–8, 115; and perception of P. Tandon 16–17, 122, 130; perception of the Baghdad Pact and SEATO 35; and perceptions of the United Nations 34–7, 47, 126; and 'Plan Balkan' 25; and Sheikh Abdullah 30, 34, 126; and socialism in India 19, 22–3, 123–4; and the significance of Jammu and Kashmir for India 30–4, 37, 49; and the 1950 Treaty of Friendship with Nepal 38, 47, 115, 127; and view of B.P. Koirala 41, 127–8

Nepal: and diplomatic relations with China 42–6, 128; and the Rana regime 38, 40–2, 127; and the Indian military mission 42–3

Nixon, Richard 62, 68, 74–5, 132–3

Non-Proliferation Treaty (NPT) 119, 146

Pakistan: and formal recognition of Bangladesh 66, 70; and its founding ideas 2, 12–19, 29–30, 69–70, 125; and the issue of the princely states

24–5, 29–30; and the role of the ISI 110–13, 145; and the Simla Agreement 66–8, 73–5, 102, 116, 132–4
Patel, Vallabhbhai 9, 14, 22, 121, 123–4, 138

Rahman, Sheikh Mujibur 108
Rao, Narasimha 77, 135, 144
Rashtriya Swayamsevak Sangh (RSS) 87–91, 97, 106–7, 117, 137–8

Sangh Parivar 7, 86, 106, 137
Savarkar, V.D. 86–7, 89–91, 97, 99, 117, 137
Shariff, Nawaz: and Bill Clinton 104, 142; and 'bus diplomacy' 101, 141; and the Lahore Declaration 101–3, 106, 141–2
Shourie, Arun 109, 144
Siachen Glacier 104
Sikhs 14, 86
Simla Agreement 10, 66–9, 73–6, 102, 116, 132–3
Singh, Hari: and Earl Louis Mountbatten 33–4; and the Instrument of Accession 31, 33–4, 129
Singh, Jaswant 100, 103, 107, 141–3
Southeast Asian Treaty Organization (SEATO) 35, 126
Soviet Union 46, 72, 74–5, 126, 135
Sri Lanka: and India's Tamil community 76–9, 84; and the 'Indira Doctrine' 80, 83

Subrahmanyam, K. 143
Swami, Praveen 143

Tandon, P. 16–17, 122, 130
Tibet 40, 45–6

uniform civil code 20–1, 91–2, 138
United Nations: and the East Pakistan crisis 70–2, 133; and the Kashmir dispute 34–7, 47, 67, 103, 107, 126; and Tamil demands in Sri Lanka 77, 83
United Progressive Alliance (UPA) 119
United States: and the Cuban Missile Crisis 9; and Indira Gandhi 55, 62–3, 68, 74–5; and the Kashmir dispute 32, 36, 43, 126; and Nepal 42–4, 46; and Sri Lanka 81–3, 136; and the Kargil War 102–4, 107, 141–2, 144

Vajpayee, Atal Bihari: and 'bus diplomacy' 101, 141; as foreign minister in the Janata Dal government 88–9, 137; and the Kargil War 101, 141; and his position within the BJP 10, 89, 137
Vishva Hindu Parishad (VHP) 94, 140
Voice of America 81–2

West Bengal 61, 109–10, 112–13, 144–5

Zhou En-Lai 44, 128